Computers
For Seniors
FOR
DUMMIES

A Wiley Brand

by **Nancy C. Muir**

FOR
DUMMIES
A Wiley Brand

Computers For Seniors For Dummies®, Fourth Edition

Published by:
John Wiley & Sons, Inc.
111 River Street
Hoboken, NJ 07030-5774
www.wiley.com

Copyright © 2015 by John Wiley & Sons, Inc., Hoboken, New Jersey

Published simultaneously in Canada

For general information on our other products and services, please contact our Customer Care Department within the U.S. at 877-762-2974, outside the U.S. at 317-572-3993, or fax 317-572-4002. For technical support, please visit www.wiley.com/techsupport.

Wiley publishes in a variety of print and electronic formats and by print-on-demand. Some material included with standard print versions of this book may not be included in e-books or in print-on-demand. If this book refers to media such as a CD or DVD that is not included in the version you purchased, you may download this material at http://booksupport.wiley.com. For more information about Wiley products, visit www.wiley.com.

Library of Congress Control Number: 2015949692

ISBN 978-1-119-04955-5 (pbk); ISBN 978-1-119-04950-0 (ebk); ISBN 978-1-119-04954-8 (ebk)

Manufactured in the United States of America

10 9 8 7 6 5 4 3 2 1

Contents at a Glance

Table of Contents

Computers for consumers have come a long way in just 25 years or so. They're now at the heart of the way many people communicate, shop, and learn. They provide useful tools for tracking information, organizing finances, and being creative.

During the rapid growth of the personal computer, you might have been too busy to jump in and learn the ropes, but you now realize how useful and fun working with a computer can be.

This book can help you get going with computers quickly and painlessly.

About This Book

This book is specifically written for mature people like you — folks who are relatively new to using a computer and want to discover the basics of buying a computer, working with software, and getting on the Internet. In writing this book, I've tried to take into account the types of activities that might interest a 55-plus-year-old who's discovering computers for the first time.

Foolish Assumptions

This book is organized by sets of tasks. These tasks start from the very beginning, assuming you know little about computers, and guide you through the most basic steps in easy-to-understand language. Because I assume you're new to computers, the book provides explanations or definitions of technical terms to help you out.

All computers are run by software called an *operating system,* such as Windows. The latest version is Windows 10. Because Microsoft Windows–based personal computers (PCs) are the most common type, the book focuses mostly on Windows 10 functionality.

Beyond the Book

Extra online content supplements this book to help you go further. Go online to take advantage of three features:

Cheat Sheet (www.dummies.com/cheatsheet/computersforseniors**):** This book's Cheat Sheet offers a list of Windows 10 shortcut keys you can use to perform common operations more quickly and a checklist of what to look for when buying a computer.

Dummies.com online articles: The Parts pages of this book provide links to helpful articles on Dummies.com. These articles are listed on the book's Extras page at www.dummies.com/extras/computersforseniors. Topics include Tips for Creating Strong Passwords and Ten or So Great Apps for Seniors.

Where to Go from Here

Whether you need to start from square one and buy yourself a computer or you're ready to just start enjoying the tools and toys your current computer makes available, it's time to get going, get online, and get computer savvy.

Part I
Get Going!

Settings	— □ ×

⚙ **SETTINGS**　　　　　　　　　　　　　　　　 | Find a setting 🔍 |

System
Display, notifications,
apps, power

Devices
Bluetooth, printers,
mouse

Network & Internet
Wi-Fi, airplane mode,
VPN

Personalization
Background, lock
screen, colors

Accounts
Your account, sync
settings, work, family

Time & language
Speech, region, date

Ease of Access
Narrator, magnifier,
high contrast

Privacy
Location, camera

Update & security
Windows Update,
recovery, backup

Visit www.dummies.com for more great content online.

Buying a Computer

*I*f you've never owned a computer and now face purchasing one for the first time, deciding what to get can be a somewhat daunting experience. There are lots of technical terms to figure out and various pieces of *hardware* (the physical pieces of your computer such as the monitor and keyboard) and *software* (the brains of the computer that help you create documents and play games, for example) that you need to understand.

In this chapter, I introduce you to the world of activities your new computer makes available to you, and I provide the information you need to choose just the right computer for you. Remember as you read through this chapter that figuring out what you want to do with your computer is an important step in determining which computer you should buy. You have to consider how much money you want to spend, how you'll connect your computer to the Internet, and how much power and performance you need from your computer.

Understand All You Can Do with Computers

Congratulations — in your life you've been witness to a remarkable revolution. In just a few decades, computers have moved from being expensive behemoths that lived in corporate basements to being personal productivity and entertainment tools. They've empowered people to connect around the world in unprecedented ways, and they've made common tasks much easier to handle.

The following list walks you through some of the things your computer will enable you to do. Depending on what activities are important to you, you can make a more-informed purchasing choice.

→ **Keep in touch with friends and family.** The Internet makes it possible to communicate with other people via email; share video images using built-in video recorders or webcams (tiny, inexpensive video cameras that capture and send your image to another computer); and make phone and video calls using your computer and Internet connection to place calls with services such as Skype. You can also chat with others by typing messages and sending them through your computer using a technology called *instant messaging* (IM). These messages are exchanged in real time, so that you and your grandchild, for example, can see and reply to text or share images immediately. Part III of this book explains these topics in more detail.

→ **Research any topic from the comfort of your home.** Online, you can find many reputable websites that help you get information on anything from expert medical advice to the best travel deals. You can read news from around the corner or around the world. You can visit government websites to get information about your taxes and Social Security benefits, and go to entertainment sites to look up your local television listings or movie reviews.

→ **Create greeting cards, letters, or home inventories.** Whether you're organizing your holiday card list, tracking sales for your home business, or figuring out a monthly budget, computer programs can help. For example, **Figure 1-1** shows a graph that the Excel program created from data in a spreadsheet.

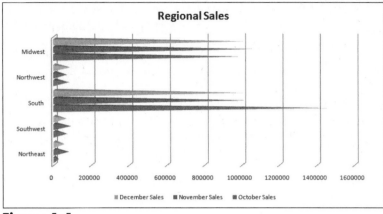

Figure 1-1

➠ **Pursue hobbies such as genealogy or sports.** You can research your favorite team online (see **Figure 1-2**) or connect with people who have the same interests. The online world is full of special-interest discussion groups where you can talk about a wide variety of topics with others.

Figure 1-2

➠ **Play interactive games with others over the Internet.** You can play everything from shuffleboard to poker and even participate in action games in virtual worlds.

➠ **Share and create photos, drawings, and videos.** If you have a digital camera, you can transfer photos to your computer (called *uploading*) or copy photos off the Internet (if their copyright permits it) and share them in emails or use them to create your own greeting cards. If you're artistically inclined, you can create digital drawings. Many popular websites make sharing your homemade videos easy, too. If you have a digital video camera and editing software, you can use editing tools to make a movie and share it with others via video-sharing sites such as YouTube or by email. Steven Spielberg, look out!

➠ **Shop online and compare products easily, day or night.** You can shop for anything from a garden shed to travel deals or a new camera. Using handy shopping site features, you can easily compare prices from several stores or read customer product reviews. Many websites, such as www.nextag.com, list product prices from a variety of vendors on one web page, so you can find the best deals. Beyond the convenience, all this information can help you save money.

➠ **Manage your financial life.** You can do your banking or investing online and get up-to-the-minute data about your bank account, credit card balances, and investments. And, if you're online savvy, you can do this all without fear of having your financial data stolen. (See Chapter 13 for more about online safety.)

Overview Hardware

Your computing experience consists of interactions with hardware and software. The *hardware* is all the tangible computer equipment, such as the monitor, central processing unit, keyboard, and mouse.

Your computer hardware consists of

➡ **A central processing unit (CPU),** which is the very small, very high-tech semiconductor *chip* that acts as the brains of your computer. The CPU is stored in a computer tower — or in all-in-one computer models, laptops, and tablets, in a single unit along with the monitor. The CPU also contains other nuts and bolts used to run your computer.

➡ **A monitor,** which displays images on its screen such as the Microsoft Windows desktop, a video you watch from an online entertainment site, or a document in a software program. Today, more and more computers sport touchscreen monitors, which allow you to use your finger on the screen to provide input to the computer.

➡ **A keyboard,** which is similar to a typewriter keyboard. In addition to typing words, you can use a keyboard to give the computer commands such as selecting, copying, and pasting text.

➡ **A mouse,** which you also use to give your computer commands. This little device is a more free-flowing way of providing input than your keyboard. You move the mouse around your desk with your hand, which moves a pointer around onscreen. Using this pointer, you can click an item — an onscreen button, for example — that causes an action, or click on the screen and drag the mouse to select text or an object to perform an action on it (such as deleting the text or making it bold). A mouse can be a separate device that is mouselike in shape, or can be built into devices like laptops in the form of a touch button or touchpad.

➡ **Peripherals,** such as printers, speakers, webcams, and headphones. These may or may not come with your computer when you buy it, but your computer does come with slots (called *ports*) where you plug in various peripherals.

Appreciate Software

Software is what makes computer hardware work and lets you get things done, such as writing documents with Microsoft Word or playing a game of solitaire. You can install software (also known as *programs, applications, or apps*) on your computer or use a version from an online website. Here are a few basics about software:

➡ **You use software to get your work done, run entertainment programs, and browse the Internet.** For example, Quicken is a financial management program you can use to balance your checkbook or keep track of your home inventory for insurance purposes.

➡ **The software used to run your computer is the operating system.** Some examples of operating systems are Apple OS X for Mac and Microsoft Windows. This book deals mainly with Windows 10 and the programs it runs.

➡ **Some programs come preinstalled on your computer; you can buy and install other programs when you need them.** For example, a computer always has an operating system because the operating system runs all the other programs. Also, some programs are included with a Windows computer, such as WordPad, a simple word-processing program, and Music and Video apps.

➡ **You can uninstall programs you no longer need.** Uninstalling unwanted programs helps to free up some space on your computer, which helps it perform better.

➡ **Software programs called *utilities* exist to keep your computer in shape.** An *antivirus* program is an example of a utility used to block or spot and erase computer viruses from your system. Your *operating system* also includes some utilities, such as those that optimize your hard drive or restore your system if it's experiencing problems.

Pick a Desktop: Tower or All-in-One?

A form of computer that has been around for quite a while is a *tower* (see **Figure 1-3**). A tower is one style of desktop computer that, because of its size, people keep on or near a table or desk. Typically, you keep the tower, which holds the hard drive, processor, and other brains of the beast, on the floor. You work with the computer via a keyboard and monitor that sit on the desk.

Figure 1-3
Courtesy of Dell, Inc.

Pros of the tower include space to expand various elements, such as memory, and fans that keep the computer cool while operating. To repair a tower, you open the metal case and replace parts.

 Compact desktops, which have the volume of a shoebox, can sit on your desktop. Check into a compact desktop, such as Intel's NCU, if you like your computer small but non-portable.

Another form of desktop computer is an *all-in-one*. With this type of computer, the brains are stored in a casing behind the monitor, so the entire computer sits on your desk or table.

All-in-ones are often sleek and modern looking, involve fewer cables, and save you from using floor space for a computer tower. However, repairing or customizing the hardware is almost impossible because opening the computer is difficult.

Both desktop towers and all-in-ones take up more surface space than a laptop computer, but if you don't need portability in your computer, a desktop may be the best choice.

 Tablets, such as iPad, and Windows-based tablets, such as Surface, offer many computing capabilities, including reading and working on simple documents, connecting to the Internet to send and receive email, playing games, listening to music, and so on. However, they have relatively small touchscreens (with a touchscreen, you provide input with your finger or a stylus); onscreen keyboards, which can be a bit challenging to use; no mouse; and often less file-management capabilities. If you just want to browse the web, read email, and play games, a tablet could be a way to go. If you want a broader range of capabilities with a larger screen size and can live with less portability, a computer is the way to go.

Choose a Laptop

A *laptop* is portable, weighing anywhere from 2 to 8 pounds. The monitor, keyboard, and mouse (in the form of a flat touchpad) are built into the laptop.

Figure 1-4 shows an example of a laptop, which is sometimes called a *notebook* computer. Choose a laptop if you want to use your computer mainly away from home or you have little space in your home for a larger computer.

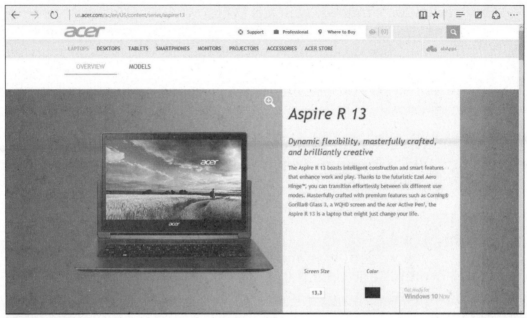

Figure 1-4

Note that if the monitor on a laptop becomes damaged, you'll pay quite a bit for a repair, or you can hook the computer up to an external monitor. Because there is less space for fans, laptops sometimes run hot to the touch.

A 2-in-1 laptop allows you to either rotate the monitor to rest on the back of the keyboard or remove the monitor so you can use the laptop like a tablet. When you have no active physical keyboard, you have to use the touchscreen feature to interact with the laptop.

 Many of today's desktops and laptops have touchscreens that allow you to interact with them using your finger or a penlike device called a stylus. See Chapter 2 for advice on using a touchscreen computer.

Select a Version of Windows

Choosing your computer's *operating system* (software that runs all the programs and organizes data on your computer) will be one of your first decisions. This book focuses on computers running the current version of Windows, which is Windows 10. Windows 10 is a radical departure from previous Windows operating systems, so if you opt for an earlier version of Windows, such as Windows 7, you would need to buy the Windows 7 edition of this book. Windows 10 comes in several versions, including two versions for home and small business users:

➠ **Windows 10 Home:** Includes apps such as Music, Video, Weather, People, Camera, and more. If you consider yourself primarily a home user, you should consider this version of Windows 10.

➠ **Windows 10 Pro:** Is great for small businesses or if you work from home. This version of Windows has ultimate security features and more administrative tools.

Upgrading to Windows 10

You can upgrade to Windows for free 10 if you have Windows 7, 8, or 8.1 on your computer. Click the Start menu and then click Settings. Click Update & Security and check for updates. This free upgrade offer is only available for one year after Windows 10's release date of 7/29/2015.

Determine Your Price Range

You can buy a computer for anywhere from about $199 to $5,000 or more, depending on your budget and computing needs. You may start with a base model, but extras such as a larger monitor or larger storage capacity can soon add hundreds to the base price. The rule of thumb is to buy just as much computer as you need.

You can shop in a retail store for a computer or shop online using a friend's computer (and perhaps get his or her help if you're brand new to using a computer). Consider researching different models and prices online with the help of a computer-savvy friend and using that information to get the best buy. Be aware, however, that most retail stores have a small selection compared to all you can find online on a website such as Amazon.com and NewEgg.com. Additionally, retail stores sometimes carry slightly older models than those available online.

Buying a computer can be confusing, but here are some guidelines to help you find a computer at the price that's right for you:

⟶ **Determine how often you will use your computer.** If you'll be working on it eight hours a day running a home business, you will need a better-quality computer to withstand the use and provide good performance. If you turn on the computer once or twice a week, it doesn't have to be the priciest model in the shop.

⟶ **Consider the features that you need.** Do you want (or have room for) a 20-inch monitor? Do you need the computer to run very fast and run several programs at once, or do you need to store tons of data? (I cover computer speed and storage later in this chapter.) Understand what you need before you buy. Each feature or upgrade adds dollars to your computer's price.

⟶ **Shop wisely.** If you walk from store to store or do your shopping online, you'll find that the price for the same computer model can vary by hundreds of dollars at different stores. See if your memberships in organizations such as AAA, AARP, or Costco make you eligible for better deals. Consider shipping costs if you buy online, and keep in mind that many stores charge a restocking fee if you return a computer you aren't happy with. Some stores offer only a short time period, such as 14 days, in which you can return a computer.

➠ **Buying used or refurbished is an option, though new computers have reached such a low price point that this may not save you much.** In addition, technology gets out of date so quickly that you might be disappointed buying an older model, which might not support newer software or hardware.

➠ **Online auctions are a source of new or slightly used computers at a low price.** However, be sure you're dealing with a reputable store or person by checking reviews others have posted about them or contacting the online Better Business Bureau (www.bbb.org). Be careful not to pay by check (this gives a complete stranger your bank account number); instead use the auction site's tools to have a third party handle the money until the goods are delivered in the condition promised. Check the auction site for guidance on staying safe when buying auctioned goods.

 Some websites, such as Epinions.com, allow you to compare several models of computers side by side, and others, such as Nextag.com, allow you to compare prices on a particular model from multiple stores.

Understand Displays

Monitors are the window to your computer's contents. If you're buying a desktop computer, it will come with a monitor that may or may not suit your purposes, or you might upgrade to a better monitor. The right monitor can make your computing time easier on your eyes. The crisper the image, the more impressive your vacation photos or that video of your last golf game will be.

Consider these factors when choosing a monitor:

➡ **Size:** Monitors for the average computer user come in all sizes, from tiny 9-inch screens on smaller laptops to 28-inch desktop models. Larger screens are typically more expensive. Although a larger monitor can take up more space side to side and top to bottom, many don't have a bigger *footprint* (that is, how much space their base takes up on your desk) than a smaller monitor.

➡ **Image quality:** The image quality can vary greatly. You will see terms such as LCD (liquid crystal display), LED (light emitting diode), flat screen, brightness, and resolution.

Look for an LCD or LED monitor (see **Figure 1-5**) that reduces glare. If you are thinking of purchasing a laptop computer, the monitor is built in, so consider the size and quality of the display as part of your laptop purchase.

➡ **Resolution:** A monitor's resolution represents the number of pixels that form the images you see on the screen. The higher the resolution, the crisper the image. You should look for a monitor that can provide at least a 1,366-x-768 pixel resolution.

➡ **Cost:** The least-expensive monitor might be the one that comes with your desktop computer, and many of these are perfectly adequate. You can often upgrade your monitor when you buy if you customize a system from a company such as Dell or Hewlett Packard. Monitors purchased separately from a computer can range from around $100 to $3,000 or more. Check out monitors in person to verify whether their image quality and size are worth the money.

Figure 1-5

⟹ **Touchscreen technology:** Windows 10 provides support for using a touchscreen interface, which allows you to use your fingers to provide input by tapping or swiping on the screen itself. If you opt for a touchscreen device, you can still use your keyboard and mouse to provide input, but touchscreen technology can add a wow factor when performing tasks such as using painting software or browsing around the web or an electronic book (e-book).

Explore Storage Options

In the recent past, most computers came with a DVD drive where you could insert a disc and play a movie or music. If you buy a software program, it may come on a CD or DVD, so you can use a built-in or external drive to install it.

Today, many new computers and laptops don't include an optical drive for reading DVDs. Instead, they have USB ports. USB ports accommodate a USB stick, which is a small plastic coated gadget that can hold a lot of data.

 If you want to play the latest optical discs, get a computer with a Blu-ray player. Blu-ray is a great medium for storing and playing back feature-length movies because it can store 50GB or more, about ten times as much as the average DVD.

 Recent computers come without DVD capabilities because you can download and install software or play videos and music from the *cloud* (that is, via the Internet), so it's possible to get along just fine without the ability to play DVDs. However, some software products still only come on a disc. You can connect an external optical drive to a USB port to load the software on your computer.

Choose Features for Faster Performance

Your computer contains a processor on a computer chip. The speed at which your computer runs programs or completes tasks is determined in great measure by your computer's processor speed, which is measured in *gigahertz* (GHz). The higher the GHz, the faster the processor. I won't quote the speed you should look for because these chips are constantly getting smaller and more powerful. However, when you shop, know that the higher numbers give the best performance, so factor that into your decision, depending on your needs.

Computers have traditionally used hard drives to store programs and data. Many computers use a solid state drive rather than a hard drive. The *access speed* (how fast your computer retrieves data) of solid state drives is much higher than the access speed of hard drives. If you need a computer that processes information very quickly, look for one with a solid state drive.

 The data storage capacity (measured in *gigabytes*) of a solid state drive is generally lower than a hard drive; therefore, the amount of large files you can store on a system with a solid state drive may be limited.

Another factor involved in performance is whether your processor has multiple cores. *Multiple core* means that two or more processors are involved in reading and executing software instructions as you use your computer. Most processors today are multi-core processors, such as the i3, i5, and i7 processor lines from Intel. Those with two processors are *dual-core;* those with four processors are *quad-core;* and processors with six cores are *hexa-core.* The bottom line with cores is that the more cores you have and the faster they are, the faster your computer can process instructions because all the cores can work at the same time, which makes multitasking possible. *Multitasking* is running several programs at one time, such as playing music, downloading files from the Internet, running an antivirus scan, and working in a word processor.

In addition to your processor, computers have a certain amount of storage capacity for running programs and accessing frequently used data that can affect performance. You'll see specifications for RAM when you go computer shopping. RAM, which stands for random access memory, is a measure of the capacity for running programs; the higher the RAM, the more quickly your computer can juggle multiple tasks, therefore increasing performance. RAM chips come in different types, such as DRAM, and the latest version, DDR4, but whichever type of RAM you see in the computer specs, make sure your computer contains at least 2 gigabytes (GB) of RAM memory.

Determine How You'll Connect to the Internet

You have to decide how you'll connect to the Internet. You can pay a fee to get a broadband connection such as DSL, satellite, or cable. (Check with AARP to find out if it offers discounted connections in your area.) If you want to set up a wireless connection in your home so you can connect to the Internet or have a laptop and want to access certain public networks called *hotspots,* you have to be sure to buy a computer with up-to-date wireless capabilities. Here's how these work:

➡ **Broadband:** These connections typically come through a DSL (digital subscriber line) or cable modem in your home. In both cases, you pay a fee to a provider, which might be your phone or cable company. DSL works over your phone line but doesn't prohibit you from using the phone when you're online. Cable runs over your cable TV line and is a bit faster than DSL. Typically, satellite broadband is used in rural areas that don't offer cable or DSL service. These "always-on" connections mean that you don't have to dial a phone connection or connect to a wireless network — you're always connected.

➡ **Dialup:** If you intend to use a dialup connection (that is, connect over your phone line), your computer has to have a dialup modem, either built in or external. Dialup connections can be very slow. In fact, in all but remote locations, dialup has been replaced by more current technology. While you're using a dialup connection, you can't use your phone to make or receive calls. I discourage you from using dialup unless you absolutely have to.

➡ **Wireless:** These connections require that you have a computer equipped with wireless capability. You can access the Internet wirelessly through a wireless network you set up in your home, or when you're near a wireless *hotspot* (a place that offers wireless service), and many hotspots are available at public places such as hotels, airports, and restaurants. You can also subscribe to a Wireless Wide Area Network (WWAN) service from a mobile phone provider to tap into its connection or use a technology called *tethering* to connect via your smartphone's 3G or 4G connection. Check the computer model you want to buy to be sure it's wireless enabled. There are various techy standards for Wi-Fi (wireless communications), such as 802.11a, b, g, or n. The very latest standard to look for is 802.11ac, which delivers the best wireless performance as of this writing.

See Chapter 11 for more about setting up your Internet connection.

Setting Up Your Computer

Chapter 2

*O*nce you unpack your new computer, you may need help getting it set up. Here I cover the basics: connecting your computer to a monitor, keyboard, and mouse (if you bought a laptop computer, you can skip these tasks as the hardware is built in); turning the computer on and off; mastering the basic use of your mouse, becoming familiar with some basic keystroke shortcuts, and, if you have a touchscreen, finding out how to interact with it.

Next, you can set up the date and time in your computer's internal clock so they match your time zone and you can apply daylight saving time settings properly. Finally, you get to work with your user accounts. Windows allows you to create multiple user accounts; each account saves certain settings and allows you to control files and folders separately. Child accounts allow you to have some control over what apps and online content a child can access. When each user logs on with a particular user account, it's like accessing a unique personal computer.

Here, then, are the procedures that you can follow to get going with your computer.

Get ready to . . .

Connect the Monitor, Keyboard, and Mouse

Your computer comes with a monitor, keyboard, and mouse. You should connect these before turning on the computer. Your computer will offer several types of connection ports (slots in the computer that allow you to connect other devices), with USB ports being the most common. For example, wireless keyboards and mice connect to your computer via a small receiver that you insert into a USB port. Wired keyboards and mice plug into your computer using a USB cable. If your computer does not have enough USB ports, you can use a USB hub (shown in **Figure 2-1**) which will allow you to plug extra peripheral devices into one USB port on your computer.

The setup information provided by your computer's manufacturer should help you get things connected. Use the following table to identify the function of device-to-PC connector ports.

Connection	What It's Good For
HDMI (High Definition Multimedia Interface) port	Connect your TV to your computer.
USB port	Connect various USB devices, such as a digital camera or wireless mouse.
Parallel port	Connect a non-USB printer.
Audio port	Connect external speakers, headphone, or microphones.
Ethernet port	Connect an Internet modem or router to your computer.

Figure 2-1

Log in to Windows 10

1. With your computer set up, you're ready to turn it on. Start by pressing the power button on your computer to begin the Windows 10 start-up sequence. When you first turn on a new computer, you should choose Express Settings to set up your computer.

2. In the resulting Windows 10 Welcome screen, click the bottom of the screen and drag upward to reveal the sign-in screen.

Enter your password or PIN, if you've set up one, and then press Enter on your keyboard. (If you haven't set up the password-protection feature for more than one user, you're taken directly to the Windows 10 desktop when you turn on your computer. If you have more than one user you have to choose the one you want to log on as.) Windows 10 verifies your password and displays the Windows 10 desktop, as shown in **Figure 2-2**.

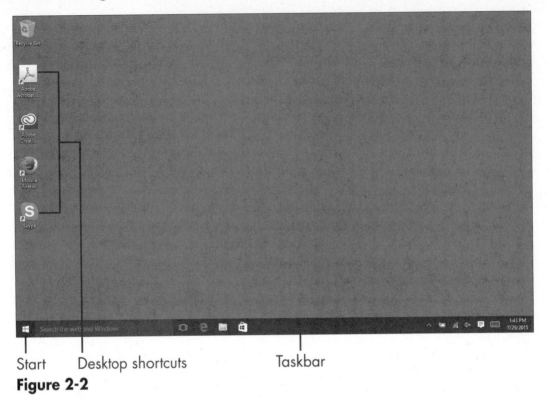

Start   Desktop shortcuts   Taskbar

Figure 2-2

Use the Mouse

Unlike using a typewriter, which sports only a keyboard to enter text into documents, with a computer you use both a keyboard and a mouse to enter text and send commands to the computer. Though you might have used a keyboard of some type before, a mouse might be new to you, and frankly, it takes a little getting used to. In effect, when you move your mouse around on your desk (or in some models, roll a ball on top of the mouse), a corresponding mouse pointer moves around your computer screen. You control the actions of that pointer by using the right and left buttons on the mouse.

Here are the main functions of a mouse and how to control them:

➡ **Click.** When people say, "click," they mean that you should move your mouse over the command or item you want to select or activate and then press and release the left mouse button.

Clicking has a variety of uses. You can click while you're in a document to move the *insertion point,* a little line that indicates where your next action will take place. For example, in a letter you're writing, you might click in front of a word you already typed and then type another word to insert it into the sentence. Clicking is also used in various windows to select check boxes or radio buttons (also called *option buttons*) to turn features on or off, to choose a command in a menu, or to select an object such as a picture or table in your document.

➠ **Right-click.** If you click the right mouse button, Windows displays a shortcut menu that's specific to the item you clicked. For example, if you right-click a picture, the menu that appears gives you options for working with the picture. If you right-click the Windows desktop, the menu that appears lets you choose commands that display a different view or change desktop properties.

➠ **Click and drag.** To click and drag, click your mouse on an item on the screen, press and continue to hold down the left mouse button, and then move (drag) the mouse to another location. For instance, you can click in a document and drag your mouse up, down, right, or left to highlight contents of your document. This highlighted text is *selected,* meaning that any action you perform, such as pressing the Delete key on your keyboard or clicking a button for bold formatting, is performed on the selected text.

➠ **Scroll.** Many mouse models have a wheel in the center that you can roll up or down to scroll through a document or website on your screen. Just roll the wheel down to move through pages going forward, or scroll up to move backward in your document.

Laptops offer a built-in touchpad, which is a flat rectangle beneath the physical keyboard. You can use a finger to tap the left or right side of the keyboard to mimic the use of the left or right side of a mouse. You can move a finger around the touchpad to move the mouse function around your screen.

Work with a Touchscreen

Windows 10 is designed to work with a touchscreen computer, though not all computers include a touchscreen feature.

If you do own a touchscreen computer or tablet device, placing and moving your finger on the screen replaces the movement of a mouse. You can tap the screen to select something, to activate features with buttons, and to make a field active so you can enter content. Windows 10 also offers an onscreen keyboard that touchscreen users can work with to enter text with the tap of a finger.

You can also use your finger to swipe to the right, left, up, or down to move from one item to another (for example, from one web page to another, one page to another in an e-reader, or from one photo to the next in the Photos app) or to move up or down on a page.

Windows 10 also offers some gestures you can make with your fingers, such as moving your fingers apart and then pinching them together to minimize elements on your screen, or swiping down from the top of the screen to close an app. If you do own a touchscreen and want to learn more, visit the Use Touch with Windows in the Get Started app (Start ⇨ Get Started ⇨ Menu ⇨ Continuum and Touch ⇨ Use Touch with Windows).

Use Shortcuts

A *keyboard shortcut* refers to a key or combinations of keys that you press and hold to perform an action. Many shortcuts involve the Windows key (the key near the bottom-left corner of your keyboard that sports the Windows logo). For example, you can press and hold the Windows key plus A (Win+A) to display the Action Center.

In Windows 10, keyboard shortcuts can be very helpful to those who don't have a touchscreen computer. Table 2-1 lists some handy shortcuts to know.

Table 2-1	Common Windows 10 Keyboard Shortcuts
Key(s)	**Result**
Windows key	Displays the Start menu
Win+S	Opens Cortana
Win+X	Displays the Desktop menu
Win+C	Opens Cortana in Listening mode
Win+L	Displays the Lock Screen
Win+A	Displays the Action Center
Win+E	Displays File Explorer
Win+I	Displays the Settings window
Win+Tab	Displays task View

Set the Date and Time

1. The calendar and clock on your computer keep good time, but if you travel, for example, you might have to provide the correct date and time for your location. Click the Start button and then click Settings.

2. Click Time & Language in the Settings window that appear, as shown in **Figure** 2-3).

3. In the Time & Language screen, set the Set Time Automatically toggle to Off, and then click the Change button under Change Date and Time.

4. In the Change Date and Time dialog box (see **Figure** 2-4), use the various drop-down fields to make different selections. For example, click the Year field and choose a different year.

5. Click Change to save the settings.

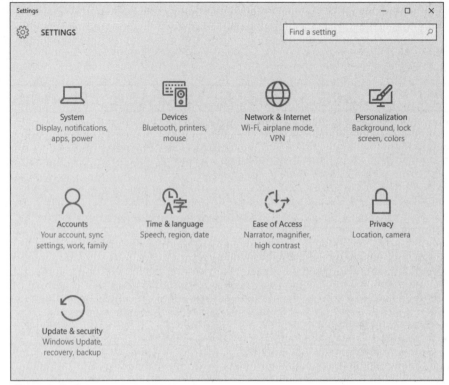

Figure 2-3

Figure 2-4

6. To change the time zone you're in, click the Time Zone drop-down menu, and then select a different time zone.

7. Click the Close button in the upper-right corner to close the Timer & Language Settings window.

Another way to display the Settings window from the desktop is to press Win+I.

Create a New User Account

1. You must have administrator status to create new users. When you first set up Windows 10, the first user created will automatically be an administrator account. This time, try a keyboard shortcut to get to the Settings window. Press Win+I.

2. Click Accounts.

3. In the Accounts screen shown in **Figure 2-5,** click Family & Other Users and then click Add Someone Else to This PC (the setting is represented by a plus sign).

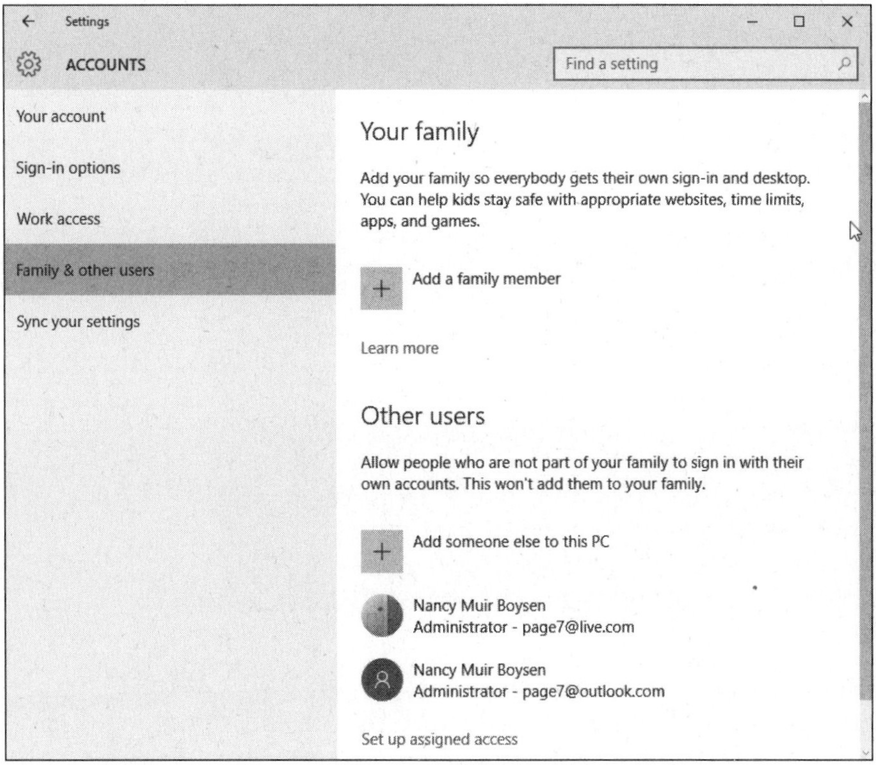

Figure 2-5

If the new user is a child, click Add a Family Member and then in the Add a Child or Adult window select Add a Child. This turns on Family Safety features and allows you to make safety settings.

4. In the resulting window, shown in **Figure 2-6**, enter a Microsoft email address. Note that if the person doesn't have a Microsoft email account, you should create a new account using the The Person I Want to Add Doesn't Have an Email Address link. Click Next.

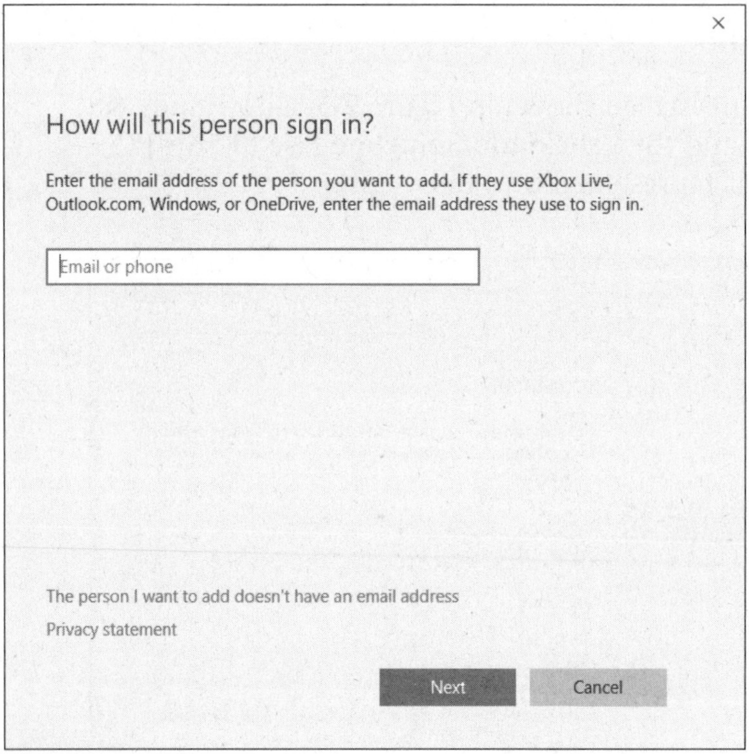

×

How will this person sign in?

Enter the email address of the person you want to add. If they use Xbox Live, Outlook.com, Windows, or OneDrive, enter the email address they use to sign in.

Email or phone

The person I want to add doesn't have an email address

Privacy statement

Next   Cancel

Figure 2-6

5. In the Good to Go dialog box, click Finish.

 After you create an account, when a user with administrative privileges is logged in he or she can make changes to the user account in the Family and Other Users settings. Click on a user Account, click Change Account Type, and then choose an account type from the drop-down list in the Edit Account dialog box.

For more on adding and changing user passwords, see Chapter 20. After you set up more than one user, before you get to the password screen, you have to click the icon for the user you want to log on as.

 If you prefer, you can log in with a four-digit PIN in place of a traditional password. This makes it quicker to sign in. When you've logged in as the user for which you want to set a PIN, go to the Accounts settings shown in Figure 2-5 and click Sign-in Options. In the PIN setting, click the Add button.

 You can set up several user accounts for your computer, which helps you save and access specific user settings and provides privacy for each user's files with passwords.

Switch User Accounts

1. To change to another user account after you've logged in, you can press Win+L to go to the Windows lock screen. Windows 10 logs off.

2. Click to display the sign-in screen.

3. Click the username you want to log in as, type the password, and press the arrow key to the right of the password field to go to the Windows desktop.

Shut down Your Computer

1. To turn off your computer when you're done, you need to initiate a shutdown sequence in your operating system instead of simply turning off the power with the power button on your computer. Click the Start button.

2. Click the Power button (refer to **Figure** 2-7). If you prefer to stop your computer running but not turn the power off, click Sleep (or simply close the lid of your laptop). If you want to reboot (turn off and turn back on) your computer, choose Restart. To shut off the power, click Shut Down.

Power button

Figure 2-7

If your computer freezes up for some reason, you can try resetting it by turning it off and then back on after a minute or so. To shut down a frozen computer, press the Power button on your computer and hold it until the computer powers off.

Don't simply turn off your computer at the power source unless you have to because of a computer dysfunction. Windows might not start up properly the next time you turn it on if you don't follow the proper shutdown procedure.

Getting around Windows 10

Chapter 3

Windows has gone through some interesting changes in recent years. With Windows 8 and 8.1, an entirely new dynamic appeared for working with a Windows computer, and frankly, that dramatic change had some users stymied. With Windows 10, you have a hybrid that includes one central desktop and a Start menu (like Windows 7) but also sophisticated tools for searching, organizing apps, and making settings, like Windows 8 and 8.1.

In this chapter, you discover the basics of getting around Windows, and using features such as the Start menu, desktop shortcuts, and the taskbar. This chapter shows you how to find and open apps with File Explorer and how to interact with a touchscreen computer. I also introduce new features, including the Action Center for receiving notifications and accessing settings, and Cortana, a personal assistant and search feature that you can use to find information, open apps, or even identify music.

Understand Changes in Windows 10

Some of the biggest changes in Windows 10 are the enhancements for those who have touchscreen-enabled computers. In fact, you could use a computer without a mouse and keyboard for the most part, if you have a touchscreen machine (although you can still use a mouse and keyboard to get anything done).

Additionally, where Windows 8 and 8.1 had two views, a desktop and a Start screen, Windows 10 focuses on a desktop as its home base (see **Figure 3-1**). This is where windows appear when you open apps or settings and where you can place desktop shortcuts to frequently-used apps.

Desktop shortcuts   Open app window

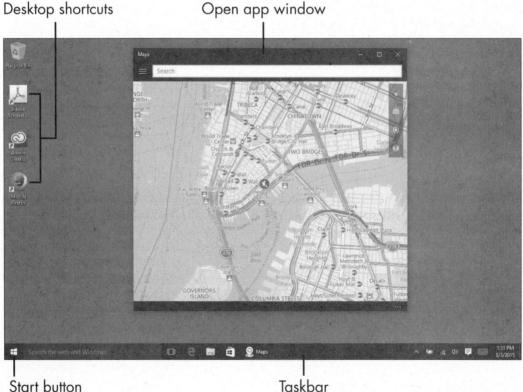

Start button   Taskbar

Figure 3-1

Additionally, the desktop contains a taskbar along the bottom that offers several tools for working with Windows settings and apps. Three items on the taskbar are new to Windows 10:

⟩ **Cortana:** This personal assistant is a sophisticated search feature that can return results from a web search, a search of your computer contents, and even apps, such as Calendar or Maps. You can also ask Cortana to take actions, such as sending email, setting an appointment, or opening an app. You can interact with Cortana by entering text or by speech.

⟩ **Task View:** This new view shows you all open apps on your desktop, and even allows you to create and view multiple desktops. For example, you might have one desktop with all your work apps open and one with all your games and entertainment apps open.

⟩ **Action Center:** This pane provides a list of notifications about such items as new emails or appointment reminders, and buttons for various settings, such as screen brightness and network connections.

Also, a Start button provides access to all apps and settings (see **Figure 3-2**).

Figure 3-2

Work with the Desktop

The desktop, your home base in Windows, is where you can get to everything Windows has to offer, any installed applications, and the Internet. **Figure 3-3** shows the desktop and some of the elements on it, including the following:

➠ The **taskbar** displays frequently used applications such as Microsoft Edge and File Explorer. It also shows currently open apps; you can click an icon to switch apps.

➠ The right end of the taskbar, the **notification area,** contains many commonly used functions such as the Action Center button, computer date and time settings, the network connections icon, and the icon to control system volume.

➠ The left end of the taskbar contains the Start button, Cortana's search field, and the Task View button.

➠ The **Recycle Bin** holds recently deleted items. It will empty itself when it reaches its maximum size (which you can modify by right-clicking the Recycle Bin and choosing Properties), or you empty it manually. Check out the task "Empty the Recycle Bin" later in this chapter for more about this.

➠ **Desktop shortcuts** are icons that reside on the desktop and provide a shortcut to opening a software program or file, much like tiles on the Start menu. Your computer usually comes with some shortcuts, such as the Recycle Bin and a browser shortcut, but you can also add or delete shortcuts. Double-click a desktop shortcut to launch the associated program. See the "Creating a Desktop Shortcut" task later in this chapter.

Start button   Task View button   Notification area

Cortana's search field

Figure 3-3

The desktop is always there as you open windows containing apps or settings to get your work done. If you make an app window as big as it can be (maximize it by clicking the Maximize button in the top-right corner, to the left of the Close button), you won't see the desktop, but you can go back to the desktop at any time by shrinking a window (minimizing it by clicking the Minimize button in the top-right corner) or closing the window (clicking the X button in the top-right corner). You can also press Alt+Tab simultaneously and to display all open apps as icons side-by-side.

Display the Start Menu

1. The Start menu provides access to all the installed apps and many of the settings for your computer. Click the Start button in the bottom-left corner of the desktop to display the Start menu (see **Figure 3**-4).

Figure 3-4

2. Click on an app, either in the list of Most Used Apps on the left of the Start menu or one of the tiles on the right to open an app. The app opens.

Use Task View to See Open Apps

1. Task View allows you to move among open apps easily and create multiple desktops. Click the Task View button to open Task View. The resulting view (see **Figure 3-5**) shows individual desktops on the bottom and all the open apps on the currently selected desktop.

 You can also open Task View by pressing Win+Tab.

2. Click any of the apps shown in Task View to work in that app.

3. When you want to switch to another open app, click the Task View button and then click the app that you want to display on the desktop.

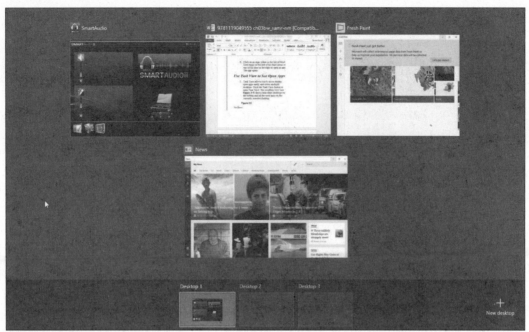

Figure 3-5

 You can also switch to another open app from the desktop by holding down the Alt key and clicking Tab repeatedly until the desired app is highlighted. Release the keys to work in the highlighted app.

Use the Snap Feature to Organize Apps on the Desktop

1. Windows 10 has a feature called Snap used to organize open apps on the desktop. Click the Task View button and then click an app you want to work with.

2. Press Win+→; the app window snaps to the right half of the screen and thumbnail images of any other open apps appear on the left half of the screen (see **Figure 3-6**).

3. Click another open app; the app window snaps to fill the left side of the screen (see **Figure 3-7**).

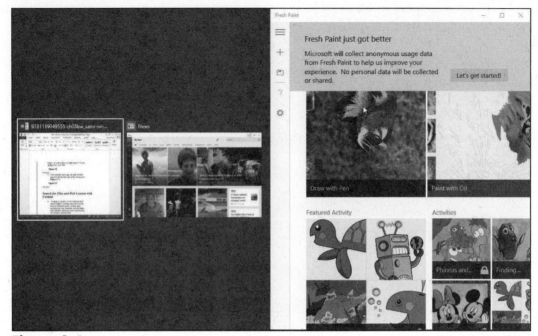

Figure 3-6

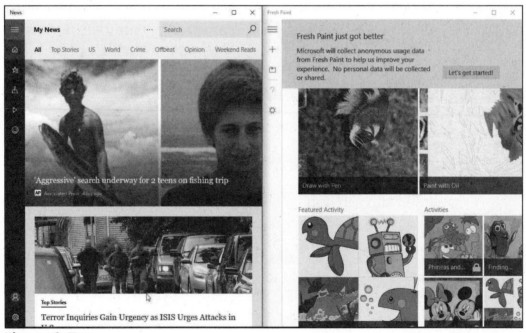

Figure 3-7

Search for Files and Web Content with Cortana

1. Cortana is, largely, a very sophisticated search feature. Cortana can return results from an Internet search, or from apps installed on your computer, such as Maps and Calendar. Begin to type a search term in Cortana's search field.

2. In the Cortana pane that appears (see **Figure** 3-8), click Search the Web or Search My Stuff (stuff stored on your computer) at the bottom of the pane if you want to narrow the search to only certain types of results.

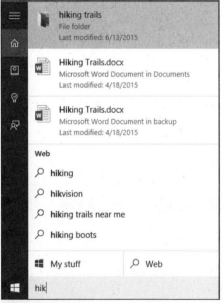

Figure 3-8

3. Click a suggested result to view an item related to the search term.

 See Chapter 7 to discover how Cortana can provide help and Chapter 9 for more about searching using Cortana, including interacting with the feature by speech.

Explore the Action Center

1. The Action Center is new in Windows 10. This pane contains notifications of events, such as appointment reminders and required system updates. From the desktop, click the Action Center button.

2. In the resulting Action Center pane (shown in **Figure** 3-9), read any notifications near the top of the pane.

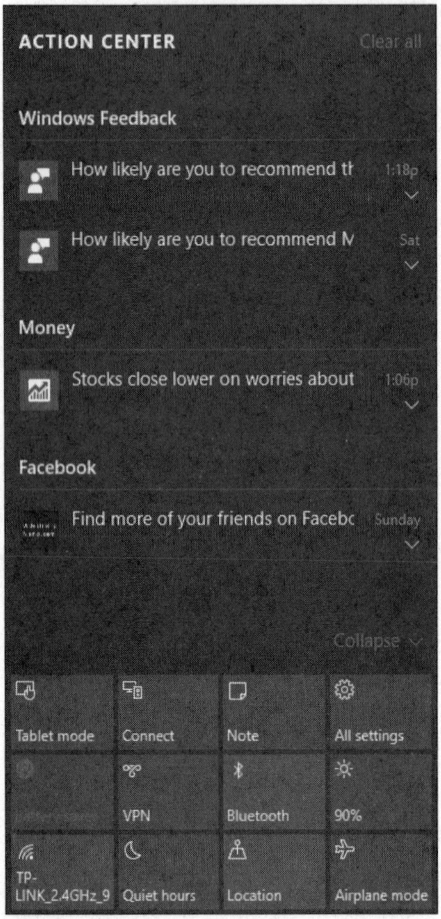

Figure 3-9

3. Click one of the Quick Action buttons near the bottom of the screen. The Quick Action buttons have the following types of functionality:

⟹ *Click a Quick Action button,* such as Tablet Mode, Wi-Fi, Bluetooth, Battery Saver, Location, Rotation Lock, or Airplane Mode to turn a feature on or off.

⟹ *Click Brightness* to raise or lower the brightness level.

⟹ *Click a Quick Action button,* such as All Settings or VPN to work with more settings in that category.

Find a File or Open an Application with File Explorer

1. File Explorer is a program you can use to find a file or folder by navigating through an outline of folders and subfolders. It's a great way to look for files on your computer. From the desktop, click the File Explorer button on the taskbar (it looks like a set of folders.)

2. In the resulting File Explorer window (shown in **Figure 3-10**), double-click a folder in the main window or in the list along the left side to open the folder.

3. The folder's contents are displayed. If necessary, open a series of folders in this manner until you locate the file you want.

4. When you find the file you want, double-click it to open it.

 To see different perspectives and information about files in File Explorer, click the View tab and choose one of the following options: Extra Large Icons, Large Icons, Medium Icons, or Small Icons for graphical displays, or choose Details to show details such as the last date files were modified.

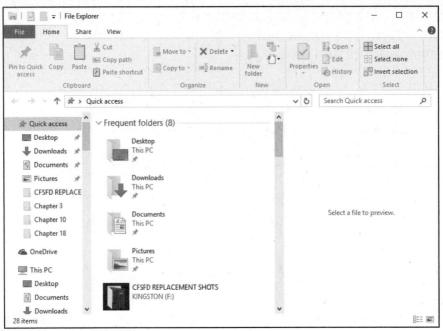

Figure 3-10

Work with Windows 10 Using a Touchscreen

If you have a touchscreen device, either a desktop computer, laptop, or tablet, you'll be glad to hear that Windows 10 is designed, to a great degree, to be used with a touchscreen. Table 3-1 lists several of the ways you can interact with your touchscreen computing device.

If you are using a 2-in-1 laptop, which allows you to remove the monitor from the keyboard, a pop-up message will ask if you want to enter Tablet mode. After clicking this pop-up, apps and the Start menu will display full-screen to make them more usable on the tablet. If you want to use this mode on a standard laptop or computer, click the Tablet Mode Quick Action button in Action Center.

Table 3-1	Touchscreen Gestures for Windows 10
Gesture	*Result*
Swipe up or down.	Move up or down on a web page.
Swipe left or right.	Move to the right or left to reveal additional content that extends beyond the screen in Windows or an app.
Swipe the right edge of the screen.	Display the Action Center.
Pinch to zoom in or out.	Zoom in or out on a page.
Tap.	Select an item.
Right-click.	Hold the screen until a small pop-up appears and then lift your finger to reveal the context-specific menu.
Swipe the left edge of the screen.	Open Task View.

Create Additional Desktops

1. If the work you do on your computer requires different sets of apps, you'll be glad to hear that you can create different desktops. For example, you might want one desktop containing financial apps and calculators, and another containing the Music app, an online radio app, and iTunes. To create multiple desktops, click the Task View button and then click the + button in the lower-right corner of the Task View.

2. In the resulting window (see **Figure 3-11**), you see thumbnails on the bottom of the window representing each desktop. Click the desktop you just created and then open the apps you want to appear in the new desktop.

 To return to another desktop, click the Task View button and then click the desired desktop button.

 Task View displays a button for each desktop you create. If there are more than six desktops, you can use right and left arrows, as shown in **Figure 3-12,** to scroll through the desktop thumbnails until you find the desktop you want.

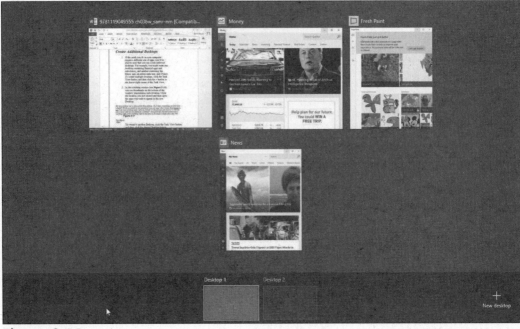

Figure 3-11

Figure 3-12

View All Apps in the Start Menu

1. Click the Start button to open the Start menu.

2. Click the All Apps button in the lower-left corner. In the resulting screen (see **Figure 3-13**), an alphabetical list of all apps installed on your computer is shown on the left side of the Start menu.

3. Scroll to find an app and click to open it.

 Some items in the All Apps list, for example Windows Accessories, have a downward arrow next to them, indicating that there are multiple apps in that category. Click the arrow to view the apps.

Figure 3-13

Empty the Recycle Bin

1. When you throw away junk mail, it's still in the house —
it's just in the Recycle Bin instead of on your desk. That's
the idea behind the Windows Recycle Bin. Your old files
sit there, and you can retrieve them until you empty it —
or until it reaches its size limit and Windows dumps a
few files. Right-click the Recycle Bin icon on the
Windows desktop and choose Empty Recycle Bin from
the menu that appears (see **Figure 3-14**).

2. In the confirmation dialog box that appears (see
Figure 3-15), click Yes. A progress dialog box appears,
indicating the contents are being deleted.

 After you empty the Recycle Bin, all files that were in it
are unavailable to you.

Figure 3-14

 Up until the moment you permanently delete items by performing the preceding steps, you can retrieve them from the Recycle Bin by double-clicking the Recycle Bin desktop icon. Select the item you want to retrieve and then click the Restore the Selected Items link on the Manage tab of the Recycle Bin ribbon.

Figure 3-15

 You can modify the Recycle Bin properties by right-clicking it and choosing Properties. In the dialog box that appears, you can change the maximum size for the Recycle Bin and whether to immediately delete files you move to the Recycle Bin. You can also deselect the option of having a confirmation dialog box appear when you delete Recycle Bin contents.

Add an App to the Start Menu

1. Click the Start button and then click All Apps.

2. Scroll to an app and right click it.

3. In the menu that appears (see **Figure** 3-16), click Pin to Start. A tile representing the app appears in the tile region of the Start menu

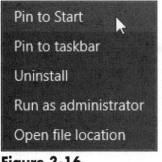

Pin to Start

Pin to taskbar

Uninstall

Run as administrator

Open file location

Figure 3-16

Creating a Desktop Shortcut

1. Shortcuts are handy little icons you can put on the desktop for quick access to items you use on a frequent basis. (See the earlier task, "Work with the Desktop," for an introduction to shortcuts.) To create a new shortcut, first click the Start button on the taskbar.

2. Locate an app and then click and drag it to the desktop, as shown in **Figure** 3-17.

3. Click and drag the shortcut that appears to the preferred location on the desktop (see **Figure** 3-18). Double-click the icon to open the app.

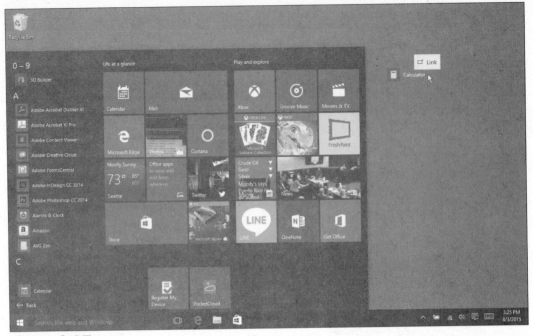

Figure 3-17

Figure 3-18

You can create a shortcut for a brand-new item by right-clicking the desktop, clicking New, and then clicking Shortcut. A dialog box opens that allows you to select an item to place there, such as a text document, an image, or a folder. Then double-click the shortcut that appears to open the item.

 If you want to remove a shortcut from the desktop, right click the shortcut and, in the menu that appears, click Delete.

Resize Windows

1. When you open an application window, it can be maximized to fill the whole screen, restored down to a smaller window, or minimized to an icon on the taskbar. With an application open and maximized, click the Restore Down button (the icon showing two overlapping windows) in the top-right corner of the program window (see **Figure 3-19**). The window reduces in size.

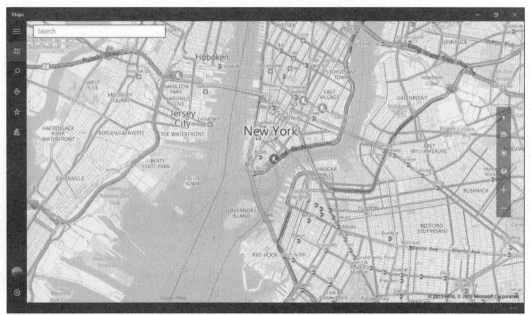

Figure 3-19

2. To enlarge a window that has been restored down, to again fill the screen, click the Maximize button. (*Note:* This button is in the same location as the Restore Down button; this button changes its name to one or the other, depending on whether you have the screen reduced in size or maximized. For many apps, a ScreenTip identifies the button when you hover your mouse pointer over it.)

3. Click the Minimize button (it's to the left of the Restore Down/Maximize button and looks like a dash or under-line) to minimize the window to an icon on the taskbar. To open the window again, just click the taskbar icon.

 With a window maximized, you can't move the win-dow. If you reduce a window in size, you can then click and hold the title bar to drag the window around the desktop, which is one way to view more than one window on your screen at the same time. You can also click and drag the corners of a reduced window to resize it to any size you want.

Setting Up Your Display

Chapter 4

You chose your designer Day Planner, paper clip holder, and solid maple inbox for your real-world desktop, right? Why shouldn't the Windows desktop give you the same flexibility to make things look the way you like? After all, this is the main work area of Windows, space that you traverse many, many times in a typical day. Take it from somebody who spends many hours in front of a computer: Customizing your computer interface pays off in increased productivity as well as decreased eyestrain.

You can modify tiles in the Start menu to rearrange them, resize them, or create tile groups. In addition, the desktop offers several customization options. To customize the desktop, you can do the following:

➠ Set up the desktop and lock screen to display background images and colors.

➠ Use screen saver settings to switch to a pretty animation when you've stopped working for a time.

➠ You can modify your *screen resolution* setting, which controls the visual crispness of the images your screen displays. (See Chapter 5 for more about resolution settings that help those with visual challenges.)

Customize Windows's Appearance

When you take your computer out of the box, Windows comes with certain preset, or default, settings such as the appearance of the desktop and a color scheme for items you see on your screen. Here are some of the things you can change about the Windows environment and why you might want to change them:

➡ **Desktop lock screen background:** As you work with your computer, you might find that changing the appearance of various elements on your screen not only makes them more pleasant to look at, but also helps you see the text and images more easily. You can change the graphic shown as the desktop background, even displaying your own picture there, and choose from a collection of background images for your lock screen.

➡ **Screen resolution:** You can adjust your screen resolution to not only affect the crispness of images on your screen but also cause the items on your screen to appear larger, which could help you if you have visual challenges. (See Chapter 5 for more about Windows features that help people with visual, hearing, or dexterity challenges.)

➡ **Themes:** Windows has built-in desktop *themes* that you can apply quickly. Themes save sets of elements that include menu appearance, background colors or patterns, screen savers, and even mouse cursors and system sounds. If you choose a theme and then modify the way your computer looks in some way — for example, by changing the color scheme — that change overrides the setting in the theme you last applied.

➡ **Screen savers:** These animations appear after your computer remains inactive for a specified time. In the early days of personal computers, screen savers helped to keep monitors from burning out from constant use. Today, people use screen savers to automatically conceal what they're doing from passersby or just to enjoy the pretty picture when they take a break.

Set Your Screen's Resolution

1. Changing screen resolution can make items onscreen easier to see. Right-click the desktop.

2. In the menu that appears, click Display Settings.

3. In the resulting window, scroll down and click Advanced Display Settings.

4. In the resulting Advanced Display Settings window, click the arrow in the Resolution drop-down box (shown in **Figure 4-1**), select a higher or lower resolution, and then click Apply.

5. In the box that appears, click Keep Changes to accept the new screen resolution and then click the Close button to close the window.

 Higher resolutions, such as 1400 x 1250, produce smaller, crisper images. Lower resolutions, such as 800 x 600, produce larger, somewhat jagged images. The upside of higher resolution is that more fits on your screen; the downside is that words and graphics are smaller and can therefore be hard to see.

 The Advanced Display Settings window contains links under Related Settings that take you to a window where you can work with color management and monitor settings.

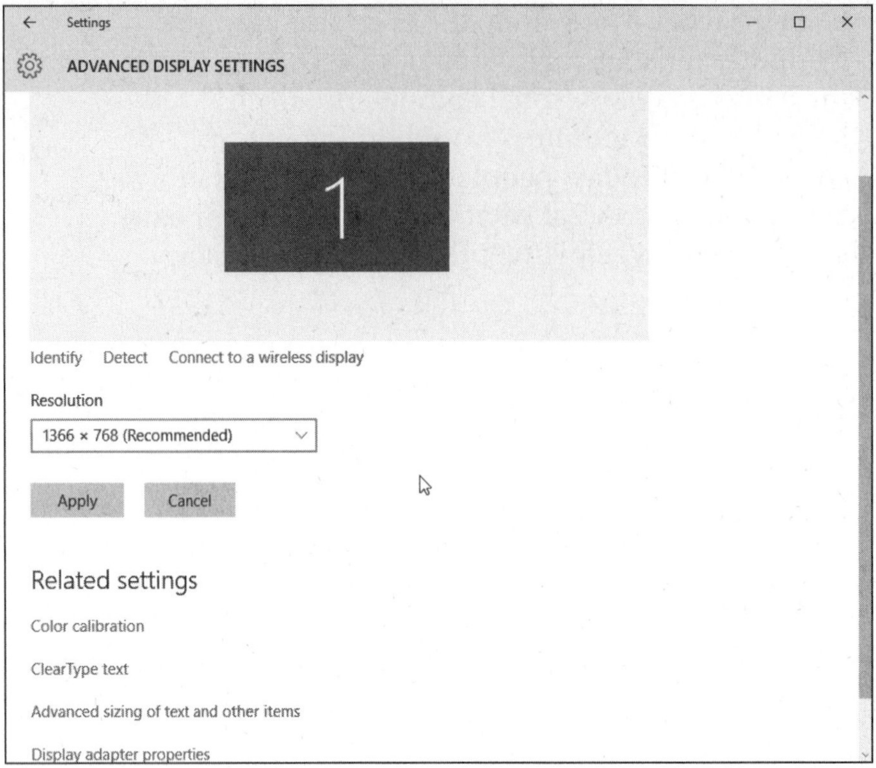

Settings

⚙ ADVANCED DISPLAY SETTINGS

— □ ×

1

Identify   Detect   Connect to a wireless display

Resolution

1366 × 768 (Recommended)   ⌄

[Apply]   [Cancel]

Related settings

Color calibration

ClearType text

Advanced sizing of text and other items

Display adapter properties

Figure 4-1

Remember that you can also use your View settings in most software programs to get a larger or smaller view of your documents without having to change your screen's resolution.

Change the Desktop Background and Color

1. Windows 10 offers several preset background patterns and color sets you can choose from the PC Settings. Click the Start button and then click Settings.

2. In the Settings window, click Personalization. In the resulting Personalization window, click Background in the left panel. (See **Figure 4-2**.)

3. Click the Background drop-down list and choose a category, such as Solid Color or Picture.

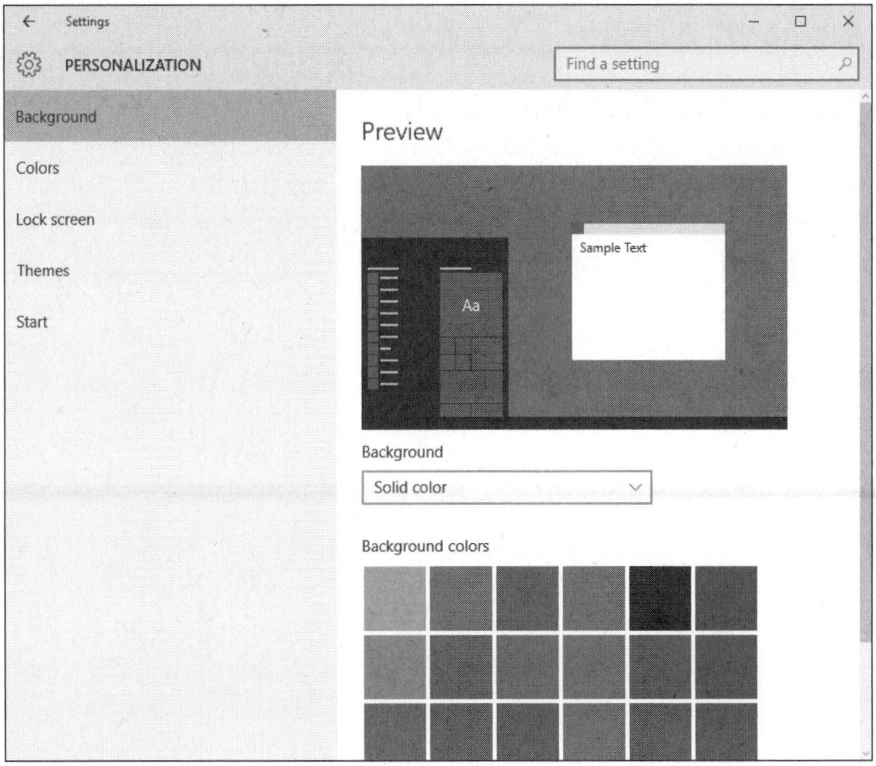

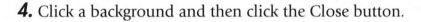

Figure 4-2

4. Click a background and then click the Close button.

 Some colors are easier on the eyes than others. For example, green is more restful to look at than purple. Choose a color scheme that's pleasant to look at and easy on the eyes!

 You can change the background color of the Start menu, Taskbar, and Action Center. Click the Start button ⇨ Settings ⇨ Personalization and then click Colors in the left panel. Click to turn Automatically Pick an Accent Color from My Background to Off and then select an Accent Color. This sets the Accent color throughout Windows. Click Show Color on Start, Taskbar, and Action Center to On to set the background color for these regions.

Change the Lock Screen Picture

1. You can choose a Windows 10 picture for your lock screen (the screen that appears when your computer goes to sleep) or use one of your own pictures for the lock screen background. Click the Start button⇨Settings, and then click Personalization.

2. Click Lock Screen in the left panel. Click the Background drop-down list and choose a category of background, such as Picture (to choose from Windows images or one of your own) or Windows Spotlight for the preset Windows image (see **Figure** 4-3).

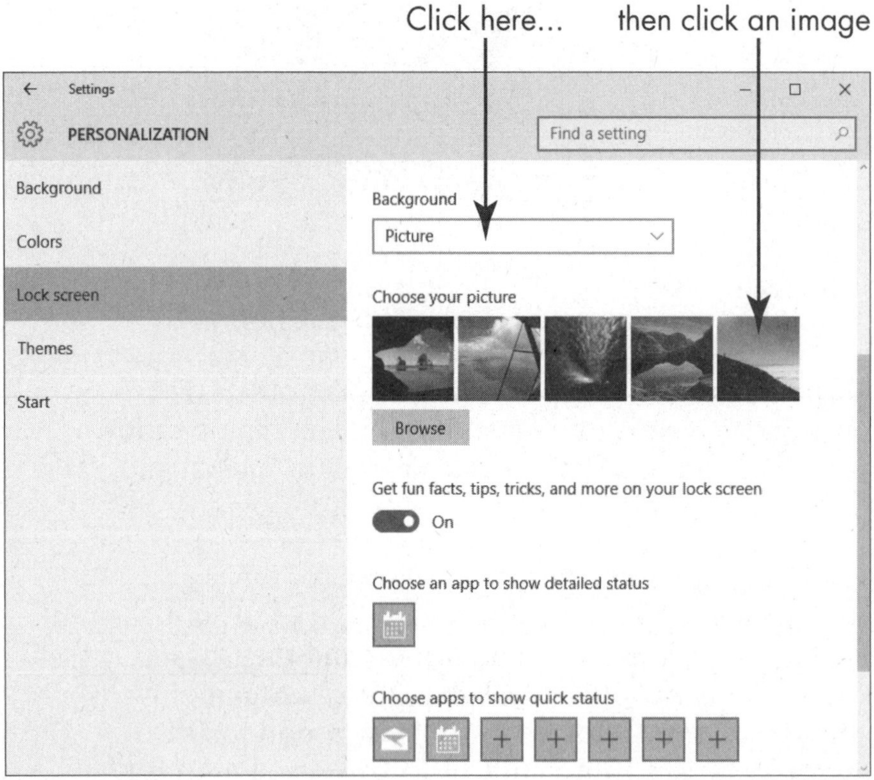

Click here...   then click an image

Figure 4-3

3. Click one of the pictures displayed, or click Browse to choose another picture.

4. If you chose to browse for one of your own pictures, from the Pictures folder that displays click a picture to use. If the picture is located in another folder, click the Go Up link to browse other folders.

5. Click the Choose Picture button.

 You can also choose a few apps that you want to keep running when your lock screen appears. On the Lock Screen tab shown in Figure 4-3, just click one of the plus signs to display the apps that are available to display, such as Calendar or Mail.

Change Your Account Picture

1. Windows 10 allows you to assign a unique picture to each user account you create. When you perform these steps, you should be logged in as the user for whom you want to change the account picture; see Chapter 2 for more about this procedure. Click the Start button and then click Settings.

2. Click Accounts. The Accounts screen appears (see **Figure** 4-4).

3. At this point, you can do one of two things:

- **Click the Browse button** and choose a picture from the files that appear (see **Figure** 4-5); click the Go Up link to explore other folders on your computer. Click the picture and then click the Choose Picture button to apply it to the active account.

Click here to choose a photo

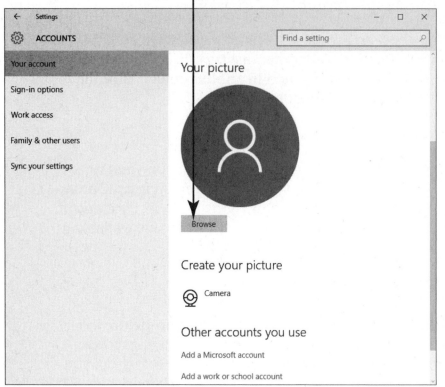

Figure 4-4

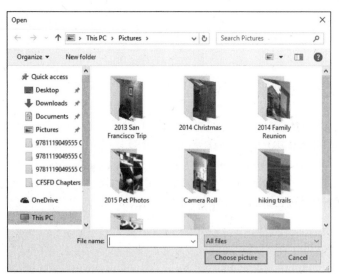

Figure 4-5

- **Click the Camera button** under Create Your Picture and in the Camera app that opens (see **Figure** 4-6) snap a picture of a person or object near your computer's *webcam* (a built-in camera device). Click the Camera button to take the picture, and then click the Apply button (shaped like a check mark) to apply it to the active account.

Figure 4-6

 Many computers allow you to switch between a front- and a rear-facing camera to give you more options for taking pictures of objects around you. While in the Camera app, just click the Change Camera button to do this — if your computer has two cameras.

Choose a Desktop Theme

1. Themes apply several color and image settings at once. Right-click the desktop and choose Personalize. In the resulting window, click Themes in the left panel and then click Theme Settings in the right panel. The Personalization window opens.

2. In the resulting Personalization window, shown in
Figure 4-7, click to select a theme. Theme categories
include the following:

- **My Themes:** Uses whatever settings you have and
  saves them with that name.

- **Windows Default Themes:** Offers you the default
  Windows theme and themes related to Nature,
  Landscapes, Light Auras, and so on.

- **High Contrast Themes** offers a variety of easy-to-
  read contrast settings in a variety of themes.

Select a desktop theme

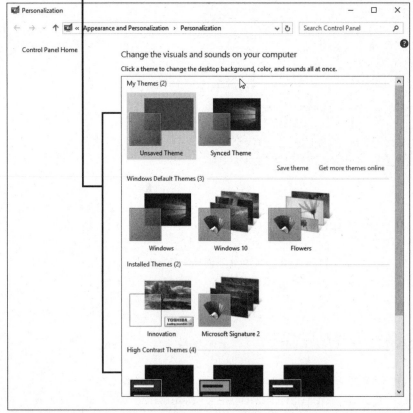

Figure 4-7

3. Click the Close button to close the dialog box.

 Themes save sets of elements that include menu appearance, background colors or patterns, screen savers, and even mouse cursors and sounds. If you modify any of these individually — for example, by changing the screen saver to another one — that change overrides the setting in the theme you last applied.

 You can save custom themes. Simply select a theme and make any changes to it using the various Appearance and Personalization settings options. Then, in the Personalization dialog box, right-click the Unsaved theme, and then click Save Theme from the menu that appears. In the resulting dialog box, give your new theme a name and click Save. It will now appear on the Theme list with that name.

Set Up a Screen Saver

1. If you want an animated sequence to appear when your computer isn't in use for a period of time, set up a screen saver. Right-click the desktop and choose Personalize. In the resulting Personalization window, click Lock Screen in the left panel, then scroll down and click Screen Saver Settings in the right panel to display the Screen Saver Settings dialog box, as shown in **Figure 4-8.**

2. From the Screen Saver drop-down list, choose a screen saver.

3. Use the arrows in the Wait *xx* Minutes text box to set the number of inactivity minutes that Windows 10 waits before displaying the screen saver.

4. Click the Preview button to peek at your screen saver of choice. When you're happy with your settings, click OK.

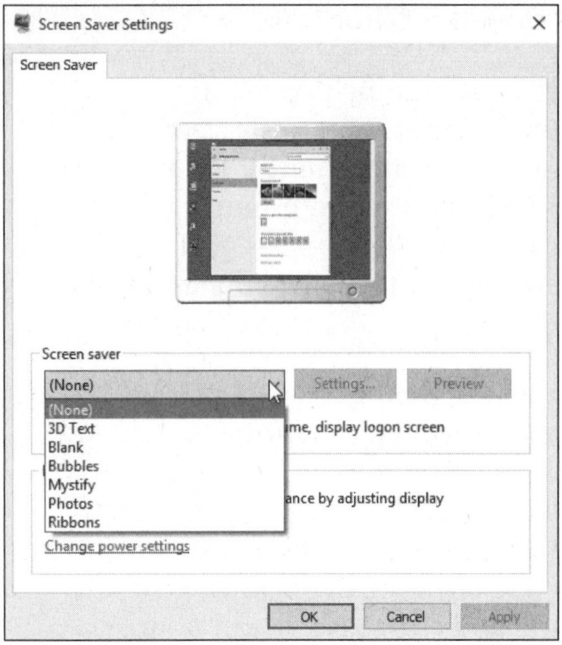

Figure 4-8

Name Tile Groups

1. In the Start menu, tiles represent apps. These tiles are organized in groups, such as Explore Windows. If you like, you can rename the group. Click the Start button to display the Start menu.

2. Click a group title; it opens for editing (see **Figure** 4-9).

3. Press the Backspace button on your keyboard to delete the current title and then type a new title.

4. Click anywhere outside the title to save the new name.

If you want to use the Start menu full screen, right-click the desktop and choose Personalize. In the resulting Personalization window, click Start in the left panel and then click the Use Start Full Screen switch to turn it on. When you click the Start button, the Start menu will open in full screen. You can click the Start button again to return to the desktop.

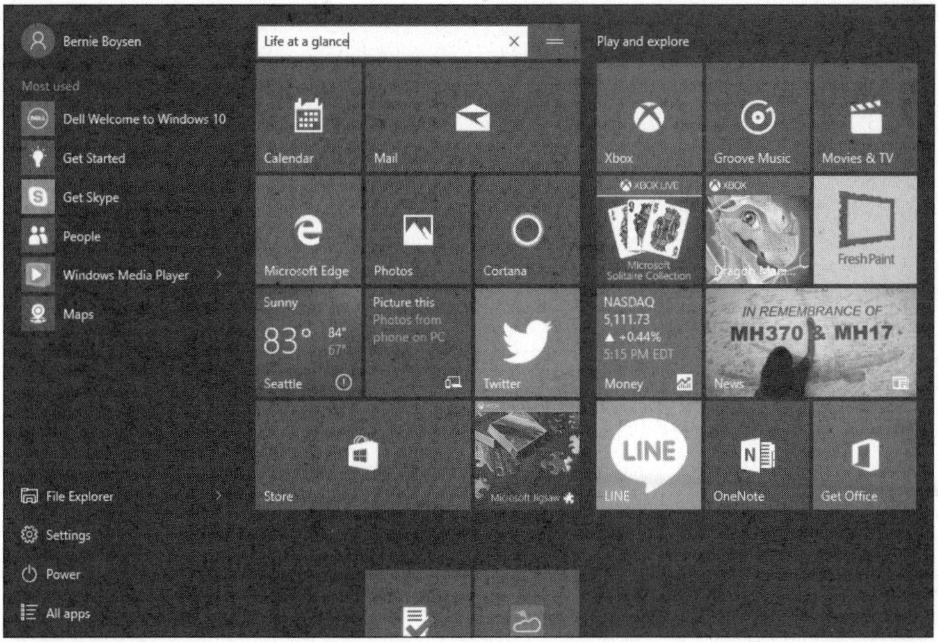

Figure 4-9

Rearrange Tiles in the Start Menu

1. If you want the apps you use most often near the top of the Start menu, you can rearrange tiles. Click the Start button to open the Start menu.

2. Click, hold, and drag a tile to a new location.

3. Release the tile and it moves to its new spot in the Start menu.

> If you want to move a whole group of tiles, click the title just above the tiles, such as Explore Windows or Everyday Apps. Click the button labelled with two stripes on the right side of the group title bar and drag the group to a new location. Release the mouse to finish the move.

Resize Tiles

1. Tiles come in different sizes by default. You may want to resize them to be smaller to fit more in the Start menu or larger to make a more frequently used app easier to find. Click the Start button to open the Start menu.

2. Right-click a tile. In the pop-up menu that appears (see **Figure 4-10**), click Resize.

3. From the side menu that appears, choose Small, Medium, Wide, or Large.

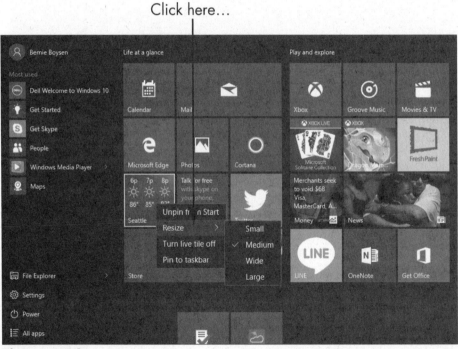

Click here…

Figure 4-10

 If you don't need a tile that Windows displays by default, it's simple to remove it from the Start menu. Right-click a tile and choose Unpin from Start in the menu shown in Figure 4-10; the tile is removed.

Getting Help with Vision, Hearing, and Dexterity Challenges

*P*eople don't always know right off the bat how to get along when they meet some-one new. Similarly, sometimes Windows has to be taught how to behave. For example, it doesn't know that somebody using it has a vision challenge that requires special help, or that a user prefers a certain mouse cursor or has difficulty using a keyboard.

Somebody taught you manners, but Windows depends on you to make settings that customize its behavior. This is good news for you because the ability to customize Windows gives you a lot of flexibility in how you interact with it.

Here's what you can do to customize Windows to work with physical challenges:

➠ Control features that help visually chal-lenged users to work with a computer, such as setting a higher contrast, using Narrator to read the onscreen text aloud, or increasing the size of text onscreen.

➠ Work with the Speech Recognition feature, which allows you to input data into a document using speech rather than a keyboard or mouse.

➠ Modify the mouse functionality for left-handed use, change the cursor to sport a certain look, or make viewing the cursor as it moves around your screen easier.

➠ Work with keyboard settings that make input easier for those who are challenged by physical conditions, such as carpal tunnel syndrome or arthritis.

Use Tools for the Visually Challenged

1. You can set up Windows to use higher screen contrast to make things easier to see, speak descriptions to you rather than make you read text, and more. In the Start menu, click Settings; in the Settings window, click Ease of Access.

2. In the Ease of Access window (as shown in **Figure 5-1**), click the Maximize button in the top-right corner and then click any of the first three categories on the left to make the following settings:

   • **Narrator:** The Narrator reads onscreen text, words you type, and announces actions you take, such as changing the Narrator speed slider. Click Narrator and then click the Narrator toggle switch in the right pane to On. Click the Choose a Voice drop-down list to display the available voices and click one. Click and drag the Speed and Pitch sliders to adjust the voice characteristics. The changes are applied immediately.

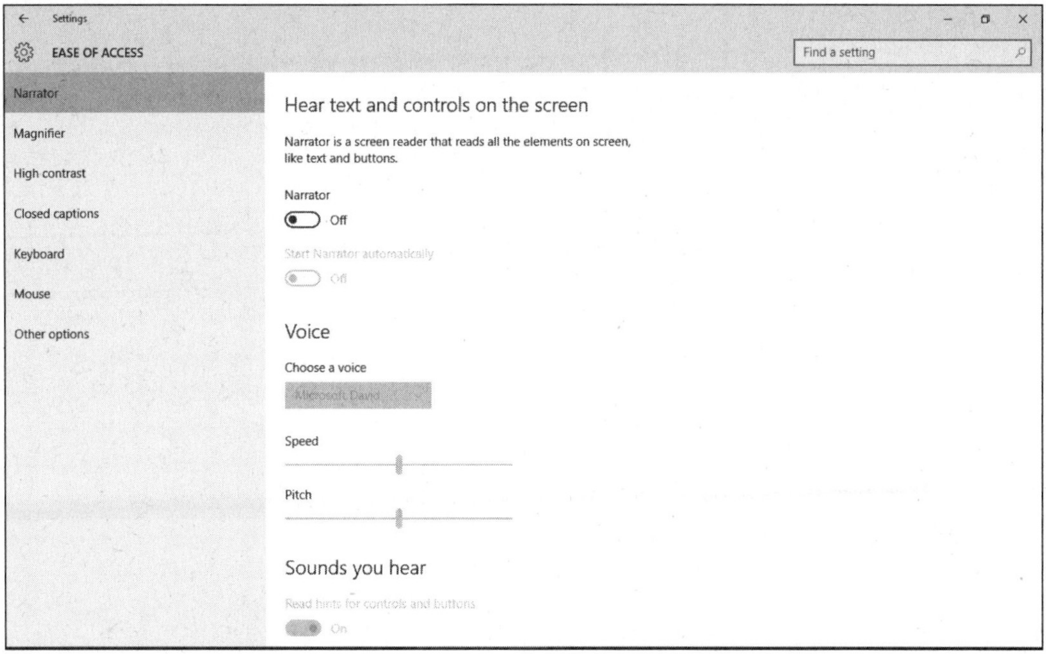

Figure 5-1

- **Magnifier:** Magnifier (see **Figure 5-2**) provides three types of magnified views. Click Magnifier in the left pane and then click the Magnifier toggle switch in the right pane to turn Magnifier on. Click the Start Magnifier Automatically toggle switch to On if you want the Magnifier to start when you sign in to Windows. To choose a view, click the Magnifying Glass icon to open the Magnifier toolbar, and then click Views. In the drop-down list, choose from among the available views:

  - *Full Screen:* The Magnifier fills the screen.

  - *Lens:* A rectangular magnification lens you can move around the screen.

  - *Docked:* A rectangular magnification region you can dock in one location.

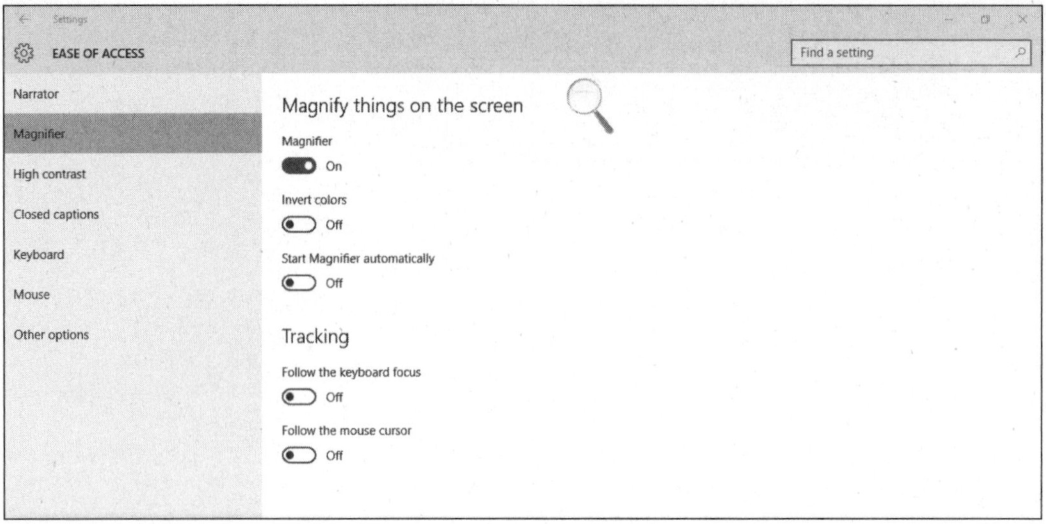

Figure 5-2

- **High Contrast:** This setting provides four color schemes that can make your screen easier to read. Click High Contrast in the left pane and then click the Choose a Theme drop-down list in the right pane to show the themes. Click one of the themes to select it, and then click Apply.

 Most keyboards include a series of function keys across the top numbered F1 through F12. Though the number of function keys varies, two of them typically are designated for adjusting the brightness of your screen up or down. Locate the keys that show an asterisk-like icon. Press the darker icon key to display a slider that you can use to dim the screen or press the lighter icon key to display a slider to brighten the display.

3. When you finish making settings, click the Close button to close the window.

Replace Sounds with Visual Cues

1. Sometimes Windows alerts you to events with sounds. If you have hearing challenges, however, you might prefer to get visual cues. Enter "Replace sounds with visual cues" in Cortana's search field and then press Enter.

2. In the resulting Use Text or Visual Alternatives for Sounds dialog box (see **Figure 5-3**), choose any of the following settings:

- **Turn On Visual Notifications for Sounds (Sound Sentry).** If you select this check box, Windows will give a visual alert when a sound plays.

- **Choose Visual Warning.** These warnings essentially flash a portion of your screen to alert you to an event. Choose one option.

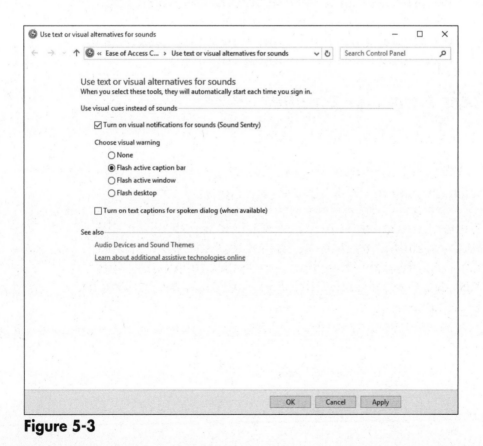

Figure 5-3

- **Turn On Text Captions for Spoken Dialog (When Available).** Select this check box to control text captions for any spoken words. *Note:* This isn't available with every application you use.

3. To save the new settings, click OK, and then click the Close button.

 Visual cues are useful if you're hard of hearing and don't always pick up system sounds alerting you to error messages or a device disconnect. After the setting is turned on, it's active until you go back to the Use Text or Visual Alternatives for Sounds dialog box and turn it off.

 This may seem obvious, but if you're hard of hearing, you may simply want to increase the volume for your speakers. You can do this by using the volume adjustment in a program such as the Groove Music app (see Chapter 18) or by modifying your system volume by tapping the Volume tool on the taskbar and then using the slider to adjust volume.

Make Text Larger or Smaller

1. In the Start menu, click Settings.

2. In the resulting Settings window, click System and then click Display in the left pane (see **Figure** 5-4).

3. Under Customize Your Display, click and drag the slider to the right to increase the size of text and other items. Click Apply; a message box appears asking if you want to sign out now or later. Click Sign Out Now to implement the change.

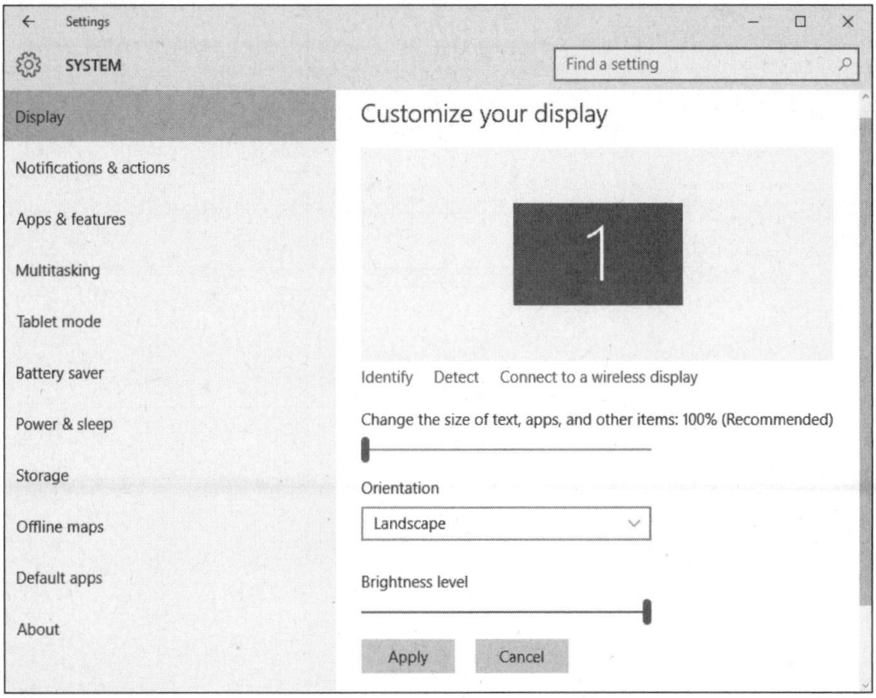

Figure 5-4

Set Up Speech Recognition

1. If you have dexterity challenges from a condition such as arthritis, you might prefer to speak commands, using a technology called *speech recognition,* rather than type them. Attach a desktop microphone or headset to your computer, enter "Speech recognition" in Cortana's search field, and then press Enter.

2. The Welcome to Speech Recognition message (see **Figure 5-5**) appears; click Next to continue. (*Note:* If you've used Speech Recognition before, this message won't appear. These steps are for first-time setup).

3. In the resulting window (shown in **Figure 5-6**), select the type of microphone that you're using and then click Next. The next screen tells you how to place and use the microphone for optimum results. Click Next.

× Set up Speech Recognition

Welcome to Speech Recognition

Speech Recognition allows you to control your computer by voice.

Using only your voice, you can start programs, open menus, click buttons and other objects on the screen, dictate text into documents, and write and send e-mails. Just about everything you do with your keyboard and mouse can be done with only your voice.

First, you will set up this computer to recognize your voice.

Note: You will be able to control your computer by voice once you have completed this setup wizard.

Next   Cancel

Figure 5-5

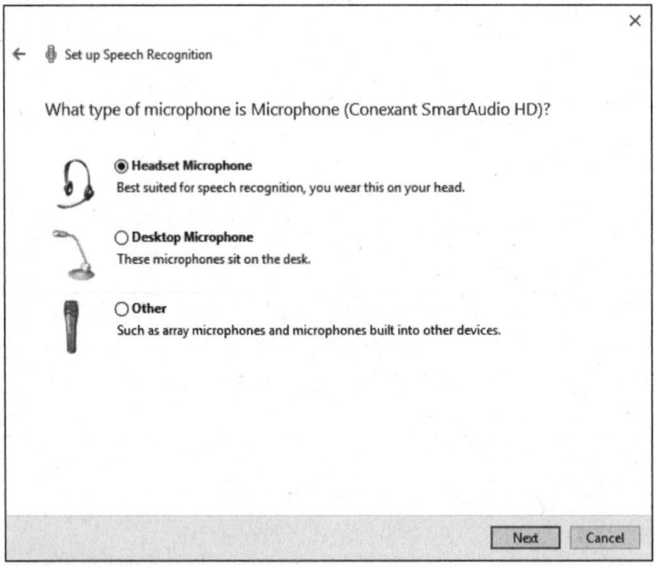

× Set up Speech Recognition

What type of microphone is Microphone (Conexant SmartAudio HD)?

◉ **Headset Microphone**
Best suited for speech recognition, you wear this on your head.

○ **Desktop Microphone**
These microphones sit on the desk.

○ **Other**
Such as array microphones and microphones built into other devices.

Next   Cancel

Figure 5-6

4. In the following window (see **Figure 5-7**), read the sample sentence aloud. When you're done, click Next. A dialog box appears telling you that your microphone is now set up. Click Next.

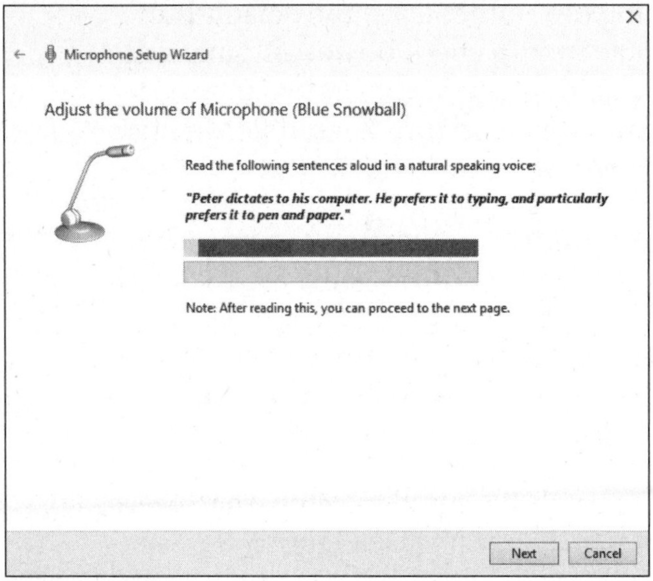

Figure 5-7

> During the Speech Recognition setup procedure, you're given the option of printing out commonly used commands. It's a good idea to do this, as speech commands aren't always second nature!

5. A dialog box confirms that your microphone is set up. Click Next. In the resulting dialog box, choose whether to enable or disable *document review,* in which Windows examines your documents and email to help it recognize your speech patterns. Click Next.

6. In the resulting dialog box, choose either manual activation mode, where you can use a mouse, pen, or keyboard to turn the feature on, or voice activation, which is useful if you have difficulty manipulating devices because of arthritis or a hand injury. Click Next.

7. In the resulting screen, if you want to view and/or print a list of Speech Recognition commands, click the View Reference Sheet button and read or print the reference information, and then click the Close button to close that window. Click Next to proceed.

8. In the resulting dialog box, either leave the default Run Speech Recognition at Startup check box to automatically turn on Speech Recognition when you start your computer or deselect that setting and turn Speech Recognition on manually each time you need it. Click Next.

9. The final dialog box informs you that you can now control the computer by voice, and offers you a Start Tutorial button to help you practice voice commands. Click that button and follow the instructions to move through it, or click Skip Tutorial to skip the tutorial and leave the Speech Recognition setup.

10. When you leave the Speech Recognition setup, the Speech Recognition control panel appears (see **Figure 5-8**). Say, "Start listening" to activate the feature if you used voice activation, or click the Microphone on the Speech Recognition control panel if you chose manual activation. You can now begin using spoken commands to work with your computer.

Figure 5-8

 To stop Speech Recognition, say, "Stop listening" or click the Microphone button on the Speech Recognition control panel. To start the Speech Recognition feature again, click the Microphone button on the Speech Recognition control panel.

Modify How Your Keyboard Works

1. If your hands are a bit stiff or you have carpal tunnel problems, you might look into changing how your keyboard works. Open the Start menu, and click Settings ⇨ Ease of Access ⇨ Keyboard.

2. In the resulting dialog box (see **Figure 5-9**), make any of
these settings:

- **Sticky Keys:** Enable this setting if you'd like to
  press keys in keystroke combinations one at a
  time, rather than in combination.

- **Toggle Keys:** You can set up Windows to play a
  sound when you press Caps Lock, Num Lock, or
  Scroll Lock (which I do all the time by mistake!).

- **Filter Keys:** If you sometimes press a key very
  lightly or press it so hard it activates twice, you can
  use the **Turn On Filter Keys** setting to change
  repeat rates to adjust for that. Use the Set Up Filter
  Keys link to fine-tune settings if you make this
  choice.

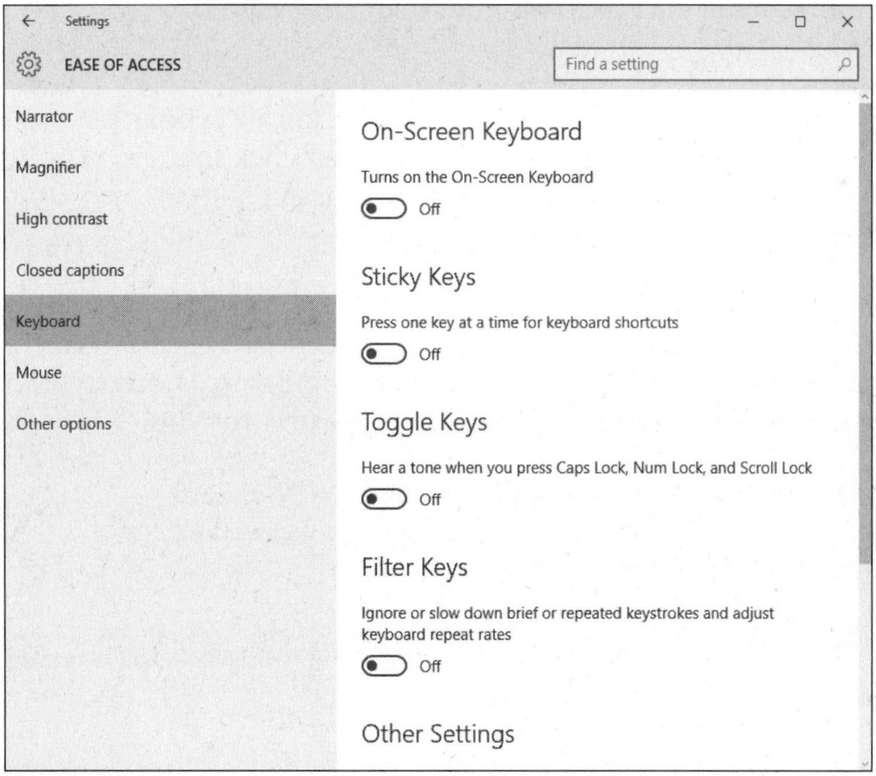

Figure 5-9

3. Click the Close button to close the Ease of Access Center.

 You can visit the Types of Assistive Technology Products page on the Microsoft website (www. microsoft.com/enable/at/types.aspx) and find out about products that might help you if you have a visual, hearing, or input-related disability.

 Every keyboard has its own unique feel. If your keyboard isn't responsive and you have a keyboard-challenging condition, you might also try different keyboards to see if one works better for you than another.

Use the Onscreen Keyboard Feature

1. Clicking keys with your mouse may be easier than using a regular keyboard. To use the onscreen keyboard, open the Start menu, click Settings, and then click Ease of Access.

2. In the resulting Ease of Access dialog box, click Keyboard in the left pane (see **Figure 5-10**), and then click the On-Screen Keyboard toggle to On. The onscreen keyboard appears (see **Figure 5-11**).

 The onscreen keyboard that displays after the previous steps has different features than the standard onscreen keyboard used on touchscreen computers. If you have a touchscreen computer, try both styles of onscreen keyboard to decide which works best for you.

3. Open a document in any application where you can enter text, and then click the keys on the onscreen keyboard to make entries.

 To use keystroke combinations (such as Ctrl+Z), click the first key (in this case, Ctrl), and then click the second key (Z). You don't have to hold down the first key as you do with a regular keyboard.

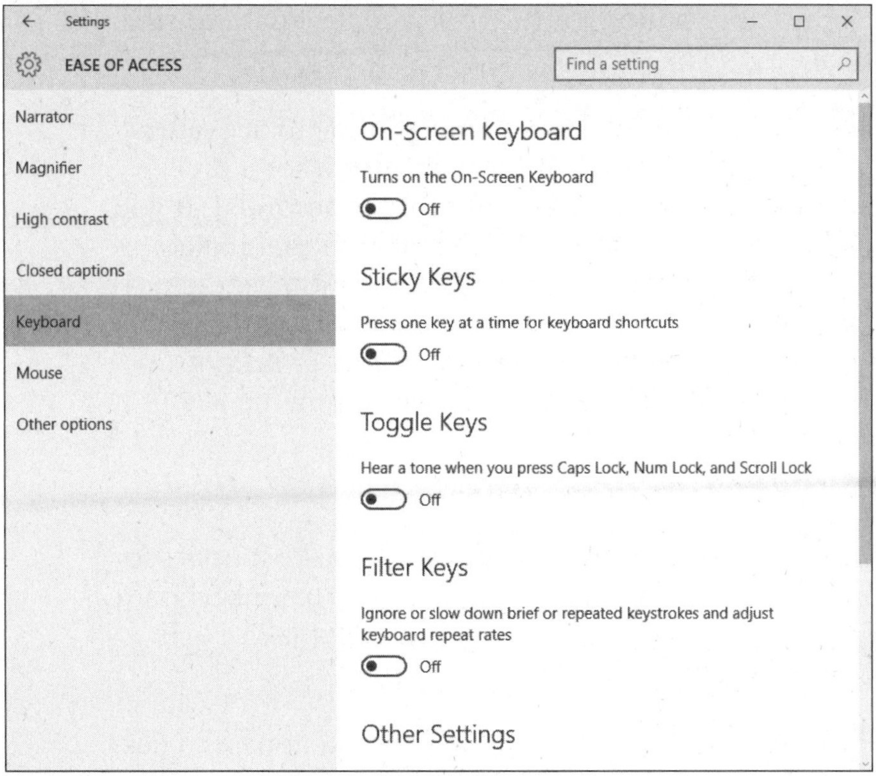

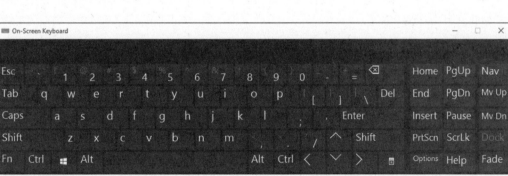

Figure 5-10

Figure 5-11

_4._ To change settings, such as turning on the numeric keypad or hearing a click sound when you press a key, click the Options key on the onscreen keyboard, choose one of the options shown in the Options dialog box, and then click OK.

5. Click the Close button on the onscreen keyboard to stop using it.

 You can set up the Hover typing mode to activate a key after you hover your mouse over it for a pre-defined period of time (*x* number of seconds). If you have arthritis or some other condition that makes clicking your mouse difficult, this option can help you enter text. Click the Hover over Keys item in the Options dialog box and use the slider to set how long you have to hover before activating the key.

Set Up Keyboard Repeat Rates

1. Adjusting your keyboard settings might make it easier for people with dexterity challenges to type. To see keyboard options, enter "Keyboard settings" in Cortana's search field and then press Enter.

2. In the Keyboard Properties dialog box that appears, click the Speed tab (see **Figure 5-12**) and drag the sliders to adjust the two Character Repeat settings, which do the following:

- **Repeat Delay:** Affects the amount of time it takes before a typed character is typed again when you hold down a key.

- **Repeat Rate:** Adjusts how quickly a character repeats when you hold down a key after the first repeat character appears.

 If you want to see how the Character Repeat settings work in action, click in the text box below the two settings and hold down a key to see a demonstration.

3. Drag the slider in the Cursor Blink Rate section. This affects cursors, such as the insertion line that appears in text.

Figure 5-12

4. Click OK to save and apply changes and close the dialog box.

If you have trouble with motion (for example, because of arthritis or carpal tunnel syndrome), you might find that you can adjust these settings to make it easier for you to get your work done. For example, if you can't pick up your finger quickly from a key, a slower repeat rate might save you from typing more instances of a character than you'd intended.

Customize Mouse Behavior

1. To avoid having to move your mouse too often, instead of moving your mouse with your hand, you can use your keyboard to move the mouse cursor. In the Start menu, click Settings ⇨ Ease of Access, and then click Mouse in the left pane. The dialog box shown in **Figure 5-13** opens.

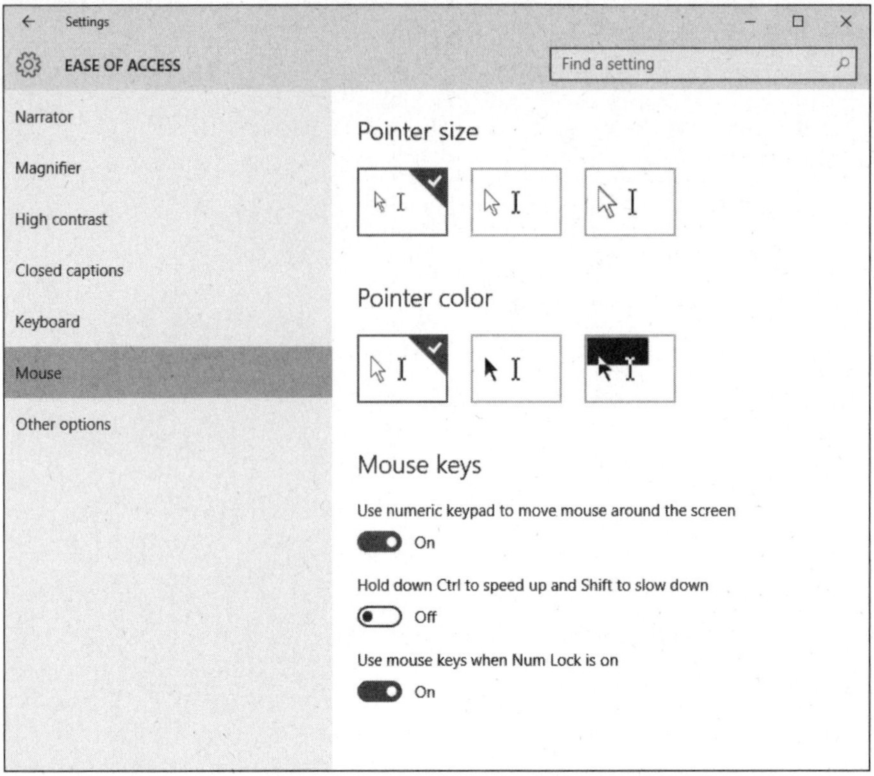

← Settings   − □ ×

⚙ EASE OF ACCESS   Find a setting   🔎

Narrator

Magnifier   Pointer size

High contrast

Closed captions

Keyboard   Pointer color

Mouse

Other options

                                   Mouse keys

                                   Use numeric keypad to move mouse around the screen
                                   ⬤▭ On

                                   Hold down Ctrl to speed up and Shift to slow down
                                   ▭⬤ Off

                                   Use mouse keys when Num Lock is on
                                   ⬤▭ On

Figure 5-13

2. To use the numeric keypad to move your mouse cursor on your screen, click the toggle setting labeled Use Numeric Keypad to Move Mouse around the Screen to On.

 To understand how to use the numeric keypad to move the mouse, visit the Microsoft Accessibility Tutorial web page at www.microsoft.com/enable/training/windows10/use-numeric-keypad.aspx.

3. To control the speed at which the cursor moves on the screen, turn on the Hold Down Ctrl to Speed Up and Shift to Slow Down toggle settings.

4. Click the Close button.

 If you're left-handed, in the Start Menu click Settings ⇨ Devices ⇨ Mouse & Touchpad. In the resulting dialog box, click the Select Your Primary

Button drop-down menu and click to select Right. This setting makes the right mouse button handle all the usual left-button functions, such as clicking and dragging, and the left button handle the typical right-hand functions, such as displaying shortcut menus. This helps left-handed people use the mouse more easily.

 If you want to modify the behavior of the mouse pointer, in the Start menu click Settings ⇨ Devices ⇨ Mouse & Touchpad and then scroll down and click Additional Mouse Options. In the resulting Mouse Properties dialog box, click the Pointer Options tab to set the *pointer speed* (how quickly you can drag the mouse pointer around your screen), activate the Snap To feature that automatically moves the mouse cursor to the default choice in a dialog box, or modify the little trails that appear when you drag the pointer.

Change the Cursor

1. If you're having trouble finding the mouse cursor on your screen, you might want to enlarge it or change its color. In the Start menu, click Settings. In the Settings window, click Ease of Access, and then click Mouse in the left pane.

2. In the resulting dialog box, as shown in **Figure** 5-14, click one of the Pointer Size icons to set the size of the cursor. The size of the cursor changes.

3. Click one of the Pointer Color icons to set the cursor color. The cursor changes immediately.

4. Click the Close button to close the Mouse dialog box.

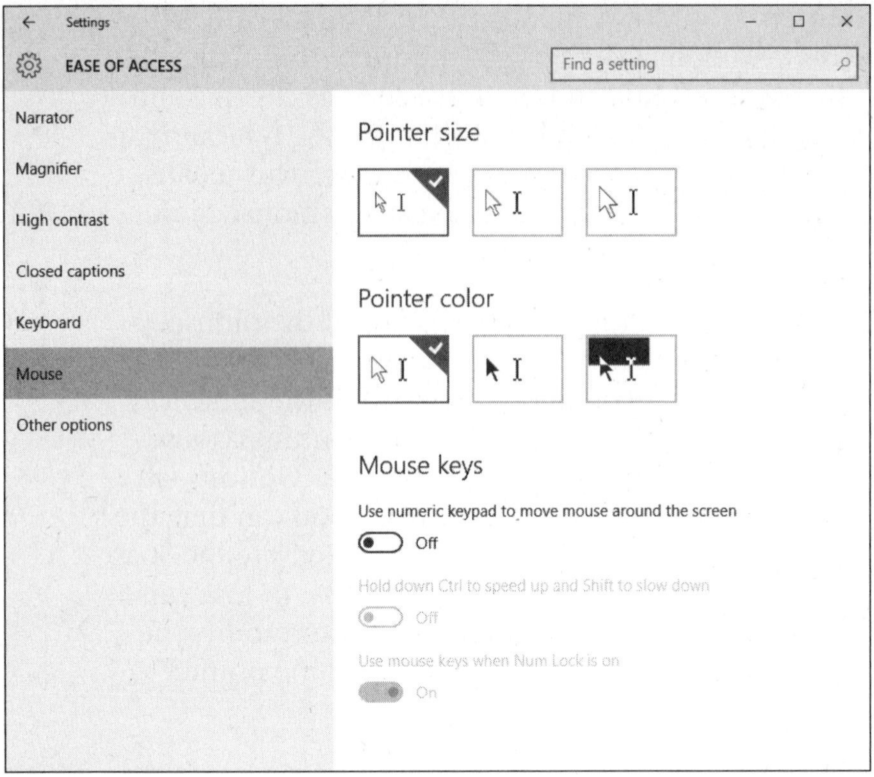

Figure 5-14

Make Your Touch Visible

1. If you're having trouble touching the correct check box on your touchscreen monitor, you can enable a visual feedback feature that shows where you touched the screen. Open the Start menu, click Settings ⇨ Ease of Access, and then click Other Options in the left pane.

2. In the resulting dialog box, shown in **Figure 5-15,** scroll down to Touch Feedback and then click the Show Visual Feedback When I Click the Screen toggle switch to On. The Touch Feedback feature is turned on.

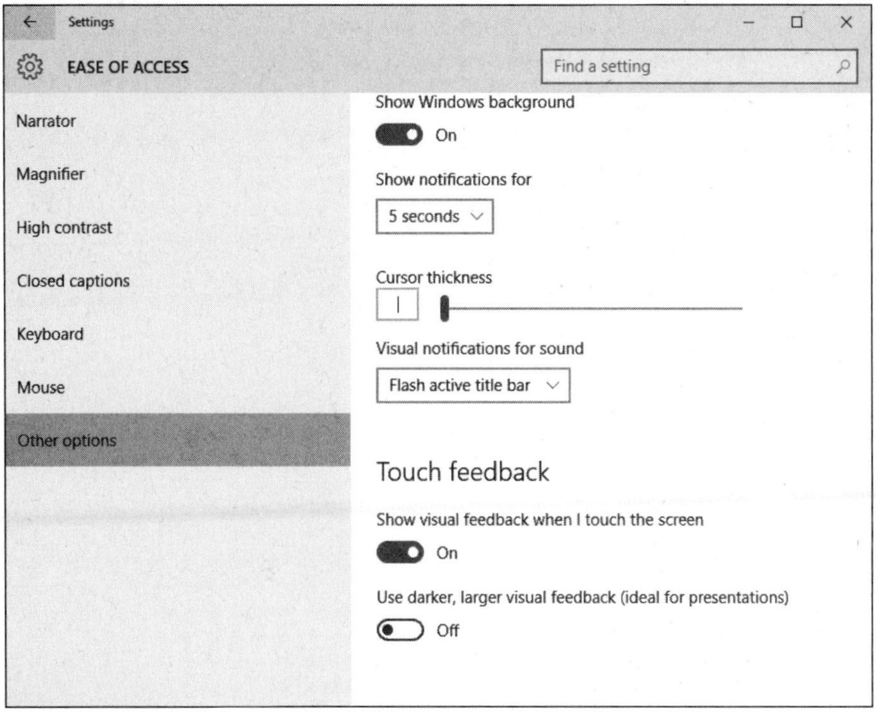

Figure 5-15

3. To make the visual feedback darker and larger so you more easily spot it, click the Use Darker, Larger Visual Feedback toggle switch to On.

4. Click the Close button to close the dialog box.

Setting Up Printers and Scanners

A computer is a great storehouse for data, images, and other digital information, but sometimes you need ways to turn printed documents into electronic files you can work with on your computer by scanning them, or sometimes you need to print *hard copies* (a fancy term for paper printouts) of electronic documents and images. Here are a few key ways to do just that:

⟹ **Printers** allow you to create hard copies of your files on paper, transparencies, or whatever materials your printer can accommodate. To use a printer, you have to install software called a *printer driver* and use certain settings to tell your computer how to identify your printer and what to print.

⟹ You use a **scanner** to create electronic files — pictures, essentially — from hard copies such as newspaper clippings, your birth certificate or driver's license, photos, or whatever will fit in your scanner. You can then work with the electronic files, send them to others as an email attachment, and modify and print them.

Scanners also require that you install a driver, which is typically provided by your scanner's manufacturer. Note that several all-in-one printer models feature both a printer and a scanner; therefore, many of the steps in this chapter that refer to printers also apply to scanners.

Install a Printer

1. Read the instructions that came with the printer. Some printers require that you install software before connecting them, but others can be connected right away and use drivers stored in Windows.

2. Turn on your computer and then follow the option that fits your needs:

- If your printer is a plug-and-play device (most are these days), you can connect it and power it on; Windows installs any required drivers automatically. If you have a printer that can connect to your computer using a wireless signal over a network (no wires required), be sure your wireless printer is turned on and available.

- Connect your printer as instructed in the accompanying materials, insert the disc that came with the device, and follow the onscreen instructions.

3. If neither of these procedures works, you can try adding a printer. Begin by choosing Settings from the Start menu.

4. Click Devices ➪ Printers & Scanners ➪ Add A Printer or Scanner and let Windows 10 search for any available devices (see **Figure 6-1**).

5. When it discovers your printer, select it, click Next, and follow the instructions.

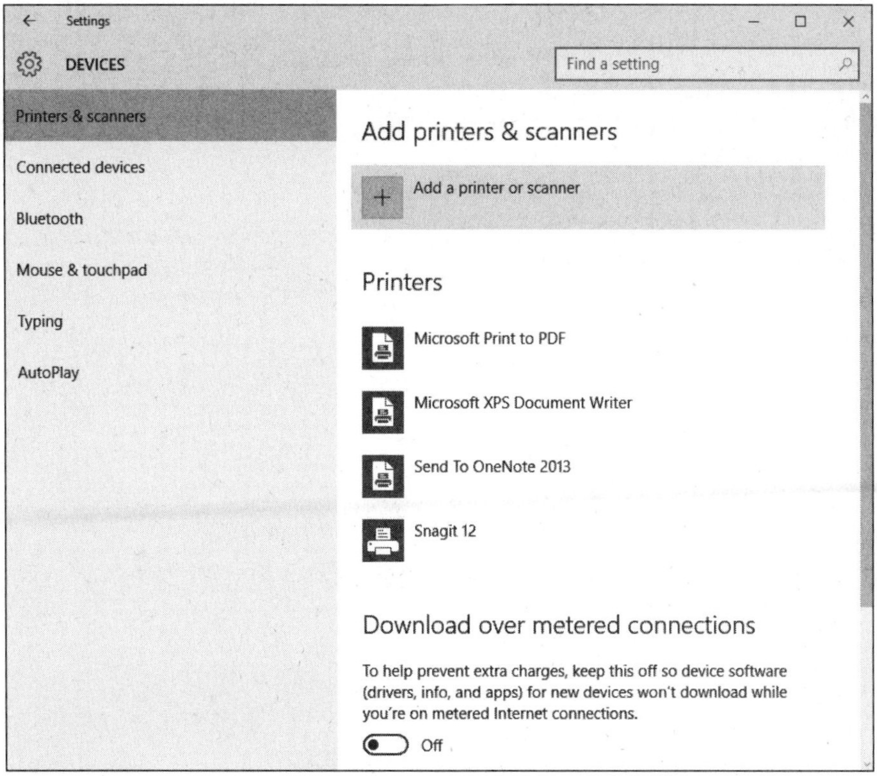

Figure 6-1

Add a Printer Manually

1. If the previous procedure doesn't work, go to the Start menu and click Settings ⇨ Devices. In the left panel of the window that appears, click Printers & Scanners and then click the Add a Printer or Scanner link near the top.

2. In the resulting Add Printer Wizard shown in **Figure 6-2**, if Windows 10 again doesn't find your printer, click the The Printer That I Want Isn't Listed link.

3. In the following window, click the Add a Local Printer or Network Printer with Manual Settings option and then click Next.

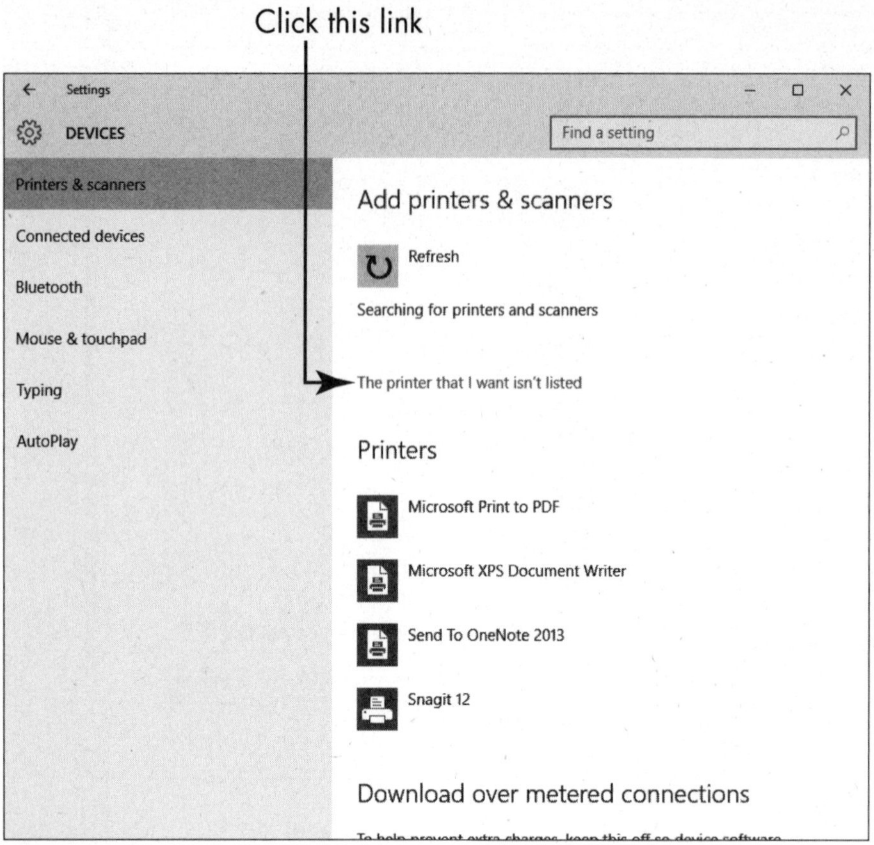

Click this link

Figure 6-2

4. In the following dialog box, shown in **Figure 6-3,** click the down arrow on the Use an Existing Port field and select a port, or just use the recommended port setting that Windows selects for you. Click Next.

5. In the next wizard window, choose a manufacturer in the list on the left and then choose a printer model in the list on the right. You then have two options:

  • If you have the manufacturer's disc, insert it in the appropriate CD/DVD drive now and click the Have Disk button. Click Next.

  • If you don't have the manufacturer's disc, click the Windows Update button to see a list of printer drivers that you can download from the Microsoft website. Click Next.

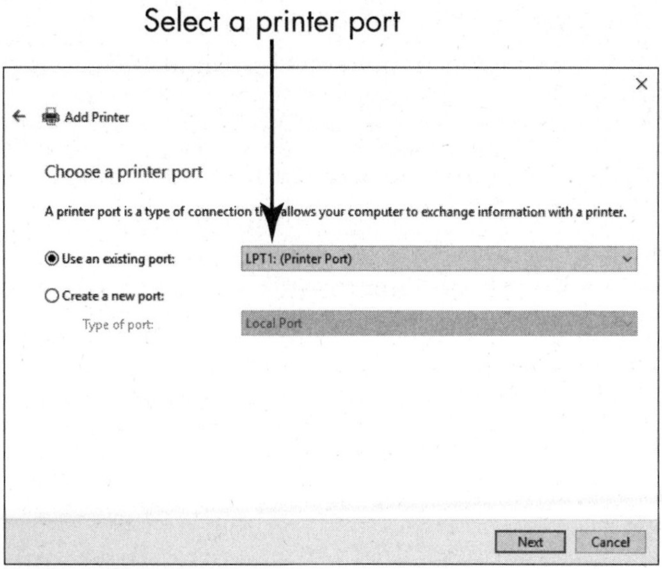

Select a printer port

Figure 6-3

6. In the resulting dialog box titled Type a Printer Name (see **Figure** 6-4), enter a printer name, or accept the default name that's entered already. Click Next.

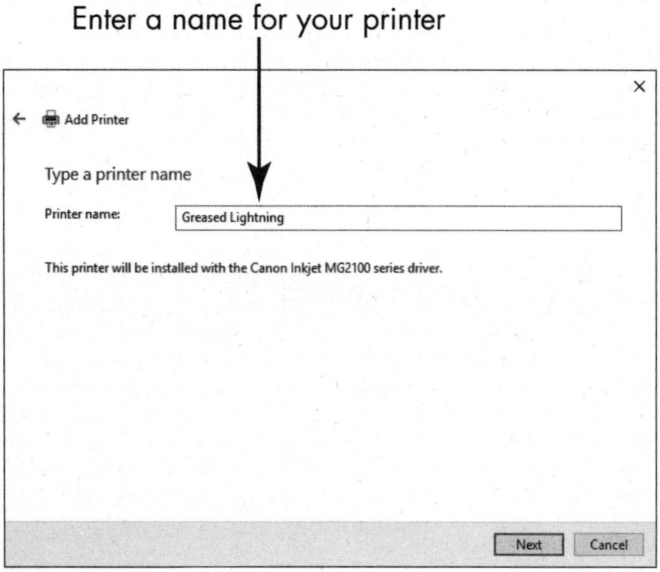

Enter a name for your printer

Figure 6-4

7. In the resulting dialog box, click the Print a Test Page button and, if the test works, click Finish to complete the Add Printer Wizard.

 If your computer is on a network, after Step 6, you get additional dialog boxes in the wizard, including one that allows you to share the printer on your network. Select the Do Not Share This Printer option to stop others from using the printer, or select the Share Name option and enter a printer name to share the printer on your network. This means that others can see and select this printer to print to.

Set a Default Printer

1. You can set up a default printer that will be used every time you print, so you don't have to select a printer each time. In the Start menu, click Settings⇨Devices⇨Printers & Scanners. Scroll down and click the Devices and Printers link.

2. In the resulting Devices and Printers window (shown in **Figure 6-5**), the current default printer is indicated by a check mark.

3. Right-click any printer that isn't set as the default and choose Set as Default Printer from the shortcut menu, as shown in **Figure 6-6**.

4. Click the Close button in the Devices and Printers window.

The default printer is checked

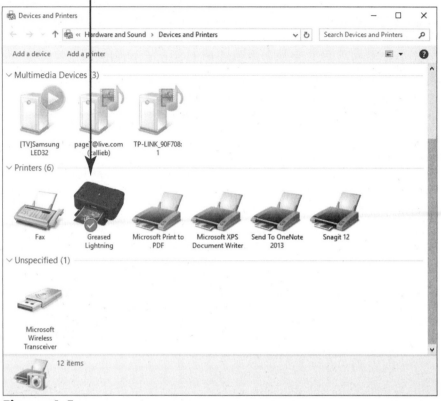

Figure 6-5

Choose this option

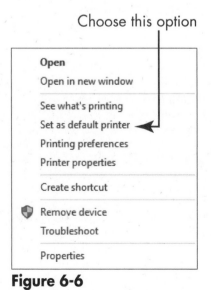

Figure 6-6

Set Printer Preferences

1. Your printer might have capabilities such as being able to print in color or black and white, or print in draft quality (which uses less ink) or high quality (which produces a darker, crisper image). To modify these settings for all documents you print, in the Start menu click Settings ➪ Devices ➪ Printers & Scanners, and then scroll down and click the Devices and Printers link.

2. In the resulting Devices and Printers window, any printers you've installed are listed. Right-click a printer and then choose Printing Preferences.

3. In the Printing Preferences dialog box that appears (shown in **Figure 6-7**), click any of the tabs to display various settings, such as Page Setup (see **Figure 6-8**). Note that different printers might display different choices and different tabs in this dialog box, but common settings include

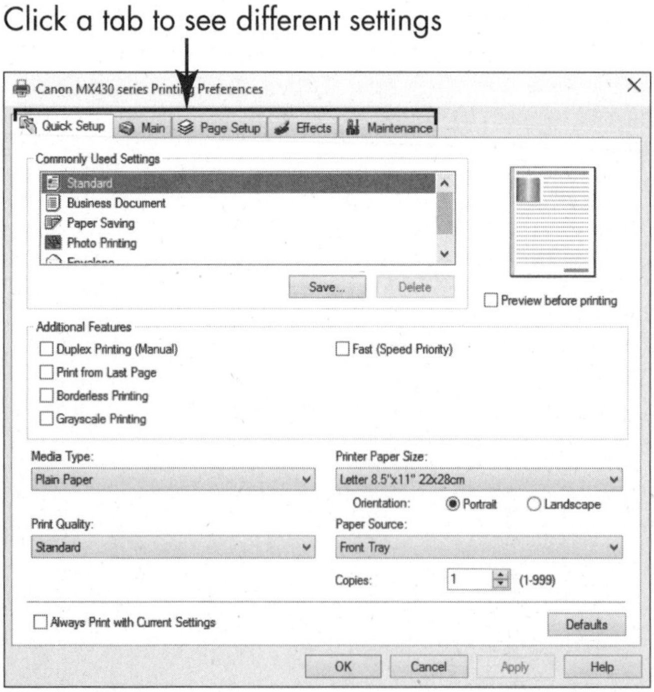

Click a tab to see different settings

Figure 6-7

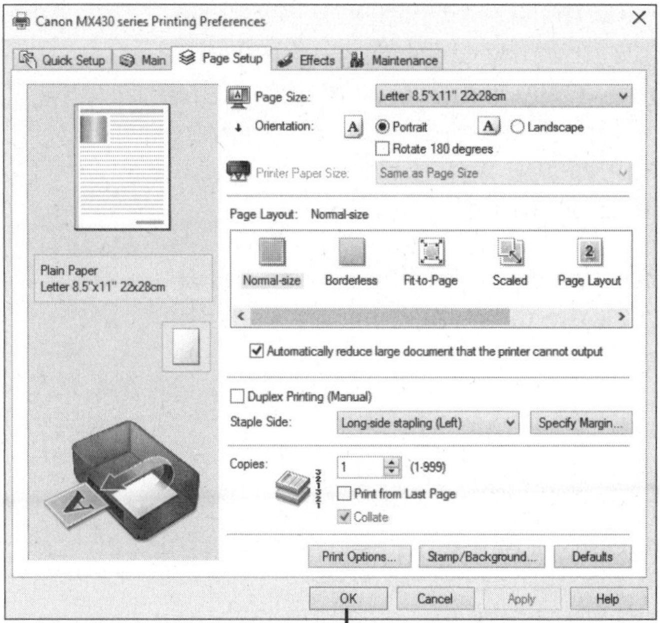

Figure 6-8

Click OK to save settings

- **Color/Grayscale:** If you have a color printer, you have the option of printing in color. The grayscale option uses only black ink. When printing a draft of a color document, you can save colored ink by printing in grayscale, for example.

- **Quality:** If you want, you can print in fast or draft quality (these settings may have different names depending on your printer's manufacturer) to save ink or you can print in a higher or best quality for your finished documents. Some printers offer a dpi (dots-per-inch) setting for quality — the higher the dpi setting, the better the quality.

- **Paper Source:** If you have a printer with more than one paper tray, you can select which tray to use for printing. For example, you might have 8½-x-11-inch paper (letter sized) in one tray and 8½-x-14-inch (legal sized) in another.

- **Paper Size:** Choose the size of paper or envelope you're printing to. In many cases, this option displays a preview that shows you which way to insert the paper. A preview can be especially handy if you're printing to envelopes and need help figuring out how to insert them in your printer.

4. Click the OK button to close the dialog box and save settings, and then click the Close button to close other open windows.

 There's a reason why settings in the Printing Preferences dialog box may differ slightly depending on your printer model; color printers offer different options than black-and-white printers, for example.

 Whatever settings you make using the procedure in this task are your default settings for all printing you do. However, when you're printing a document from within a program — for instance, Microsoft Works — the Print dialog box that displays gives you the opportunity to change the printer settings for that document only.

View Currently Installed Printers

1. Over time, you might install multiple printers, in which case you may want to remind yourself of the capabilities of each or view the documents you've sent to be printed. To view the printers you've installed and view any documents currently in line for printing, from the Start menu click Settings ⇨ Devices ⇨ Printers & Scanners, and then scroll down and click the Devices and Printers link.

2. In the resulting Devices and Printers window (see **Figure 6-9**), a list of installed printers appears. If a printer has documents in its print queue, the number of documents is listed at the bottom of the window in the Status field. If you want more detail about the documents or want to cancel a print job, select the printer and click the See What's Printing button at the top of the window. In the window that appears, click a document and choose Document⇨Cancel, and then click Yes to stop the printing. Click the Close button to return to the Devices and Printers window.

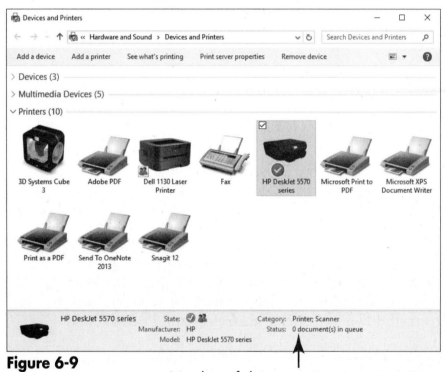

Figure 6-9

Number of documents in queue to print

3. You can right-click any printer and then choose Properties (see **Figure 6-10**) to see details about it, such as which port it's plugged into or whether it can scan as well as print.

4. Click the Close button (the X in the upper right) to close the Devices and Printers window.

Click this option

Figure 6-10

Remove a Printer

1. Over time, you might upgrade to a new printer and chuck the old one. When you do, you might want to remove the older printer driver from your computer also so your Printers window isn't cluttered with printers you don't need anymore. To remove a printer, from the Start menu click Settings ➪ Devices ➪ Printers & Scanners, and then scroll down and click the Devices and Printers link.

2. In the resulting Devices and Printers window (refer to Figure 6-9), right-click a printer and choose Remove Device. (*Note:* You can also select the printer and click the Remove Device button at the top of the window.)

3. In the Printers dialog box that appears, click Yes; the Remove Device window closes, and your printer is removed from the printer list.

 If you remove a printer, it's removed from the list of installed printers, and if it was the default printer, Windows assigns default status to another printer you've installed. You can no longer print to it unless you install it again. See the earlier task, "Install a

Printer," if you decide you want to print to that printer again.

Modify Scanner Settings

1. After you've set up a printer/scanner, you might want to look at or change the scanner default settings. To do so, with your printer/scanner attached to your computer, click All Apps in the Start menu, scroll down, and then click Scan.

2. In the resulting Scan window, click Show More.

3. In the resulting window (see **Figure 6-11**), click the arrow in the drop-down lists for Source, File Type, Color Mode (to fine-tune the way color is scanned) or Resolution (the higher the resolution, the crisper and cleaner your electronic document, but the more time it may take to scan) to view the available choices.

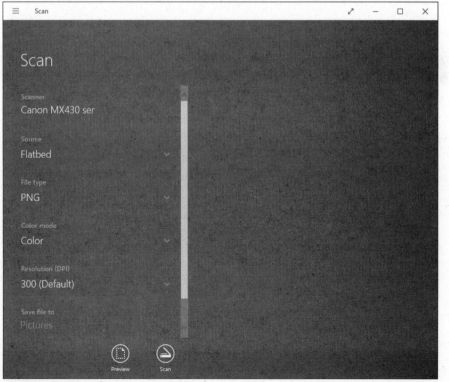

Figure 6-11

When you're ready to run a scan, place the item to be scanned in your scanner. Depending on your model, the item may be placed on a flat bed with a hinged cover or fed through a tray. Click All Apps in the Start menu, scroll down, and then click Scan. In the Scan window, click the Scan button. After you begin the scan, your computer displays a dialog box showing you the scan progress and allowing you to view and save the scanned item.

Connecting with Cortana

Cortana is a personal assistant feature introduced in Windows 10. Cortana resembles apps on smartphones that reply to your voice requests for directions, a list of nearby restaurants, current weather conditions, and more.

Cortana is also your central search feature in Windows 10, which can give you requested information verbally or take you to online search results.

Where Cortana goes beyond those smartphone apps is in integrating your daily activities and interests to anticipate the type of information you might need. You can set up your preferences in Cortana, help her learn your voice, and have her integrate with apps such as Calendar, Mail, Music, and more.

Overview Cortana

When you open Cortana, you see information in the Cortana panel that might be useful (see **Figure 7-1**), depending on settings you've made, such as your local weather or traffic conditions or sports teams.

Beyond that, Cortana is kind of like the computer in a *Star Trek* movie that you can command to do various tasks. Although Cortana can't fire a photon torpedo or transport you to a nearby planet, it can make your life easier. Here are just some of the things Cortana can do, from either a voice command or text that you enter in her search box:

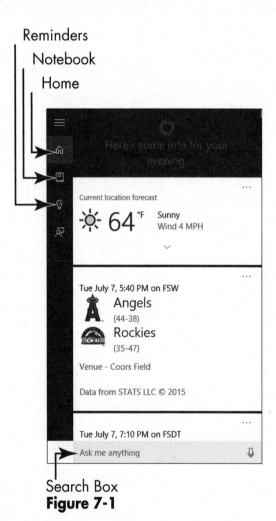

Reminders

Notebook

Home

Current location forecast

☀ 64 °F Sunny
Wind 4 MPH

Tue July 7, 5:40 PM on FSW
Angels
(44-38)
Rockies
(35-47)
Venue - Coors Field

Data from STATS LLC © 2015

Tue July 7, 7:10 PM on FSDT

Ask me anything

Search Box
Figure 7-1

➠ Set appointments and reminders

➠ Search for information online

➠ Open apps

➠ Play and identify music

➠ Search for files on your computer

➠ Get directions from the Maps app

➠ Send an email

Set Up Cortana

1. When you first open Cortana, you will be asked questions used to set up Cortana, such as what you want Cortana to call you (your nickname). You can access Cortana's settings later if you want to change how Cortana is working. Click in Cortana's search box to open Cortana. When the panel appears, click the Notebook button, and in the resulting Notebook panel (see **Figure 7-2**), click About Me.

2. In the resulting About Me panel, you can change your name or your favorite places. Click Edit Favorites and then, in the Places panel, click the Add button (the + shaped button in lower-right corner) to add a Favorite.

3. In the resulting panel's Add a Favorite text box, begin to type a location, such as your workplace. Click to select the correct location from the search results.

4. In the resulting panel (see **Figure 7-3**), click the Set as Work setting to On and click the Save button at the lower right.

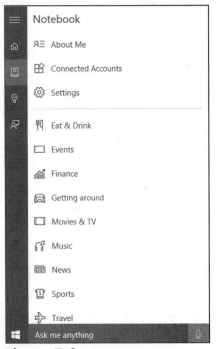

Figure 7-2

Figure 7-3

5. Click the Notebook button again and then click Settings. The Settings options shown in **Figure** 7-4 open. Settings allows you to control whether Cortana responds to the spoken phrase "Hey Cortana," responds to anyone's voice or just yours, finds tracking information in your email and other messages, and enables Taskbar Tidbits (occasional tidbits of information that appear in Cortana's search box).

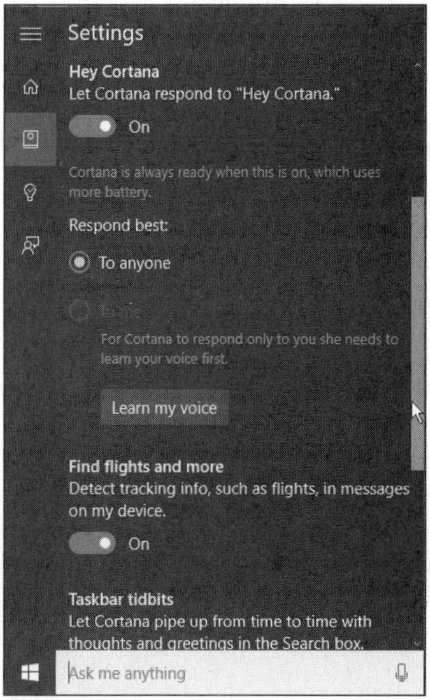

![Settings panel showing Hey Cortana, Respond best, Find flights and more, and Taskbar tidbits options]

Figure 7-4

6. If the Let Cortana Respond to "Hey Cortana" switch is set to Off, click to turn it On. If you are the only one who uses the computer, click the Learn My Voice button, and then repeat the six phrases that Cortana supplies.

 To turn Cortana off while keeping any contents or settings in the Notebook, click the first On/Off setting labeled Cortana Can Give You Suggestions.

 After you open the Cortana panel, you can close it by clicking the Escape button on your keyboard.

Set Up Cortana's Notebook

1. You can access Cortana's Notebook to customize how Cortana deals with different topics. For example, you can make settings for Events, Finance, News, Getting Around, and more. To explore any of these categories, click in Cortana's search box to open Cortana's panel, click the Notebook button, and then click a category, in this example, Sports.

2. In the resulting Notebook panel (see **Figure 7-5**) if you want to add a team to track, click Add a Team under the Teams You're Tracking heading, and then type a team name in the Search For a Team text box.

3. Select a team from the search results and then click Add.

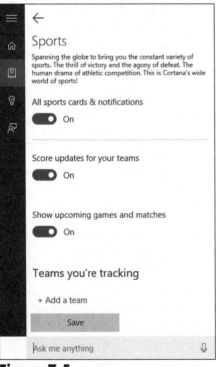

Figure 7-5

4. By default, Score Updates for Your Teams and Show
Upcoming Games and Matches are set to On. If you
want to change this, click the switch to Off, and then
click Save.

 You can control the pieces of information that appear in Cortana's
Home panel when you first open it by choosing to display Cards. To
control what information is included, click the Notebook button, click
a topic such as Sports or Eat & Drink, and then turn the Cards setting
for that topic on or off.

Interact with Cortana

You can interact with Cortana through speech or text. You can speak
to Cortana, starting with the phrase "Hey Cortana" or by clicking the
microphone button in her search box. With the speech feature active,
you can then state a request such as, "Open the Music App" or "What
is the Diameter of the Earth?" You can also type a request in the
Cortana search box.

Results will vary based on how you asked the question and what the
request was. If you use speech, she may respond verbally or may display search results in the Cortana panel or in Bing. If you type a question, she won't respond verbally, but may show you her response in
the panel or in Bing. If you have requested an action, such as adding
an appointment to your calendar, she may display a form in her panel
(see **Figure 7-6**) that you can use to provide additional information.

 Over time, Cortana should learn more about you and respond more
appropriately to your requests. You can also go through a procedure
to help her learn your voice, which is discussed in the "Setting Up
Cortana" section earlier in this chapter. Bottom line: Play around
with Cortana using both speech and text and see what results she
provides.

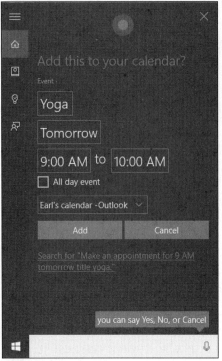

Figure 7-6

Set Reminders

1. Click in Cortana's search box to open Cortana and then click the Reminders button. (If you need an indication of which button is Reminders, just click the More button at the top of the Navigation bar). The Reminders panel opens.

2. Click the Add button (the + shaped button in the bottom right of the panel) and then in the resulting panel (see **Figure 7-7**) fill in the details of what you want to be reminded to do, including the date and time. When you click a field such as People, you might be taken to an app to make a choice. Click the Remind button.

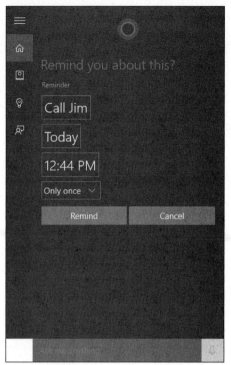

Figure 7-7

3. At the time you set to display a reminder, it appears in the bottom-right corner of the desktop. Click either the Snooze or Complete button to allow the reminder to appear a bit later or to indicate the reminder is no longer needed because the task is complete.

Search with Cortana

1. You can ask Cortana to look up facts; for example, say, "Hey Cortana, how tall is the Washington Monument?" The result is shown in **Figure 7-8**.

2. You can also use text or speech to ask Cortana to provide a list of results using the Bing search engine. Say or enter the phrase "The Russian Revolution." Cortana will search using Bing and return a list of matches to your request, as shown in **Figure 7-9**.

Figure 7-8

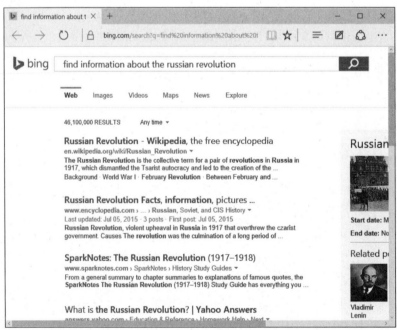

Figure 7-9

Cortana's results aren't limited to facts and figures. Try asking her to find the best nearby pizza restaurant or to tell you a joke. You can also ask for help with using Windows 10 features. See Chapter 12 for more about searching using Cortana.

Identify Music with Cortana

1. If you hear a song playing that you don't recognize, Cortana can identify it for you. Say, "Hey Cortana, what music is playing?" and Cortana will open in a "Listening for Music" mode. After a few moments, if she recognizes the song, Cortana provides the name of the song, album, and artist, as shown in **Figure 7-10**.

2. Click the song title and the Store opens so that you can buy the song or album if you wish. See Chapter 18 more about buying and playing music.

Figure 7-10

Part II
Getting Things Done with Software

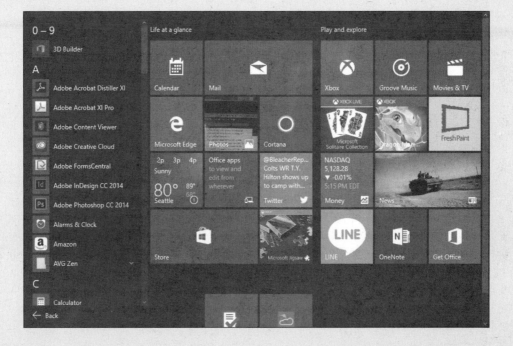

Visit www.dummies.com/extras/computersforseniors for information about working with the View Ribbon.

Working with Software Programs

Chapter
8

*Y*ou may think of Windows 10 as a set of useful accessories, such as games, music players, and a paint program for playing around with images, but Windows 10 is first an operating system. Windows 10's main purpose is to enable you to run and manage other software programs, from programs that manage your finances to a great animated game of bingo. By using the best methods for accessing and running programs with Windows 10, you save time; setting up Windows 10 in the way that works best for you can make your life easier.

In this chapter, you explore several simple and very handy techniques for launching and moving information between applications. You go through systematic procedures ranging from setting defaults for which programs to use with various document formats to uninstalling programs when you no longer need them.

Launch a Program

1. Launch a program by using any of the following methods:

- Click a tile in the Start menu. (For more about pinning apps to the Start menu, see Chapter 3.)

- Open the Start menu and click the All Apps button in the lower-left corner. This displays an alphabetical list of installed apps (as shown in **Figure 8-1**). Click an app to open it.

Figure 8-1

- Double-click a program shortcut icon on the desktop (see **Figure 8-2**).

- Click an item on the desktop taskbar to display a currently open program. The taskbar should display by default. If it doesn't, press the Windows key (on your keyboard) to display it, and then click an

icon on the taskbar (as shown in Figure 8-2).
See Chapter 3 for more about working with the
taskbar.

Figure 8-2

2. When the application opens, if it's a game, play it; if it's a
spreadsheet, enter numbers into it; if it's your email program, start deleting junk mail . . . you get the idea.

 See Chapter 10 for more about working with apps in
Windows 10.

View Open Apps in Task View

1. New to Windows 10 is Task View. Task View shows you
all the open apps and helps you switch among them.
With two or more apps open, click the Task View button
to the right of Cortana's search field.

2. Click a running app to make it the active app (see **Figure** 8-3). It will open to the size it displayed at last (full screen, minimized, etc.)

Figure 8-3

Task View button

3. Click the Maximize button near the top-right corner to expand a minimized app to full screen.

Close an App

Most mainstream apps, such as Microsoft Word and Quicken, offer a few ways to close the program. On a Windows computer, there is a Close button shaped like an X in the upper-right corner of the program window, as shown in **Figure 8-4**. Click this button. If you have an unsaved document open, you may be asked if you want to save it before closing the program, which is a good idea. If you have already saved the document, the program simply closes. You can also use the File menu command Close to close the program.

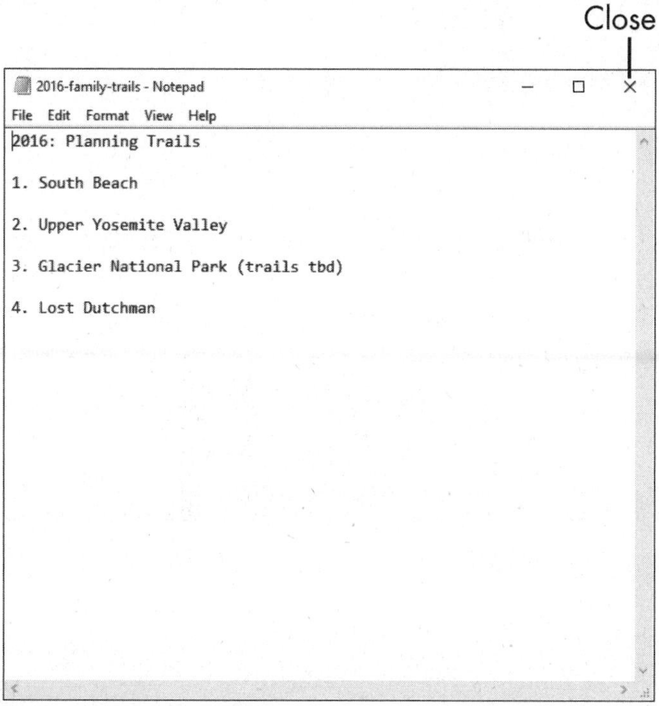

Close

Figure 8-4

In non-productivity apps, such as games or utilities like Windows Calculator, there may or may not be a Close button. If there isn't, look for a main menu and choose a command such as Exit from the choices that appear.

Move Information between Programs

1. Click the File Explorer button in the taskbar to open it.

2. Browse and open documents in two programs; in this example, open Microsoft Word and WordPad (see the earlier section for more about opening applications). Right-click the taskbar (see **Figure 8-5**) and choose Show Windows Side by Side or Show Windows Stacked.

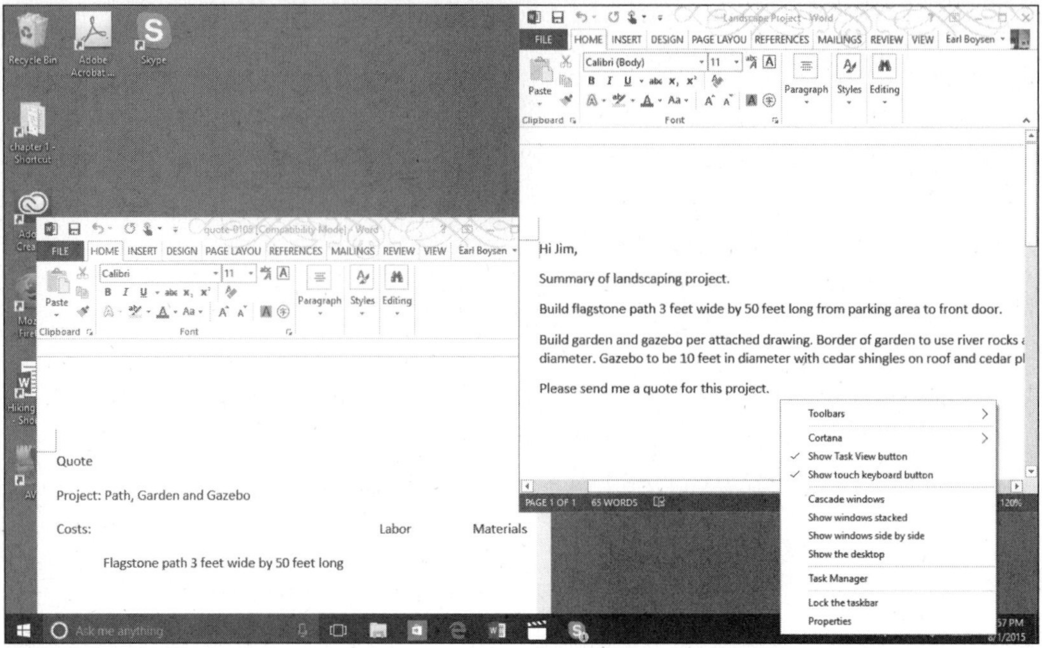

Figure 8-5

3. Select the information that you want to move (for example, click and drag your mouse to highlight text or numbers, or click on a graphical object in a document). Drag the selection to the other document window (see **Figure 8-6**).

4. Release your mouse, and the information is copied to the document in the destination window.

You can also use simple cut-and-paste or copy-and-paste keystroke shortcuts to take information from one application and move it or place a copy of it into a document in another application. To do this, first click and drag over the information in a document, and then press Ctrl+X to cut or Ctrl+C to copy the item. Click in the destination document where you want to place the item and press Ctrl+V. Alternatively, you can right-click selected content and choose Cut, Copy, or Paste commands from the menu that appears.

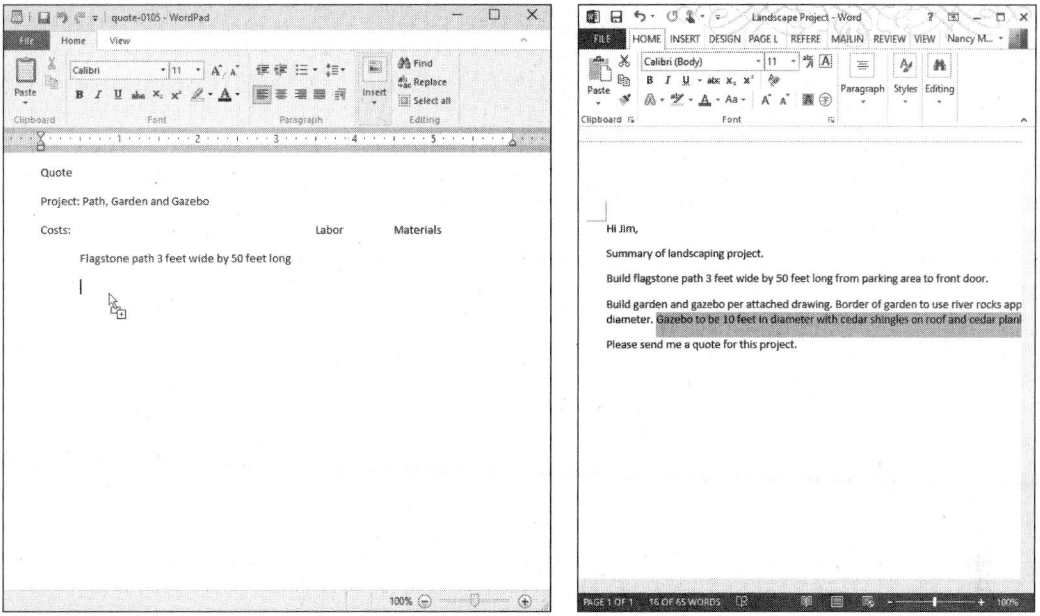

Figure 8-6

 Remember, dragging content won't work between every type of program. For example, you can't click and drag an open picture in Paint into the Windows Calendar. It will most dependably work when dragging text or objects from one Office or other standard word-processing, presentation, database, or spreadsheet program to another.

Set Program Defaults

1. To make working with files easier, you may want to control which programs are used to open files of different types by default. For example, you might always want word-processed documents to be opened by Microsoft Word or WordPad. From the Start menu, click Settings.

2. Click System ⇨ Default Apps. In the resulting window shown in **Figure 8-7**, scroll down and click the Set Defaults by App link in the right panel to see specifics about the default programs.

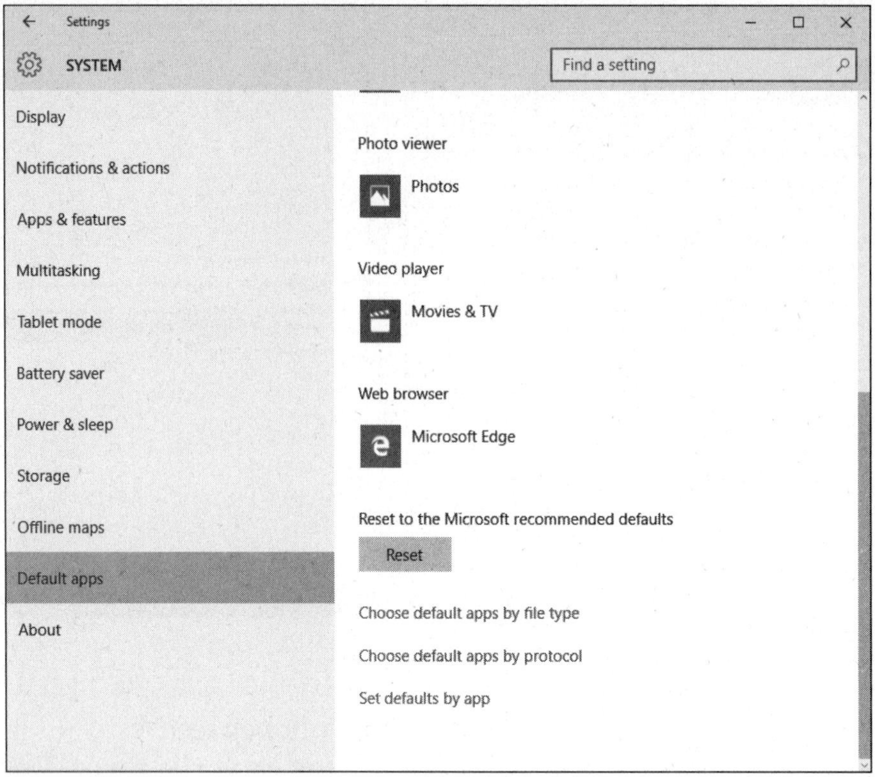

Figure 8-7

3. In the resulting Set Default Programs window, click a program in the list on the left (see **Figure 8-8**) and then click the Set This Program as Default option. You can also click Choose Defaults for This Program and select specific file types (such as the JPEG graphics file format or DOCX Word 2013 file format) to open in this program; click Save after you've made these selections.

4. In the Set Default Programs window, click OK to save your settings and then click the Close button.

 You can also choose which devices to use by default to play media such as movies or audio files by selecting Change Default Settings for Media or Devices in the Programs window you opened in Step 2.

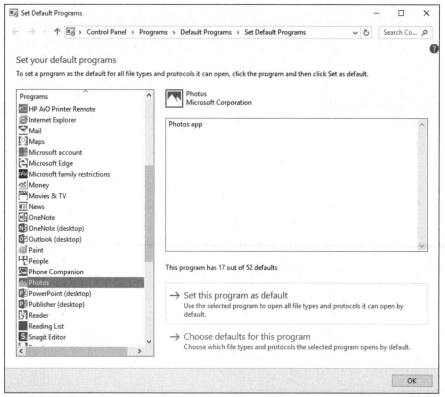

Figure 8-8

Uninstall a Program

1. If you don't need a program, removing it may help your computer's performance, which can get bogged down when your hard drive is too cluttered. From the Start Menu, click Settings ⇨ System ⇨ Apps & Features.

2. In the resulting window, shown in **Figure 8-9**, click a program and then click the Uninstall button that appears. Although some programs will display their own uninstall screen, in most cases, a confirmation dialog box appears (see **Figure 8-10**).

3. If you're sure that you want to remove the program, click Uninstall in the confirmation dialog box. A progress bar shows the status of the procedure; it disappears when the program has been removed.

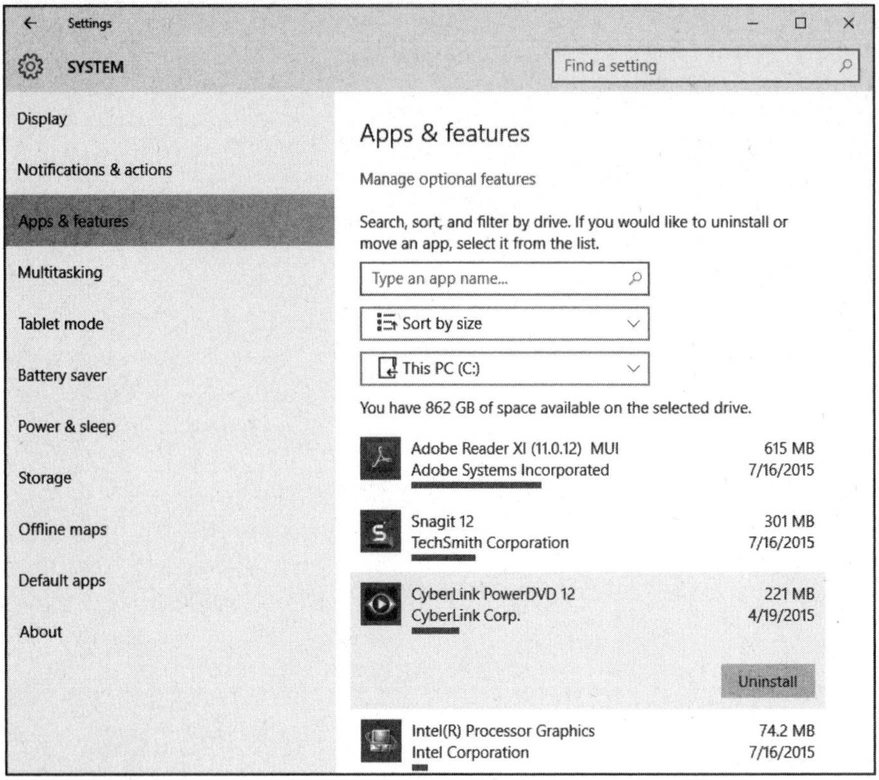

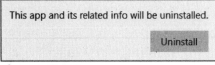

Figure 8-9

Figure 8-10

4. Click the Close button to close the window.

> If you click the Uninstall button, some programs will simply be removed with no further input from you. Be really sure that you don't need a program before you remove it, that you have the original software on disc, or that you have a product key for software you downloaded from the Internet so you can reinstall it should you need it again.

Working with Files and Folders

*J*oin me for a moment in the office of yesteryear. Notice all the metal filing cabinets and manila file folders holding paper rather than the sleek computer workstations, ubiquitous tablets, and wireless Internet connections we use today.

Fast forward: You still organize the work you do every day in files and folders, but today the metal and cardboard have given way to electronic bits and bytes. Files are the individual documents that you save from within applications, such as Word and Excel, and you use folders and subfolders to organize several files into groups or categories, such as by project or by year.

In this chapter, you find out how to organize and work with files and folders, including

➠ **Finding your way around files and folders:** This includes tasks such as locating and opening files and folders using Search or Cortana, and using some of the tools on the File Explorer Ribbon.

➠ **Manipulating files and folders:** These tasks cover moving, renaming, deleting, and printing a file.

Get ready to . . .

➡ **Squeezing a file's contents:** This involves creating a compressed folder to reduce the size of a large file or set of files to be more manageable when backing up or emailing them.

➡ **Backing up files and folders:** To avoid losing valuable data, you should know how to make backup copies of your files and folders on a recordable CD/DVD or *flash drive* (a small stick-shaped storage device that fits into a USB port on your computer).

Understand How Windows Organizes Data

When you work in a software program, such as a word processor, you save your document as a file. Files can be saved to your computer hard drive to removable storage media, such as USB flash drives (which are about the size of a stick of gum), or to recordable DVDs (small, flat discs you insert into a disc drive on your computer). (Note that you can also save files to an online storage site, such as OneDrive; this is known as storing in the cloud. Working with OneDrive and the cloud is covered in detail in Chapter 15).

You can organize files by placing them in folders that you work with in an app called File Explorer. The Windows operating system helps you organize files and folders in the following ways:

➡ **Take advantage of predefined folders.** Windows sets up some folders for you as libraries of content. For example, the first time you start Windows 10 and open File Explorer, you find folders for Documents, Music, Pictures, Downloads, and Videos already set up on your computer (see **Figure 9-1**). (See Chapter 3 for an explanation of File Explorer.)

The Documents folder is a good place to store letters, presentations for your community group, household budgets, and so on. The Pictures folder is where you store picture files, which you may transfer from a digital camera or scanner, receive in an email message from a friend or family member, or download from the Internet. Similarly, the Videos folder is a good place to put files from your camcorder or mobile phone. The Download folder is where files you download are stored by default, unless you specify a different location, and the Music folder is where you place tunes you download or transfer from a music player.

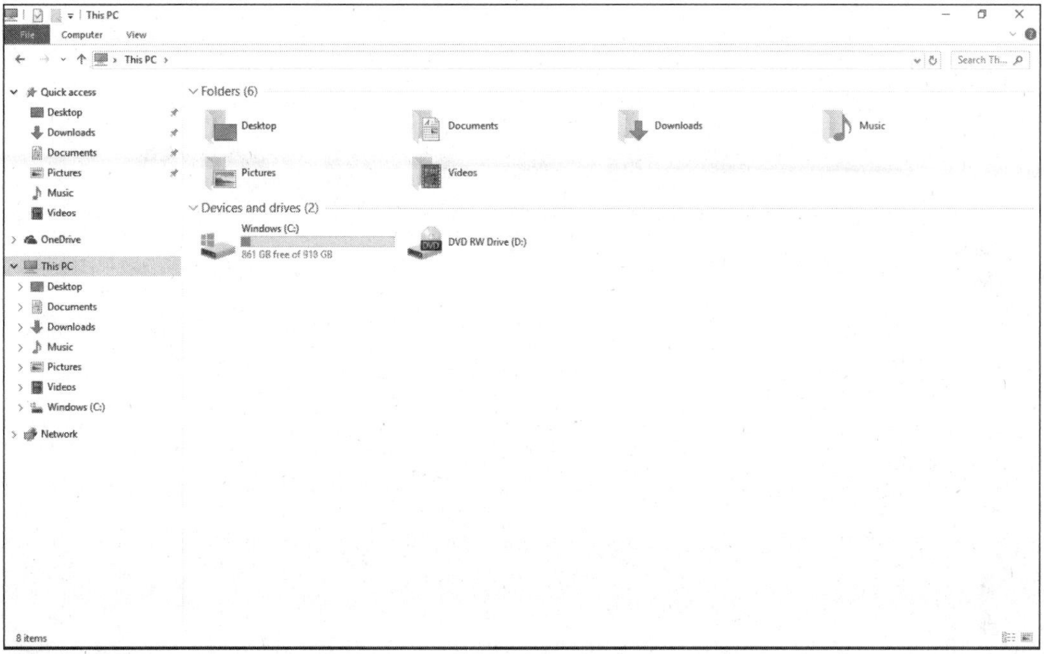

Figure 9-1

➡ **Create your own folders.** You can create any number of folders and give them a name that identifies the types of files you'll store there. For example, you might create a folder called *Digital Scrapbook* if you use your computer to create scrapbooks, or a folder called *Taxes* where you save emailed receipts for purchases and electronic tax-filing information.

➡ **Place folders within folders to further organize files.** A folder you place within another folder is called a *subfolder*. For example, in your Documents folder, you might have a subfolder called *Holiday Card List* that contains your yearly holiday newsletter and address lists. In my Pictures folder, I organize the picture files by creating subfolders that begin with the year and then a description of the event or subject, such as *2015 Home Garden Project, 2014 Christmas, 2014 San Francisco Trip, 2015 Family Reunion, 2015 Pet Photos,* and so on. In **Figure 9-2,** you can see subfolders and files stored within the Pictures folder.

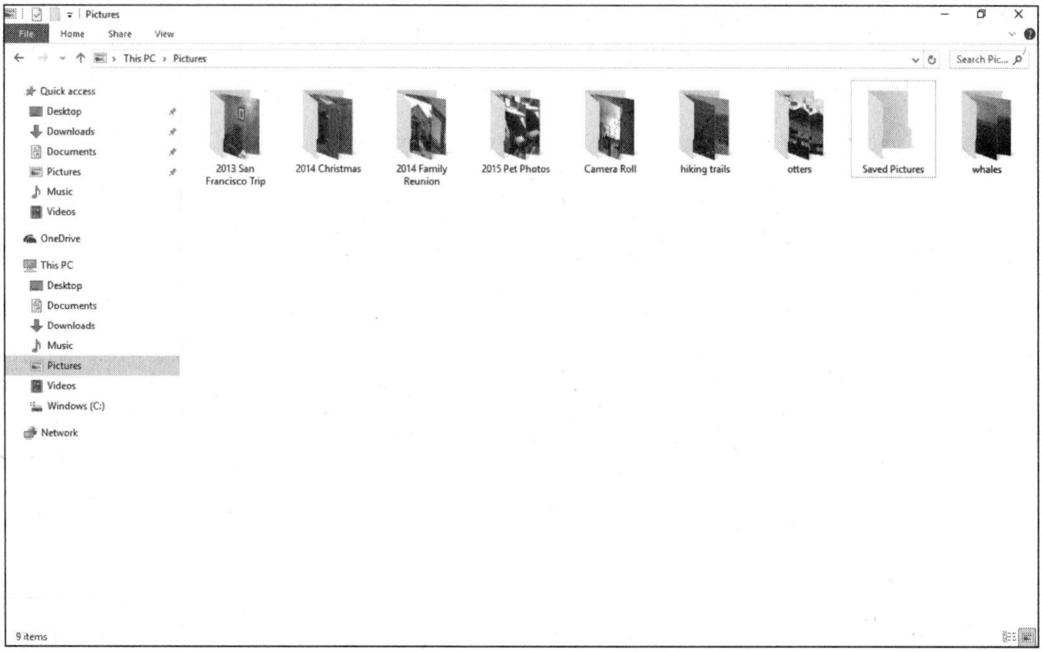

Figure 9-2

⟼ **Move files and folders from one place to another.** Being able to move files and folders helps when you decide it's time to reorganize information on your computer. For example, when you start using your computer, you might save all your documents to your Documents folder. That's okay for a while, but in time, you might have dozens of documents saved in that one folder. To make your files easier to locate, you can create subfolders by topic and move files into them.

Access Recently Used Items

1. If you worked on a file recently, File Explorer offers a shortcut to finding and opening it to work on again. Click the File Explorer button in the taskbar.

2. File Explorer opens with Quick Access displayed (see **Figure 9-3**). Quick Access contains a list of items you've accessed recently, including Recent Files and Frequent Folders.

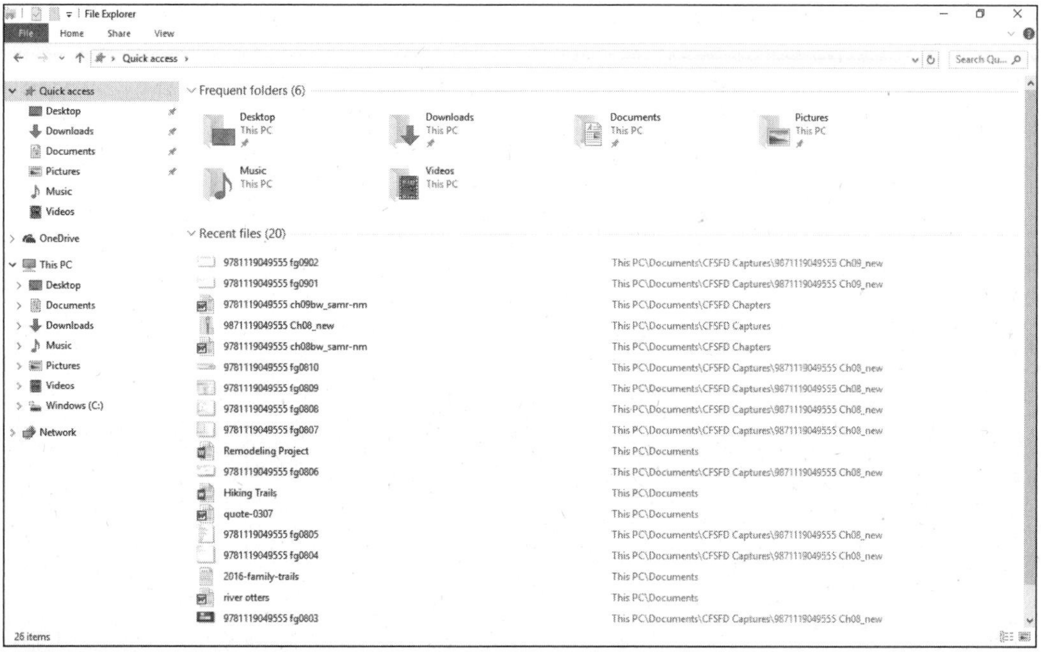

Figure 9-3

3. Double-click a file to open it.

Locate Files and Folders in Your Computer with File Explorer

1. Can't remember what you named a folder or where on your computer or storage media you saved it? You can

use File Explorer's search feature to find it. First, click the File Explore button in the taskbar to open File Explorer.

2. In the File Explorer window, click This PC in the list on the left. Click in the Search field in the upper-right corner, and begin typing the name of a file or folder.

3. In the search results that appear (see **Figure** 9-4), click a file to open it.

Figure 9-4

You can narrow your File Explorer search results to folders, such as Documents, Downloads, or Pictures, by clicking a folder before you type the search term. For instance, if you want to find the files with file names containing the word *river* in Documents, click Documents first and then type **river** in the File Explorer search field (see **Figure** 9-5).

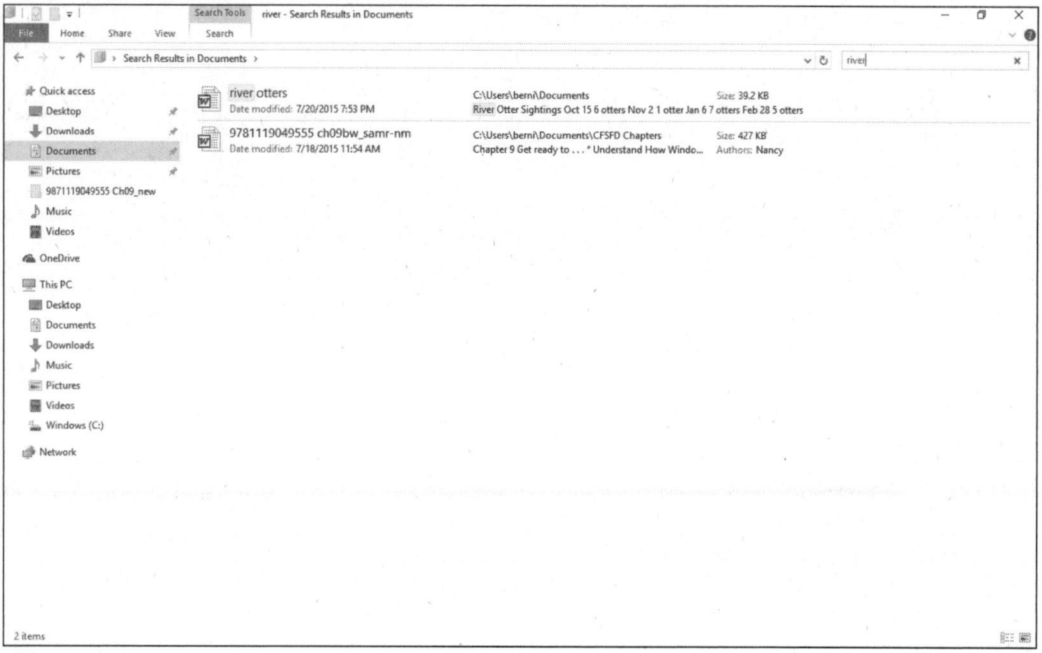

Figure 9-5

Working with the View Ribbon

1. File Explorer contains menus that display sets of tools in an area known as the Ribbon. Depending on what you have selected in File Explorer, the menus that run across the top of File Explorer may vary. All sets of menus, however, contain a View menu and a ribbon of tools that can help you find files and folders by displaying information about them in different ways. With File Explorer open, locate a file, select it, and then click the View menu.

2. In the View ribbon, click Preview Pane. A preview of the selected document opens on the right side of the window, as shown in **Figure 9-6**.

3. In the View ribbon, click the Details Pane. Information about the file appears in the right pane.

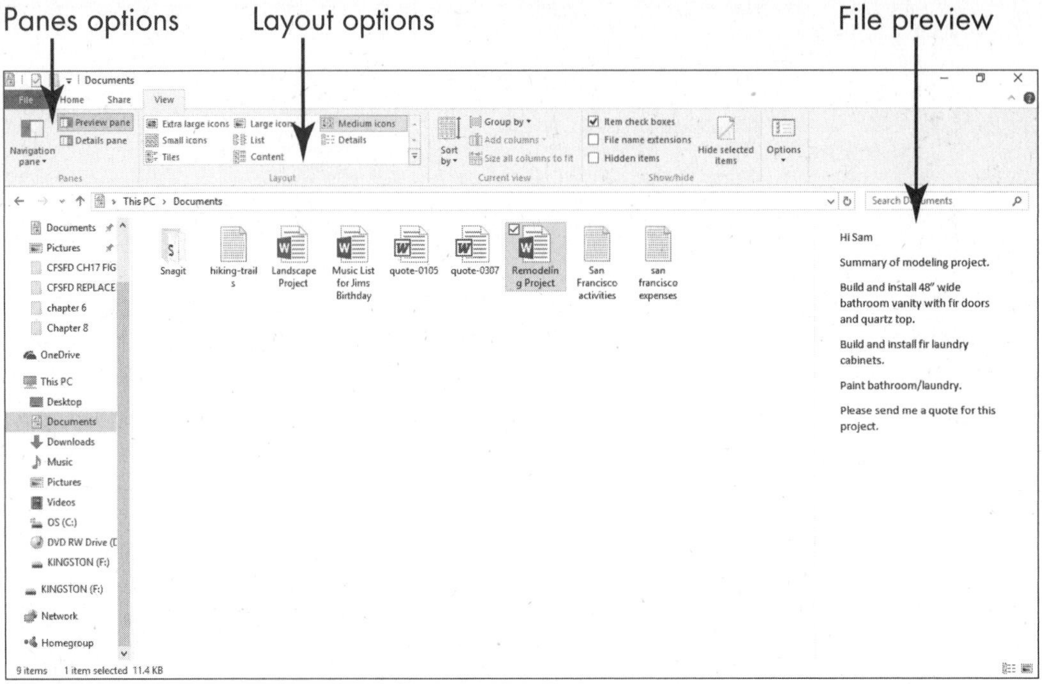

Panes options   Layout options   File preview

Figure 9-6

4. Click various options in the Layout section of the Ribbon
to display information about the file in layouts that
include information ranging from detailed file information or a simple text list of files, to icons that show a
smaller or larger representation of the file's contents.

Search with Cortana

1. If you want to locate files, you can use the Cortana search
feature. In the Cortana search field in the taskbar, begin
to type a file name.

2. Possible Search matches appear in categories, such as
Photos, Documents, or Web (see **Figure 9-7**). Click a file
to open it.

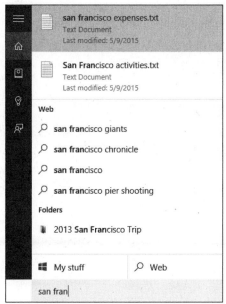

Figure 9-7

 In Cortana's search results, you can choose either My Stuff to display results from your computer, or Web to display results from the Bing search engine.

 If you type part of a file name and don't see what you want in the results, keep typing more letters until the file appears in the results list.

Move a File or Folder

1. Sometimes, you save a file or folder in one place but in reorganizing, you decide you want to move the item to another location. To move a file or folder, click the File Explorer button in the taskbar.

2. In File Explorer, click a folder to reveal its contents, or double-click a subfolder or series of subfolders to locate the file that you want to move (see **Figure 9-8**).

Figure 9-8

3. Take one of the following actions:

- **Click and drag** the file to another folder in the Navigation pane on the left side of the window.

- If you **right-click and drag,** you're offered options via a shortcut menu: You can move the file, copy it, or create a shortcut to it.

- **Right-click** the file and choose Send To. Then choose from the options shown in the submenu that appears (as shown in **Figure 9-9**); these options may vary slightly depending on the type of file you choose and your installed software.

Figure 9-9

4. Click the Close button in the upper-right corner of File Explorer to close it.

 If you want to create a copy of a file or folder in another location on your computer, right-click the item and choose Copy. Use File Explorer to navigate to the location where you want to place a copy, right-click, and choose Paste or press Ctrl+V.

Rename a File or Folder

1. You may want to change the name of a file or folder to update it or make it more easily identifiable from other files or folders. Locate the file that you want to rename by using File Explorer.

2. Right-click the file and choose Rename (see **Figure 9-10**).

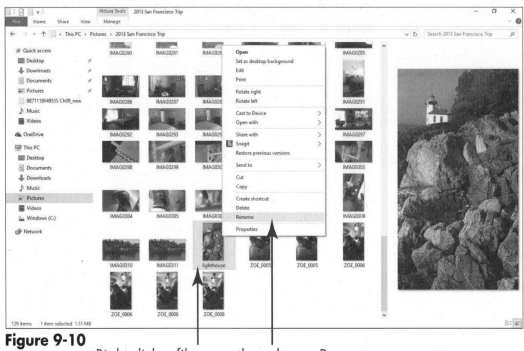

Figure 9-10

Right-click a file...   then choose Rename

3. The filename is now available for editing. Type a new name, and then click anywhere outside the filename to save the new name.

 You can't rename a file to have the same name as another file located in the same folder. To give a file the same name as another, cut it from its current location, paste it into another folder, and then follow the procedure in this task. Or open the file and save it to a new location with the same name, which creates a copy. Be careful, though: Two files with the same name can cause confusion when you search for files. If possible, use unique filenames.

Create a Shortcut to a File or Folder

You can place a shortcut to a file or folder you used recently on the desktop for quick and easy access.

1. In File Explorer, right-click the file or folder that you want and select Send To (as shown in **Figure** 9-11) and then select Desktop (Create Shortcut).

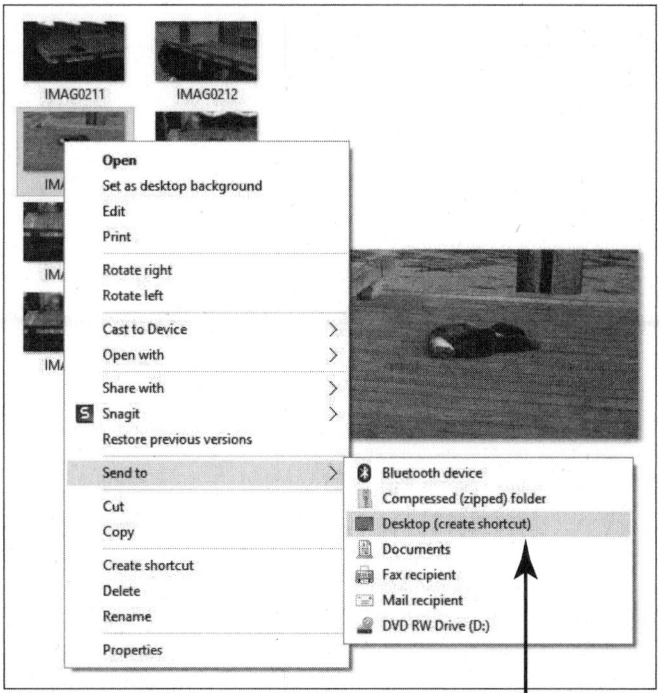

Figure 9-11

Choose Desktop (create shortcut)

2. A shortcut appears on the desktop.

> Once you've placed a shortcut on the desktop, to open the file in its originating application or open a folder in File Explorer, simply double-click the desktop shortcut icon.

Delete a File or Folder

1. If you don't need a file or folder anymore, you can clear up clutter on your computer by deleting it. Locate the file or folder by using File Explorer. Display File Explorer, and then browse to locate the file you want to delete.

2. In File Explorer, right-click the file or folder that you want to delete and then choose Delete (see **Figure** 9-12).

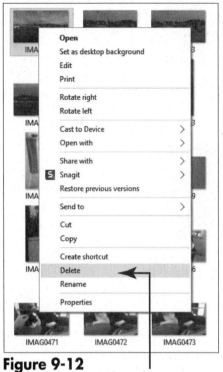

Open	
Set as desktop background	
Edit	
Print	
Rotate right	
Rotate left	
Cast to Device	>
Open with	>
Share with	>
Snagit	>
Restore previous versions	
Send to	>
Cut	
Copy	
Create shortcut	
Delete	
Rename	
Properties	

IMAG0471   IMAG0472   IMAG0473

Figure 9-12

Select this option

 When you delete a file or folder in Windows, it's not really gone. It's moved to the Recycle Bin on the desktop. Windows periodically purges older files from this folder, but you may still be able to retrieve recently deleted files and folders from it. To try to restore a deleted file or folder, double-click the Recycle Bin icon on the desktop. Right-click the file or folder and choose Restore. Windows restores the file to wherever it was before you deleted it.

 Instead of right-clicking and choosing Delete from the menu that appears in Step 2 earlier, you can click to select the file and then press the Delete key on your keyboard.

Create a Compressed File or Folder

1. To shrink the size of a file or all the files in a folder, you can compress them. This is often helpful when you're sending an item as an attachment to an email message. Locate the files or folders that you want to compress by using File Explorer. (Click the File Explorer button on the taskbar, and then browse to locate the file[s] or folder[s].)

2. In File Explorer, you can do the following (as shown in **Figure 9-13**):

- **Select a series of files or folders.** Click a file or folder, press and hold Shift to select a series of items listed consecutively in the folder, and click the final item.

- **Select nonconsecutive items.** Press and hold the Ctrl key and click the items.

Figure 9-13

3. Right-click the selected items. In the resulting shortcut menu (see **Figure 9-14**), choose Send To and then choose Compressed (Zipped) Folder. A new compressed folder appears below the last selected file in the File Explorer list.

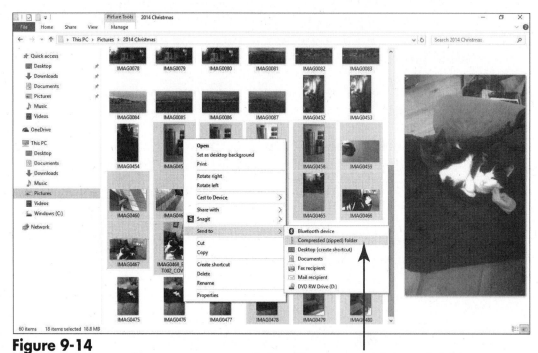

Figure 9-14

Select Compressed (zipped) folder

4. The folder icon is named after the last file you selected in the series, but you can rename it. Type a new name or click outside the item to accept the default name.

 You may want to subsequently rename a compressed folder with a name other than the one that Windows automatically assigns to it. See the task "Rename a File or Folder," earlier in this chapter, to find out just how to do that.

Add a Folder to Your Quick Access List

1. Quick Access offers a fast way to access frequently used folders. Locate the folders that you want to place in Quick Access using File Explorer.

2. In the resulting File Explorer window, right-click a folder. In the resulting short-cut menu, click Pin to Quick Access (see **Figure 9-15**). The selected folder appears in the Quick Access list.

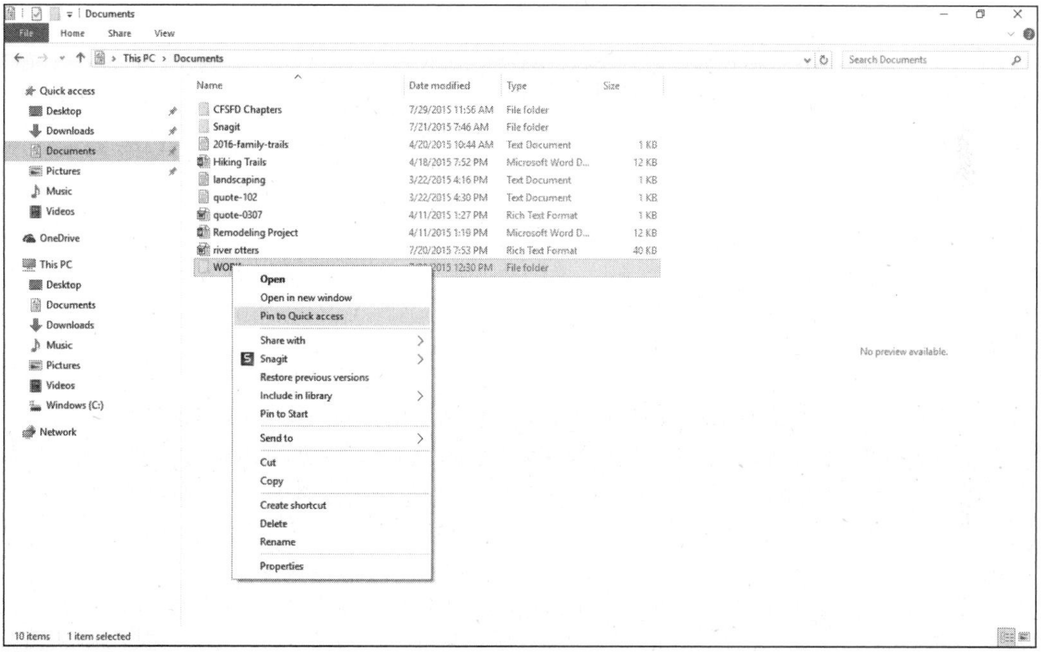

Figure 9-15

3. To see a list of folders in Quick Access, open File Explorer where you'll see folders you have pinned to Quick Access as well as frequently used folders and recently used files (see **Figure 9-16**). File Explorer opens with Quick Access selected.

4. Click on an item to open it.

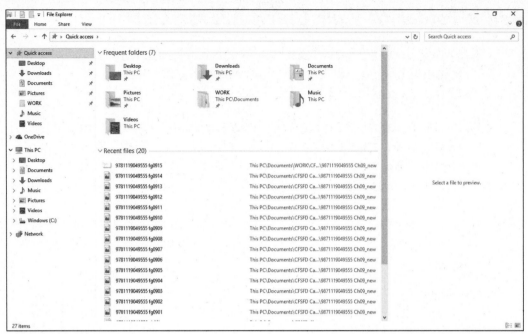

Figure 9-16

Back Up Files

1. You've put a lot of work into your files, so don't forget to back them up. If your computer is damaged or loses data, you'll then have a copy safely tucked away. Place a blank writable CD-R/RW (read/writable) or DVD-R/RW in your CD-RW or DVD-RW drive (or connect a USB drive to your USB port) and then open File Explorer.

2. Select the files or folders that you want to copy.

3. Click the Share tab on the Ribbon in File Explorer and click Burn to Disc.

 To move files to a drive, instead of burning a copy to disc on the Home tab, click Move To and then select Choose Location from the menu. In the Move Items dialog box, click the drive associated with your USB drive and then click the folder on that drive where you want to save the files. Click the Move button.

4. Select the way to use the disc (for example, USB or CD/DVD, depending on what media you are backing up to) and then click Next. Files are burned to the storage device.

5. Click the Home tab and then click the Eject button, and then click the Close button to close the Document window.

 You can also save files to OneDrive, Microsoft's online file-sharing service, as discussed in Chapter 15.

 The method discussed here is a manual way to back up files, which you can do on a regular basis. However, you can also back up to a network or another drive. From the Start menu click Settings ⇨ Update & Security ⇨ Backup, and then under Back Up Using File History, click the Add a Drive button and select a drive. Backing up to a CD/DVD or USB drive is a little different from saving a backup copy in that after you back up your files, only changes that have happened to files since you last saved are saved each subsequent time a backup is run.

Working with Windows Apps

Chapter 10

S everal apps that are preinstalled in Windows 10 can come in handy in planning your activities, finding your way around, and connecting with others. Each app is represented on the Start menu by a tile that you simply click to open.

The News app provides current headlines to keep you informed, while the Weather app can tell you whether you need to wear a raincoat or slather on the sunscreen.

The People app is your contact-management resource. You can store contact information and then use information in a contact record to send an email, view a profile, or post a message on that person's Facebook other social network page.

The Calendar app lets you view your schedule by day, week, or month, and add details about events, such as the date and time, length, and whether it's a recurring event. After you've entered information about an event, you can send yourself a reminder and even invite others to the event.

Finally, the Maps app provides maps and directions to get you where you need to go.

Get Up to Speed with the News App

1. The News app is one of the apps represented by a tile in the Start menu. Click the Start button and then click the News tile (look for the tile with the word News in the bottom-left corner). The News app opens, showing Headlines (see **Figure 10-1**) and a scrollable list of news categories, such as Top Stories, World, Technology, and Entertainment.

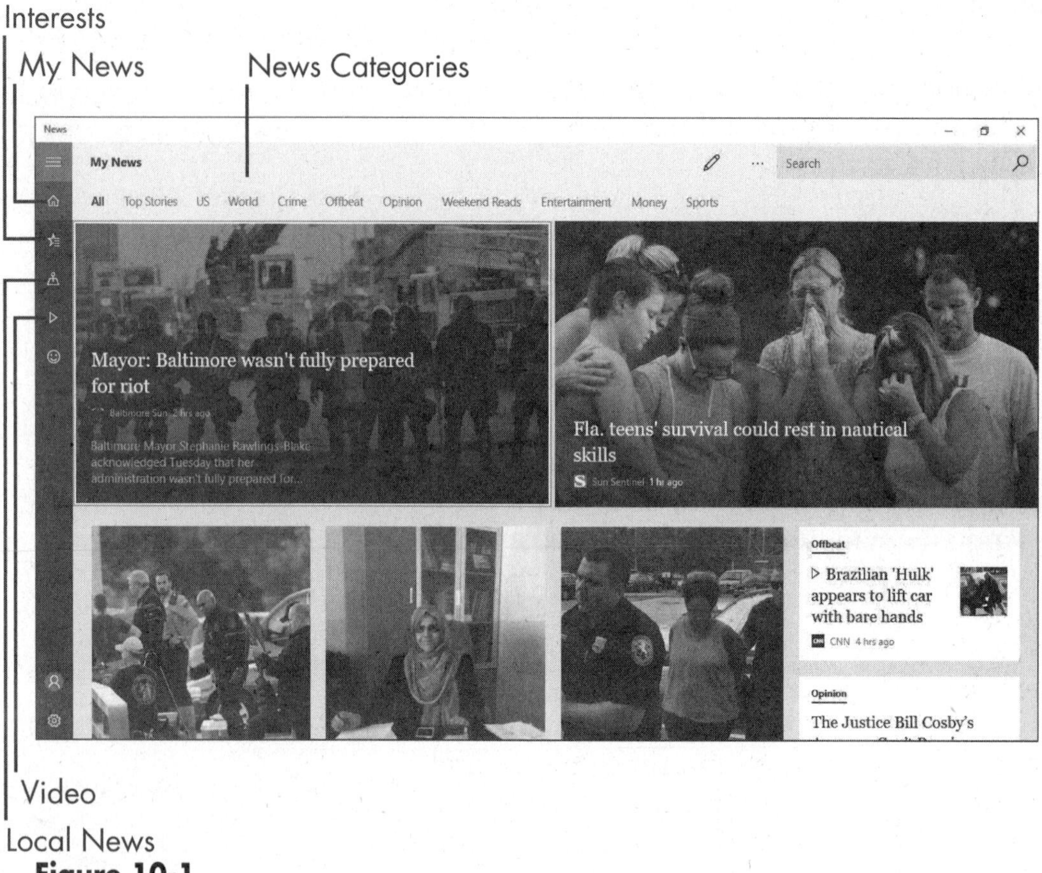

Interests
My News   News Categories

Video
Local News

Figure 10-1

2. Click a news category, such as World, Technology, Politics, and Entertainment, at the top of the screen.

3. Click and drag the vertical scroll bar on the right to scroll down and view the headlines. Click any story that sounds of interest to display it (see **Figure 10-2**).

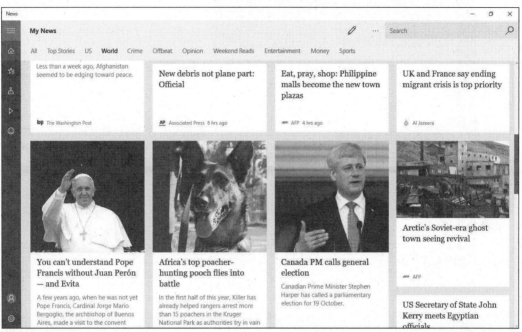

Figure 10-2

4. Use the arrows on the middle of the right and left sides to move to the next or previous page or story, and click the arrow in the top-left corner to go back to the previous story.

5. Type a term in the search field at the top right of the News app and click the search icon to see headlines related to that topic (see **Figure 10-3**). Click a story to display the entire article. To add the topic to the news categories along the top of the News app, click the Add Interest button (the star-shaped icon to the left of the search field).

6. Click the Interests button in the toolbar on the left and click the Add an Interest button; the drop-down box shown in **Figure 10-4** appears. Enter a new interest here.

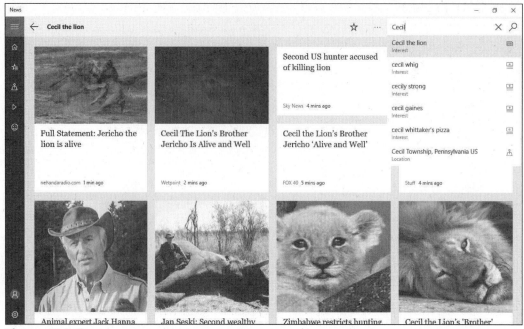

Figure 10-3

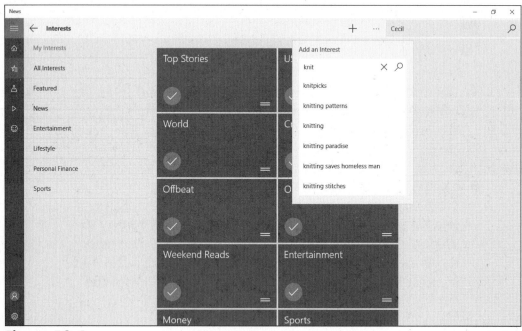

Figure 10-4

7. Click a check mark in a circle on an interest to remove it. It will no longer appear in the list of categories on the News home page.

 The News app also includes access to Local news, Videos, and Interests on the toolbar on the left side of the window.

Display Weather Views

1. Weather offers several sets of information. Click the Start button, and then click the Weather tile to open the Weather app showing the forecast for the next several days (see **Figure 10-5**). If access to your location is requested, click Yes.

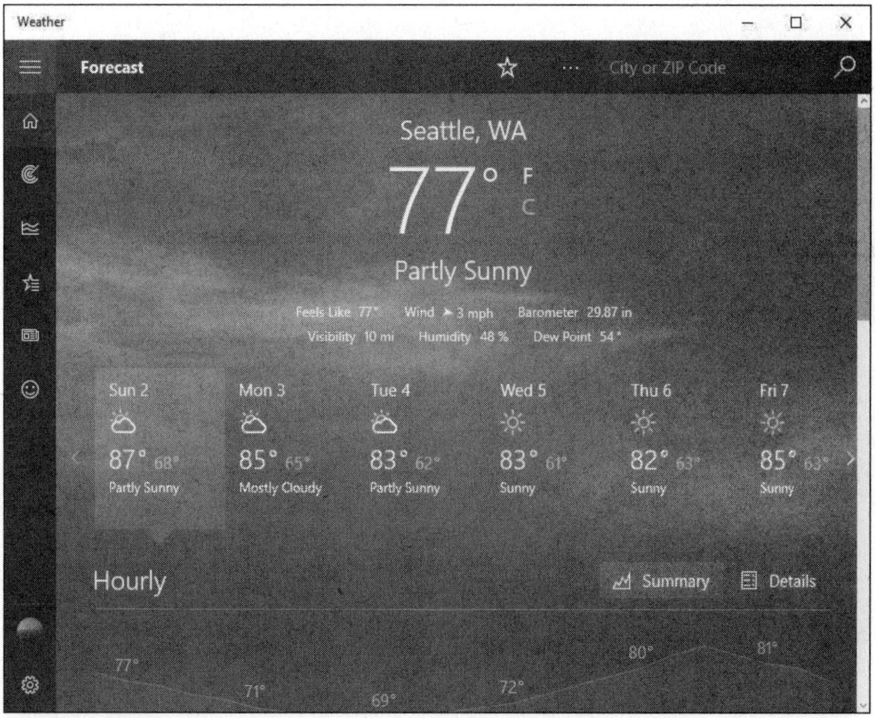

Figure 10-5

2. Scroll down to view the forecast for the next 24 hours, Day Details including Humidity, Max Wind speed, and Sunrise time, and records for this date, such as Record Rain, Record High temperature, and Record Low temperature.

3. Click the Menu button in the top-left corner of the Weather app. The choices shown in the menu in **Figure 10-6** appear.

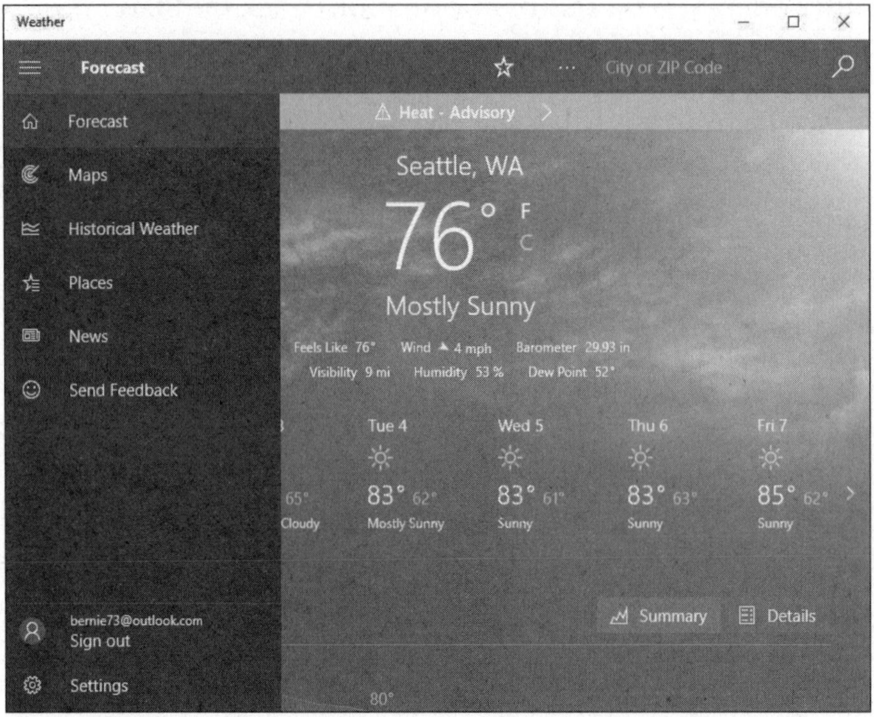

Figure 10-6

4. Click Historical Weather; a chart of historical weather trends is displayed.

5. Click Maps; a weather map for your region is shown.

6. Click Settings to set the units (Fahrenheit or Celsius) for temperature or to change your location.

Specify a Place in Weather

1. You can specify one or more favorite places and then display detailed weather information for any of those places easily. To add a place, click the Start button, and then click the Weather tile.

2. Click in the search field in the top-right corner of the Weather app and start typing a city name. Click the correct city in the search results; the forecast for that city appears in the Weather app.

3. Click the Add to Favorites button (the star-shaped icon at the top of the screen) and then click Close.

4. Click the Places button (the star in the left toolbar) to display your Favorite Places as shown in **Figure 10-7**.

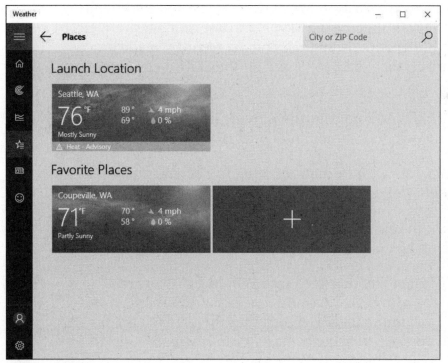

Figure 10-7

5. Click one of the Favorite places to display information for it.

 You can pin the displayed weather for a particular location to the Start menu. This creates a tile that you can click to retrieve the weather for that location. To pin a location, with the location displayed, click the Pin button (the pin-shaped button at the top of the window).

 To remove a location from your Favorite places, display the Forecast for that location and then click the Remove from Favorites button (the white star at the top of the window).

Add a Contact

1. After you've entered contacts in the People app, you can look up information about them and even send them email, call them using Skype, or post messages to their social network using their contact record. To add a new contact, click the People tile on the Start menu to open the app.

2. Click the Add button (the plus symbol) in the left pane of the window shown in **Figure 10-8**.

3. Enter contact information in the form that appears, as shown in **Figure 10-9**.

4. Click the Save button in the upper-right corner of the dialog box.

 When you're logged into Windows 10 with a Windows Live account, contacts from that account are automatically copied into the People app. It's also possible to bring contacts from other accounts into your People app. With the People app open, click the More button (three dots in a line) in the top of the left pane, and then click Settings in the drop-down

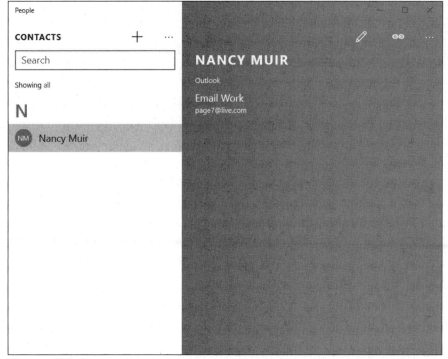

Figure 10-8

Figure 10-9

list. In the Settings window, click Add an Account. Click an email account type and sign in to the account you want to add. In the dialog box that appears, scroll down and click Accept. (Note that this not only allows the People app to import your contacts from your other account, but also allows other Windows apps access to information on calendars, email, and other info in your other account).

 You can find contacts quickly by clicking the search field at the top of the left pane of the People home screen. Type the first letter of the name, which displays a list of contacts whose names start with that letter. Continue to type until the contact's name appears in the list.

Edit Contact Information

1. Sometimes, you get new information about a contact or find that the information you've already saved to that person's profile changes. To update the information, you can edit the contact. Click the People tile on the Start menu.

2. Click a contact.

3. Click the Edit button (shaped like a pencil) in the upper-right corner of the window.

4. In the Edit Contact screen (see **Figure 10-10**), edit or add any information in text fields for the contact.

5. For any field with a + symbol next to it, click to display additional options; for example, if you click Phone, you can choose from options such as Mobile, Home, or Work.

6. Click the Save button.

 Click the Other button to add or edit a job title, significant other, website, or notes for your contact.

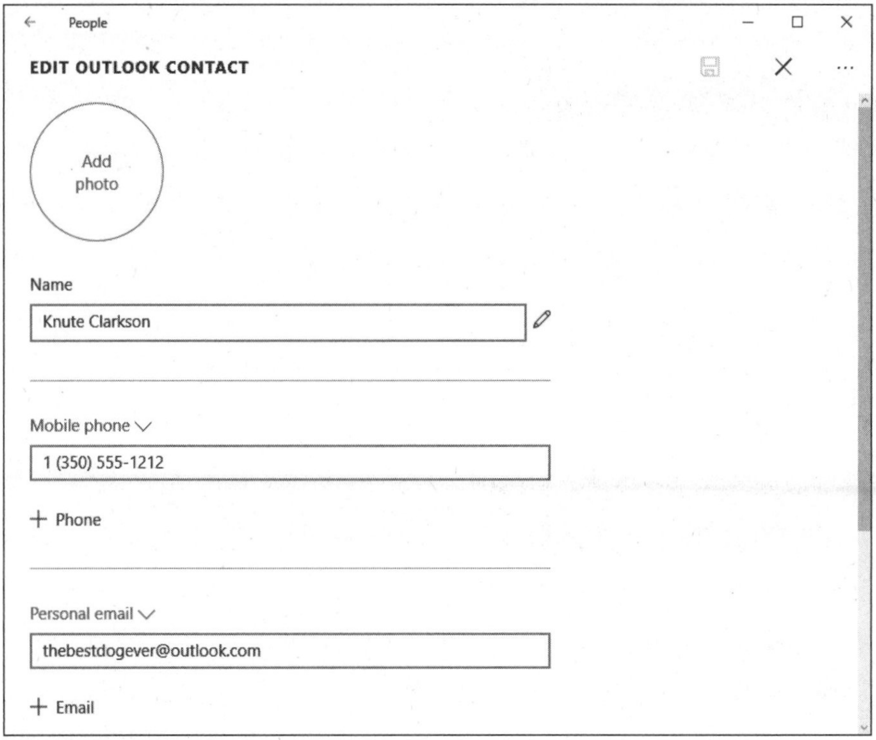

Figure 10-10

Send Email to Contacts

1. After you've added contact information, including an email address, you can use the People app to quickly address an email. Click the People app on the Start menu.

2. Click a contact.

3. Click on the contact's email address in the right panel. In the pop-up menu, click Mail and then click OK (see **Figure 10-11**). If asked which account to use, click the account you've already set up.

4. The Mail app opens with the new message form displayed. Click the Cc & Bcc button to display those fields and then enter any addresses you want to copy on the message, as shown in **Figure 10-12**.

Figure 10-11

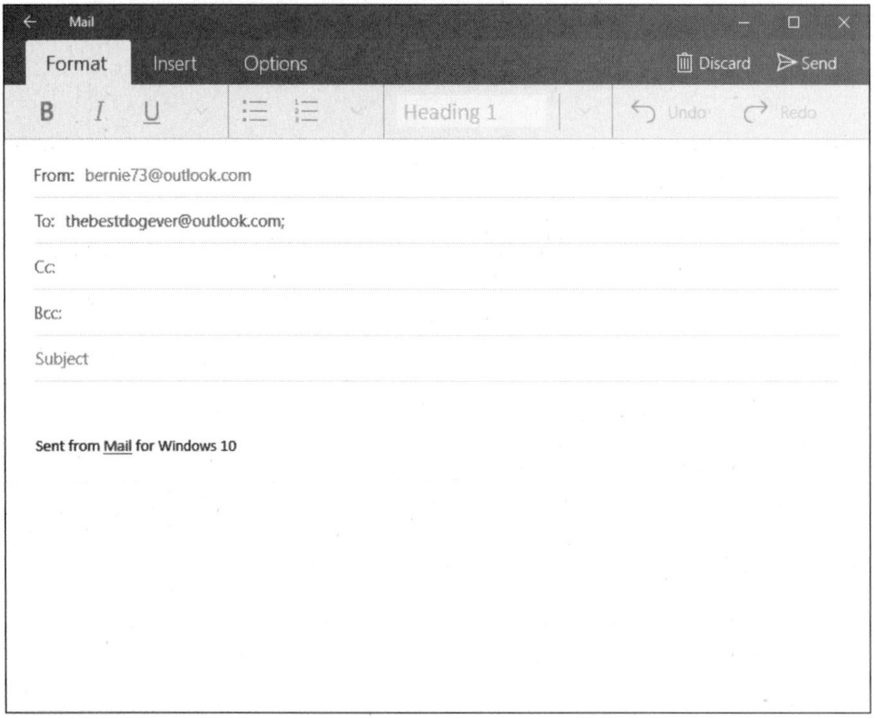

Figure 10-12

5. Click in the Subject field and enter a subject for the message.

6. Click in the message area (below the Subject) and enter your message. You can click the Format tab to access some useful text formatting tools.

7. If you want to add attachments, click the Insert tab, click Attach File, browse for a file, and then click Open.

8. Click the Send button in the upper-right corner of the window.

Add an Event to Your Calendar

1. The Calendar app is a great way to track your activities. To display and add an event to your Calendar, click the Calendar tile on the Start menu.

2. Click the view you prefer from the list at the top of the window: Day, Work Week, Week, Month, or Today (see **Figure 10-13**).

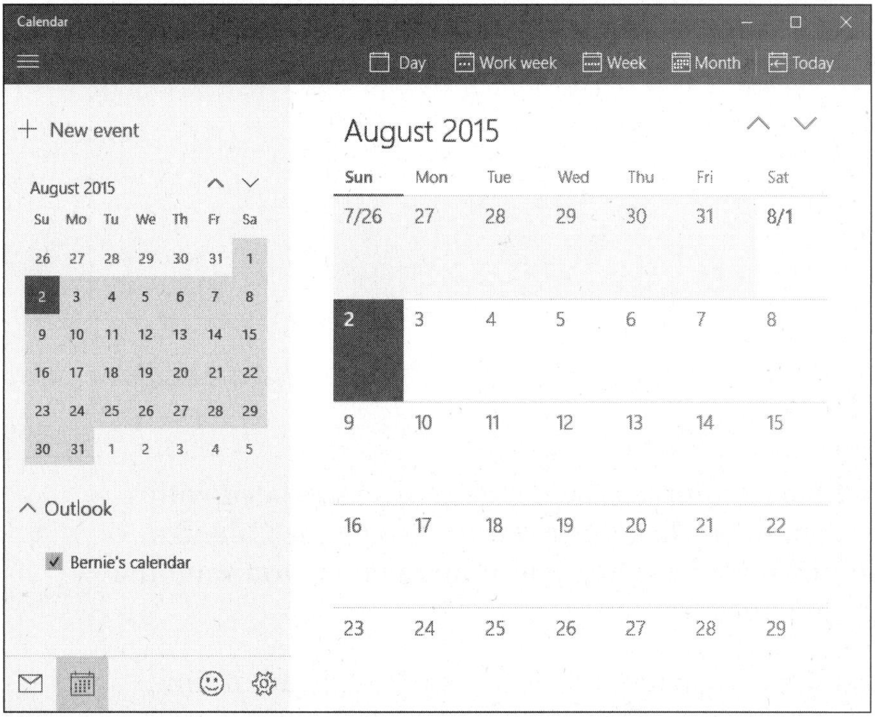

Figure 10-13

3. Click the New Event button in the upper-left corner of the window.

4. In the Details dialog box that appears (see **Figure 10-14**), enter the details of the event in text boxes (such as Event Name or Location) or choose them from drop-down calendars or lists (such as Start or End).

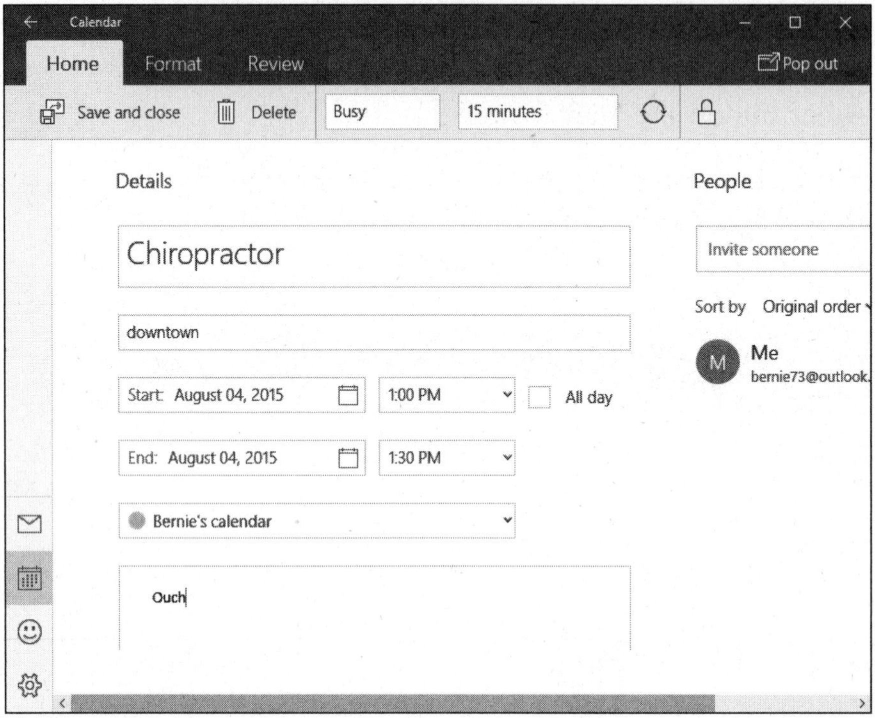

Figure 10-14

5. If you have multiple calendar accounts associated with your computer, click the arrow to display the Calendar drop-down list and then select the calendar you want the event to appear in.

6. If you want to be reminded of the event ahead of time, click the Reminder field at the top of the window (see **Figure 10-15**) and select how long before the event the reminder should occur, such as 15 minutes or 1 week.

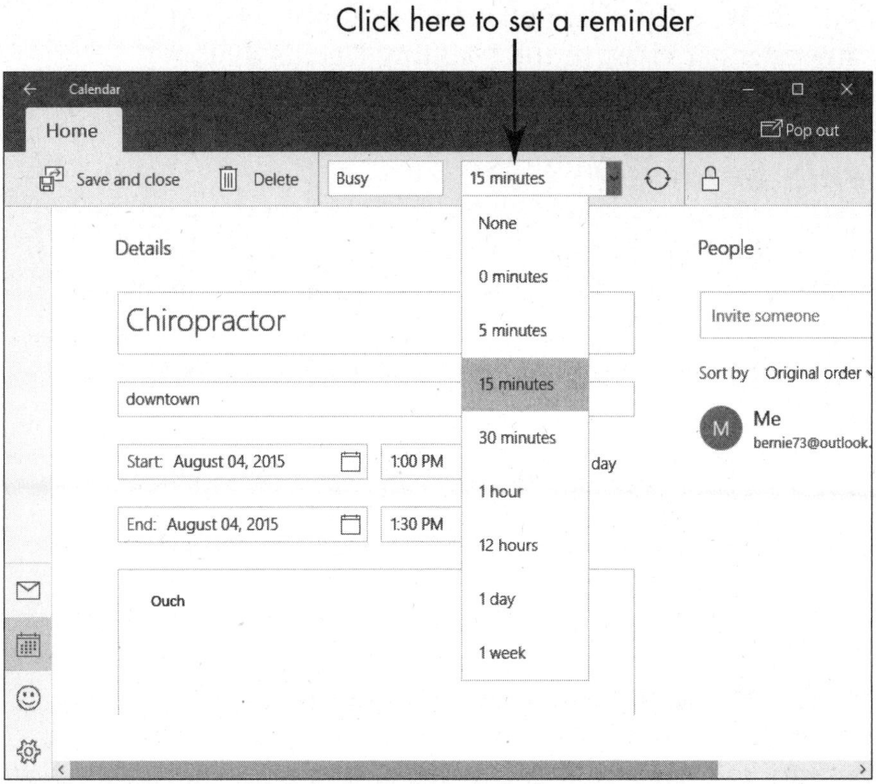

Click here to set a reminder

Figure 10-15

7. Click the Save & Close button.

If you want to create a recurring event such as a weekly meeting or monthly get-together with friends, use the Repeat button in the Details dialog box. This offers intervals ranging from every day to every year and creates multiple calendar entries accordingly.

To show events from calendars associated with your computer, such as a US Holidays calendar or the calendar from an email account, with the Calendar app open, click the drop-down list arrow for Outlook or another provider, such as Gmail, in the left pane of the window to open the list of available calendars. Click the check box for any calendar you want to show events from.

To edit an event after you create it, simply click it in any calendar view. In the resulting Details dialog box, modify the details, and then click Save & Close.

Invite People to an Event

1. If you're setting up an event, such as your neighborhood association's meeting or a party, the Calendar app offers a handy way to get the invites out to everybody involved. To create an event and invite others to it, click the New Event button.

2. In the Details dialog box that appears, enter the details of the event in text boxes (such as Event Name and Location) or choose them from drop-down lists (such as Start Time and End Time).

3. Click in the Invite Someone field and begin to enter a name. The People app will suggest people and email addresses from your contacts; click one (see **Figure 10-16**). If you want to invite another person, start to enter the name in the Invite Someone field and click the correct name from the suggested contacts.

4. Click the Send button in the upper-left corner of the dialog box. Windows sends an email with details of the event to each invitee.

 If you're browsing through the months or weeks in the Calendar app and want to quickly return to today's events, click Today in the upper-right corner of the Calendar home window.

 You can click the click the Settings button (a sprocket-shaped icon) to change Calendar Settings, such as changing the first day of the week, or adding additional accounts that will sync information with the Calendar app. You can also edit Account settings.

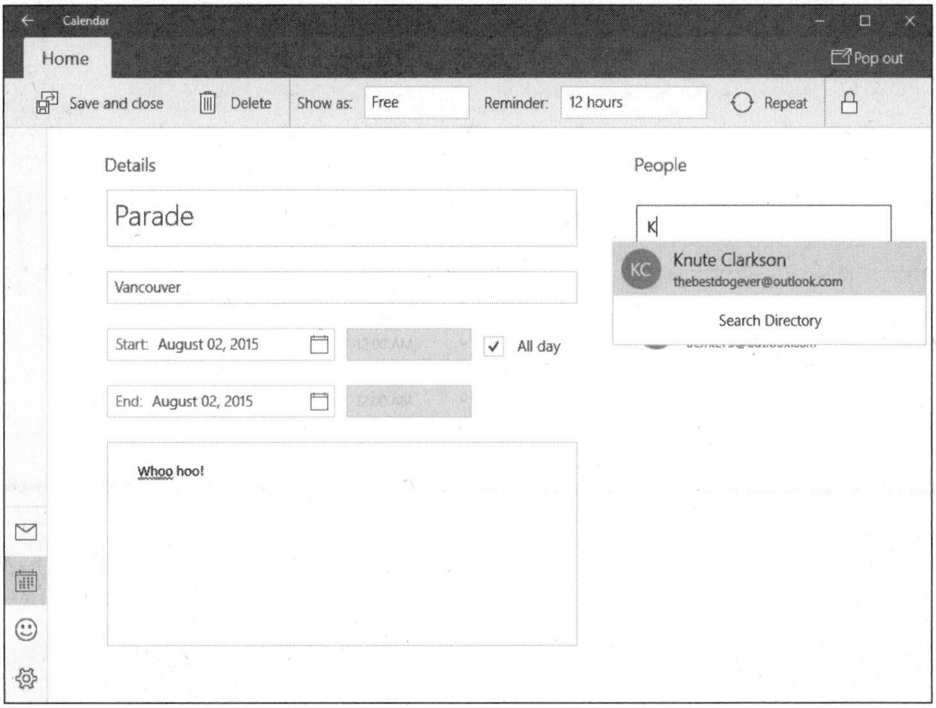

Figure 10-16

Use the Maps App

Mapping applications make use of information about your location whenever you're connected to the Internet to provide directions, updates on traffic, and even listings of local businesses, such as restaurants and gas stations. Mapping apps are really useful if you are moving outside your home or office with a laptop or tablet computer.

The Maps app is preinstalled with Windows 10. This app allows you to keep a record of favorite locations and even get 3-D views of many major cities.

Set Your Location

When you first open Maps from the Start menu, you see a message (see **Figure 10-17**) asking if Maps can use your location. If you click the No button, Maps can only estimate your location, so directions and traffic information may be less exact. If you click the Yes button,

Maps can use your location to provide more specific maps, but you are then allowing a remote service to pinpoint your location (though with Maps that affords little risk).

For example, if children use your laptop, allowing a service to pinpoint your location could also allow people to find them. However, for most folks, allowing use of your location for a service such as Maps is pretty safe, so you can click Yes to continue. The map that appears will then be specific to your location.

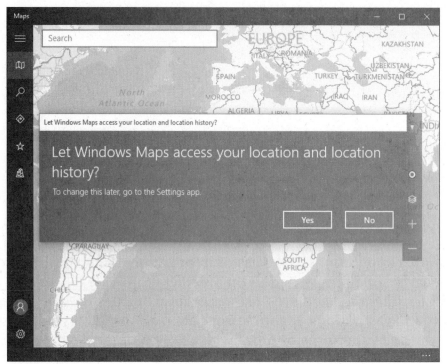

Figure 10-17

Show Traffic

1. After you open Maps, toolbars appear along the left and right sides of the app (see **Figure 10-18**). Click the Show My Location button on the right side (the third button down resembling a bull's-eye) to zoom in on your location.

Directions

Show My Location

Search

Tilt

Map

Rotate Map So North Is Up

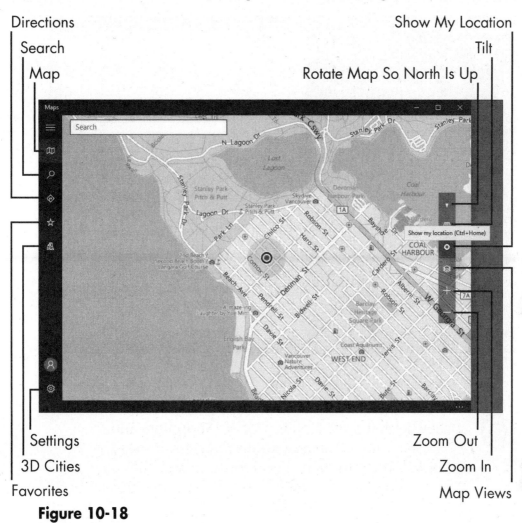

Settings

Zoom Out

3D Cities

Zoom In

Favorites

Map Views

Figure 10-18

2. Click the Map Views button on the right and then click Traffic in the pop-up that appears. Traffic alerts such as those shown in **Figure 10-19** appear.

3. Click an alert to display information about its nature and severity, start time, and estimated end time (refer to Figure 10-19).

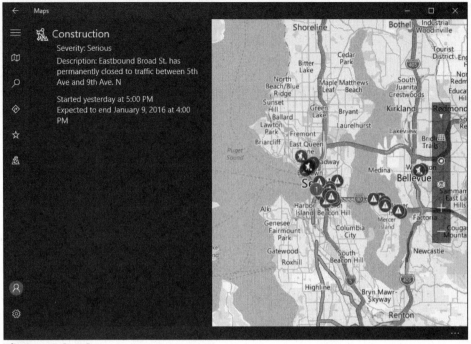

Figure 10-19

 You can click the Search tool to get a list of categories such as Restaurants, Hotels, Coffee, Shopping, and Museums. Click a category to display a list of nearby locations. You can then click a location and click links to access that business's website, get directions, or place a call to it using Skype.

Get Directions

1. With the Maps app open, click the Directions button. A Directions panel appears (see **Figure 10-20**).

2. Enter a start point in the field labeled A.

3. Enter a destination address in the field labeled B and click the arrow on the right side of that field.

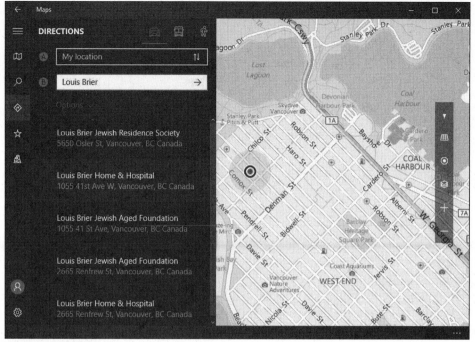

Figure 10-20

4. If you are offered a few choices for the start point or destination, click the one you want, and then click one of three icons: Drive (a car), Transit (a bus), or Walking (a person) to get directions for that mode of transportation (see **Figure 10-21**).

 When you open the Directions panel, click the Options link (refer to Figure 10-20) to choose to avoid highways, ferries, unpaved roads, tunnels, or tolls.

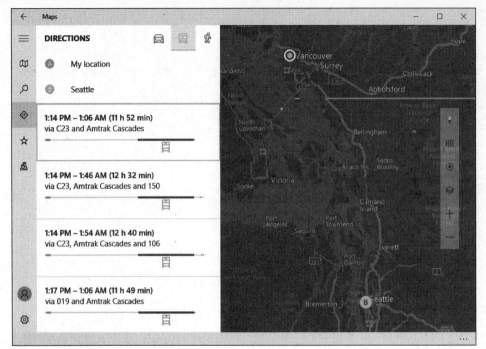

Figure 10-21

Part III
Going Online

Understanding Internet Basics

For many people, going online might be the major reason to buy a computer. You can use the Internet to check stock quotes, play interactive games with others, shop, and file your taxes, for example. For seniors especially, the Internet can provide wonderful ways to keep in touch with family and friends located around the country or on the other side of the world via email, instant messaging, or video calling. You can share photos of your grand-children or connect with others who share your hobbies or interests.

But before you begin all those wonderful activi-ities, it helps to understand some basics about the Internet and how it works.

This chapter helps you understand what the Internet and World Wide Web are, as well as some basics about connecting to the Internet and navigating it. I also tell you about the Microsoft Edge app, which is new with Windows 10.

Understand What the Internet Is

The "Internet," "links," the "web". . . . People and the media bounce around many online-related terms these days, and folks sometimes use them incorrectly. Your first step in getting familiar with the Internet is to understand what some of these terms mean.

Here's a list of common Internet-related terms:

➠ The *Internet* is a large network of computers that contain information and technology tools that anybody with an Internet connection can access. (See the next section for information about Internet connections.)

➠ Residing on that network of computers is a huge set of documents and services, which form the *World Wide Web*, usually referred to as just the *web*.

➠ The web includes *websites*, which are made up of collections of *web pages* just as a book is made up of individual pages. Websites have many purposes: For example, a website can be informational, function as a retail store, or host social networking communities where people can exchange ideas and thoughts.

➠ You can buy, sell, or bid for a wide variety of items in an entire online marketplace referred to as the world of *e-commerce*.

➠ To get around online, you use a software program called a *browser*. Many browsers are available, and they're free. Microsoft Edge is Microsoft's latest browser; other available browsers include Mozilla Firefox, Google Chrome, Safari, and Opera. Browsers offer tools to help you navigate from website to website and from one web page to another.

➠ Each web page has a unique address that you use to reach it, called a *Uniform Resource Locator (URL)*. You enter a URL in a browser's address bar to go to a website or a particular page within a site.

➡️ When you open a website, you might see colored text or graphics that represent *hyperlinks*, also referred to as *links*. You can click links to move from place to place within a web page, within a website, or between websites. **Figure 11-1** shows some hyperlinks indicated by colored text or graphics.

Graphical hyperlink

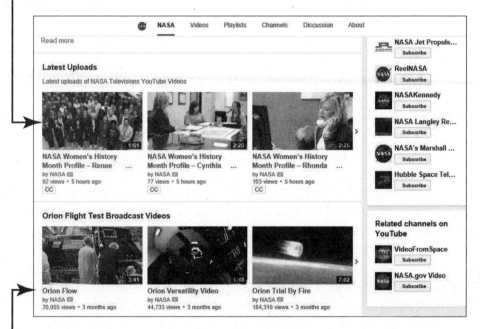

Text hyperlink

Figure 11-1

🎯 A link can be a graphic (such as a company logo or button) or text. A text link is identifiable by colored text, which is sometimes underlined and which sometimes changes color when you hover your mouse over it. After you click a link, the link itself usually changes color to indicate that you've followed the link. Some websites include tabs and drop-down lists or menus for navigation, as well.

Explore Different Types of Internet Connections

Before you can connect to the Internet for the first time, you have to have certain hardware in place and choose your *Internet service provider* (also referred to as an *ISP* or simply a *provider*). An ISP is a company that owns dedicated computers (called *servers*) that you use to access the Internet. ISPs charge a monthly fee for this service.

You can choose a type of connection to go online. The type of connection you want determines which companies you can choose from to provide the service. For example, a DSL connection might come through your phone company, whereas a cable connection is available through your cable-TV company. Not every type of connection is necessarily available in every area, so check first with phone, cable, and local Internet providers rather than national or international providers to find out your options and costs. Some ISPs offer discounts to AARP members, for example.

Each connection type offers pros and cons in terms of the quality of the signal and potential service interruptions, depending on the company and your locale, so do your homework before signing on the dotted line. Here are the most common types of connections:

➡ **Digital Subscriber Line (DSL):** This service is delivered through your phone land line, but your phone is available to you to make calls even when you're connected to the Internet. DSL is a form of broadband communication, which may use phone lines and fiber-optic cables for transmission. You have to subscribe to a broadband service (check with your phone company) and pay a monthly fee for access. Some providers also let you purchase DSL service "naked," or without telephone service if you prefer to use a mobile phone rather than a land line.

➡ **Cable:** You may instead go through your local cable company to get your Internet service via the cable that brings your TV programming. This is another type of broadband service, and it's relatively fast. Check with your cable company for monthly fees.

Many cable providers offer plans that bundle TV, phone, and Internet services.

➡ **Satellite:** Especially in rural areas, satellite Internet providers may be your only option. This requires that you install a satellite dish. HughesNet, dishNET (from Dish Network), and Exede (from WildBlue) are three providers of satellite connections to check into.

➡ **Wireless hotspots:** If you take a wireless-enabled laptop computer, tablet, or smartphone with you on a trip, you can piggyback on a connection somebody else has made. You will find wireless hotspots in many public places, such as airports, cafes, and hotels. If you're in range of such a hotspot, your computer usually finds the connection automatically, making Internet service available to you for free or for a fee. You can also buy your own portable wireless hotspot from a provider such as Verizon or, in some cases, use your smartphone to connect a computer or tablet to the Internet via a cellular network. This type of connection also requires a data plan with the mobile carrier.

 Satellite and mobile connections often restrict how much data you can download per month. Overages with mobile data plans can be expensive, so be sure to monitor your data usage once you get started with a new plan.

➡ **Dialup:** This is the slowest connection method, but it's relatively inexpensive. With a dialup connection, you use a phone line to connect to the Internet, entering some phone numbers (*local access numbers*) that your ISP provides. Using these local access numbers, you won't incur long distance charges for your connection. However, with this type of connection, you can't use a phone line for phone calls while you're connected to the Internet, so it's no longer a popular way to connect.

Internet connections have different speeds that depend partially on your computer's capabilities and partially on the connection you get from your provider. Before you choose a provider, it's important to understand how faster connection speeds can benefit you:

➡ Faster speeds allow you to send data faster — for example, to download a photo to your computer. In addition, web pages and images display faster.

➡ Dialup connection speeds run at the low end, about 56 kilobits per second, or Kbps. Most broadband connections today start at around 500 to 600 Kbps and range up to 15 Mbps (megabits per second), or more. If you have a slower connection, a file might take minutes to upload. (For example, you upload a file you're attaching to an email.) This same operation might take only seconds at a higher speed.

➡ Broadband services typically offer different plans that provide different access speeds. These plans can give you savings if you're economy minded and don't mind the lower speeds, or offer you much better speeds if you're willing to pay for them.

Depending on your type of connection, you'll need different hardware:

➡ Many desktop and laptop computers come with a built-in modem for dialup connections (though these are being left out more and more as people move to wireless connections) and are enabled for wireless.

➡ A broadband connection uses an Ethernet cable and a broadband modem, which your provider should make available. For a wired connection, the Ethernet cable connects the modem to your computer. From there, you will also need a telephone cable to connect the modem to your phone line (for DSL) or a coaxial cable to connect the modem with a cable line or incoming line from satellite dish.

➡ If you want to make your broadband connection wireless, your phone or cable company can provide you with a wireless router (usually for a price), or you can buy one from an office supply or electronics store. Instead of connecting the modem to the computer, you use the Ethernet cable to connect the broadband modem to the wireless router, which enables two-way wireless communication. A wireless adapter in the computer enables it to connect with the wireless router. Most new desktop and laptop computers now offer built-in wireless adapters that enable them to pick up wireless signals. If you have a system that doesn't have a built-in wireless modem, you can add this hardware by buying and installing an internal wireless adapter card (for desktops) or a USB adapter (for laptops).

If this all sounds like Greek to you, review your computer's system specifications for information about its networking capabilities, and then visit a computer or major office supply store and ask representatives for their advice about your specific hardware.

 Many providers offer free or low-cost setup when you open a new account. If you're not technical by nature, consider taking advantage of this when you sign up.

Set Up an Internet Connection

1. The first step is to set up a connection in Windows so you can access the Internet. Begin by clicking the Start menu button on the taskbar, and then click Settings on the Start menu.

2. Click Network & Internet.

3. In the resulting window, click Network and Sharing Center.

4. In the resulting Network and Sharing Center window (see **Figure 11-2**), click the Set Up a New Connection or Network link.

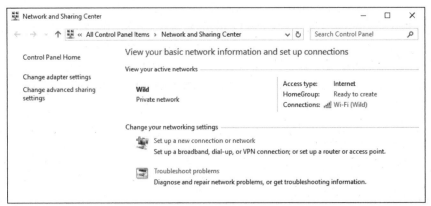

Figure 11-2

5. In the Choose a Connection Option window, click Next to accept the default option of creating a new Internet connection. If you're already connected to the Internet, a window appears; click Set Up a New Connection Anyway.

6. In the resulting dialog box, click your connection. (These steps follow the selection of Broadband.)

7. In the resulting dialog box, shown in **Figure 11-3**, enter your username and password, and change the connection name if you wish (this is optional), and then click Connect. Windows automatically detects the connection, and the Network and Sharing Center appears with your connection listed.

 In some cases, if you have a disc from your ISP, you don't need to follow the preceding steps. Just pop that DVD into your DVD-ROM drive, and in no time, a window appears that gives you the steps to follow to get set up.

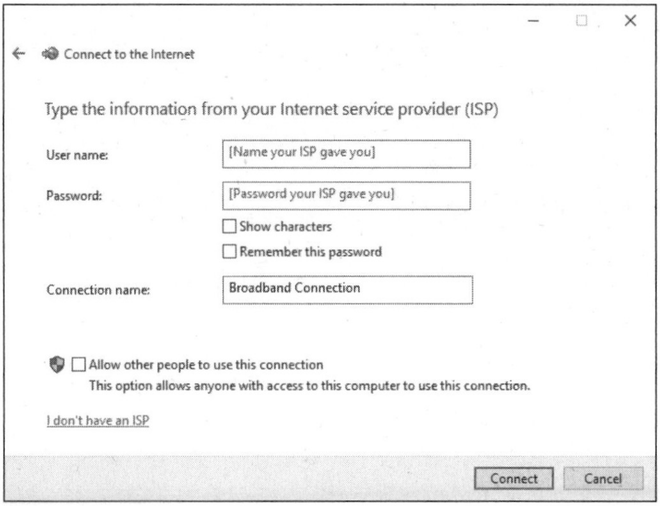

Figure 11-3

Practice Navigation Basics with the Microsoft Edge App

1. A browser is a program that you use to navigate, manage, and use features on the various pages of content on the web. You can practice how to get around the web using a browser such as the new Microsoft Edge, included with Windows 10. Open Microsoft Edge by clicking the Microsoft Edge button on the taskbar.

2. Enter a website address such as the example shown in **Figure 11-4,** http://understandingnano.com, in the Search or Enter Web Address box on the Start page, and then press Enter. (You also can click the address bar at the top, type the website address, and press Enter. This is the method to use after you've displayed the first web-site page on a tab in Microsoft Edge or if you're having Microsoft Edge display a home page when it starts up, as described later, instead of the Start page.)

3. On the resulting website, click a link to display another page. Try using navigation tools on the page (such as the What Is Nanotechnology? menu on the page in **Figure 11-4**) or enter another address in the address bar and press Enter to proceed to another page.

Enter a web address here

Figure 11-4

 A link can be text or graphics (such as an icon or photo). A text link is identifiable by colored text, sometimes blue. After you click a link, it usually changes to another color (such as purple) to show that it's been followed.

4. Click the Back button to the left of the address bar to move back to the first page that you visited. Click the Forward button just to the right of the Back button to go forward to the second page that you visited.

 The Refresh button (a curved arrow) to the right of the Forward button is useful for navigating sites. Clicking the Refresh button redisplays the current page. This is especially useful if a page, such as on a stock market site, updates information frequently. You can also use the Refresh button if a page doesn't load correctly; it might load correctly when refreshed.

You can quickly access frequently viewed sites by marking them as Favorites. See Chapter 12 for more info about marking and organizing Favorites.

Using Internet Explorer When You Need It

1. Windows 10 also includes Internet Explorer (IE) 11 to support older websites that may not be compatible with Microsoft Edge. If you encounter a website or page that won't load properly in IE, click the More Actions button (to the far right of the address bar, with three dots in a horizontal row), and then click Open with Internet Explorer (see **Figure 11-5**).

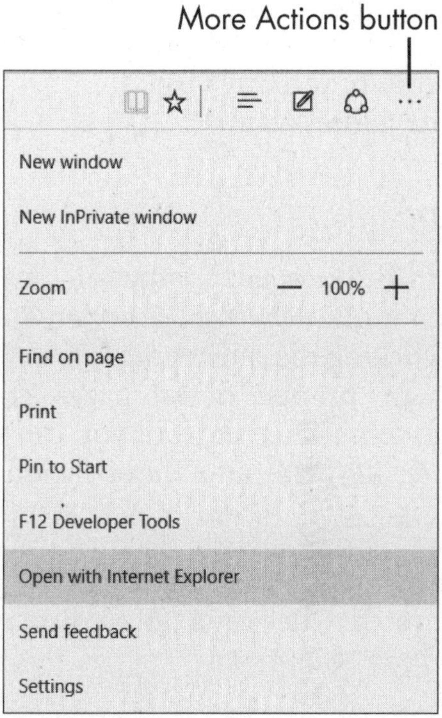

More Actions button

New window
New InPrivate window
Zoom   — 100% +
Find on page
Print
Pin to Start
F12 Developer Tools
Open with Internet Explorer
Send feedback
Settings

Figure 11-5

Note: In some cases, Microsoft Edge may display a message that a website needs Internet Explorer. When that happens, click the Open with Internet Explorer button that appears on the message page. To open IE 11 from the Windows desktop, click in the Cortana search box on the taskbar, type **internet explorer,** and click Internet Explorer in the search results.

2. From there, browsing is similar to browsing in Microsoft Edge. Enter an address such as www.microsoft.com in the address bar, and press Enter. Note you can also enter a search term here to search for online content.

3. Click the Previous button to return to the page you just left.

4. Click the Next button to go back to the second site you visited.

 Both Microsoft Edge and IE use tabs to load multiple websites at one time. See the next section, "Understand Tabs in Browsers," for more about using them.

 In IE 11, you can display a history of recently visited sites by clicking the arrow in the address bar.

Understand Tabs in Browsers

Several browsers use tabs (**Figure 11-6** shows tabs in the Microsoft Edge app), which allow you to keep multiple web pages open at once and easily switch among them by clicking the tabs. A *tab* is a sort of window you can use to navigate to any number of web pages. You don't have to create a new tab to go to another site, but you can more quickly switch between two or more sites without a lot of clicking around or entering URLs.

In Microsoft Edge and IE, for example, tabs across the top of the page look like tabs used to divide index cards. Click on a tab to display that page.

To add a new tab in Microsoft Edge or IE, click the New Tab button to the right of the current far-right tab, or press Ctrl+T. Type the URL you want to show in the Search or Enter Web Address box (Microsoft Edge only) or address bar for the new tab, and then press Enter. (See **Figure 11-7.**) To close a tab, click the Close Tab (X) button on the right end of the tab. Pressing Ctrl+W closes the current tab. To go to another open tab, simply click anywhere on the tab away from the Close Tab button.

Open tab   Active tab you're on   New Tab button

Figure 11-6

Enter web address here   Close Tab button New Tab button

Figure 11-7

Understand Start and Home Pages

When you open Microsoft Edge, the first page you see by default is the Start page. In addition to offering the Search or Enter Web Address box for you to use to begin browsing, it displays current news from MSN. If you want to make changes to this page, you can click the Customize link at the upper right. In the screen that appears, you can change the default language, and click the news topics that you want to appear at the top of the Start page news feed. Click Save to apply your changes.

In contrast, in most browsers the first page you see when you open the browser is your home page, which you can choose. In fact, you can even choose to reload the tab(s) you had open during your last browser session, or load a blank tab page, as your home page(s). Your home page(s) appears automatically every time you open Microsoft Edge, so choose a site that you go to often for this setting. For example, if you like to start your day by reading the news from the online version of your local paper, you could set that up as your home page. Or, if you prefer to start the day by going to a financial site and checking stock quotes and news, you could make that website your home page. See the next task, where I tell you how to set this up.

Set Up a Home Page in Microsoft Edge

1. Open Microsoft Edge. Click the More Actions button at upper right, and choose Settings from the menu.

2. In the resulting Settings pane, under the Open With section, click the option button for the type of home page you want:

- **New Tab Page:** Opens a blank tab as your home page. You can customize what appears on new tabs using the Open New Tabs With drop-down list.

- **Previous Pages:** Sets the prior pages that you had open during your last browsing session as your home pages.

- **A Specific Page or Pages:** Lets you choose a specific home page. When you click this option, a drop-down list appears beneath it. Click the list, and in the menu that appears, click MSN, Bing, or Custom. If you click Custom, an Enter a Web Address text box appears. Enter a website address to use as your home page, as shown in **Figure 11-8,** and then click the Add (plus) button to the right of the box. (You can even use the box and the Add button to add additional home pages.)

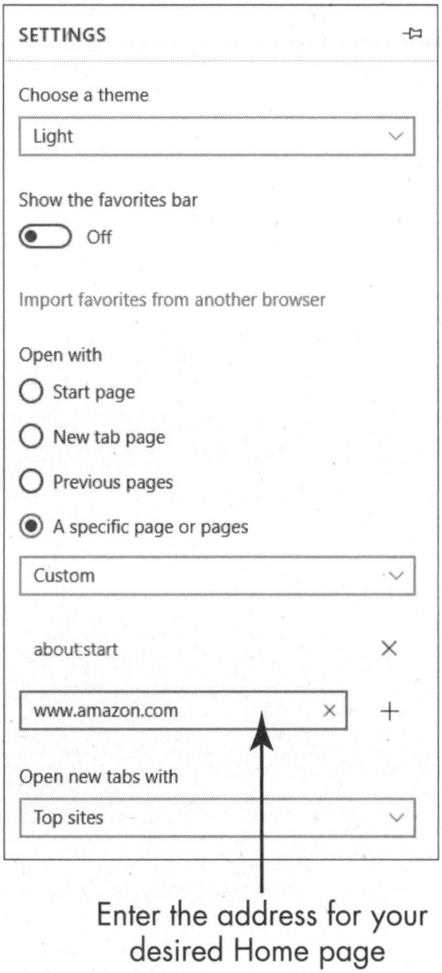

SETTINGS

Choose a theme

Light

Show the favorites bar

Off

Import favorites from another browser

Open with

○ Start page

○ New tab page

○ Previous pages

◉ A specific page or pages

Custom

about:start   ✕

www.amazon.com   ✕   ＋

Open new tabs with

Top sites

Enter the address for your
desired Home page

Figure 11-8

3. After you choose a home page setting, press Esc to close the Settings pane. Then close and restart Microsoft Edge to go to your home page.

 To remove a specific home page that you've set up, go to the Settings pane mentioned in Step 2 and, under the A Specific Page or Pages option, click the web page, and then click the Remove (X) button beside it. Set another home page as needed, and then press Esc to close the pane.

Browsing the Web

Chapter

12

A *browser* is a program that you can use to move from one web page to another, but you can also use it to perform searches for information and images. Most browsers, such as Microsoft Edge, Google Chrome, and Mozilla Firefox, are available for free. Macintosh computers come with a browser called Safari preinstalled with the operating system.

Chapter 11 introduced browser basics, such as how to go directly to a site when you know the web address, how to use the Back and Forward buttons to move among sites you've visited, and how to set up the home page that opens automatically when you launch your browser.

In this chapter, you discover the ins and outs of using Microsoft Edge — the latest new browser included with Windows 10.

By using Microsoft Edge, you can

➠ **Navigate all around the web.** Use the Microsoft Edge navigation features to go back to places you've been (via the Favorites and History features), and use Bing or Cortana to search for new places to visit.

Get ready to . . .

➡ **Take advantage of reading and note-taking features.** You can create a list of articles you'd like to read later, view them in Reading view for a more natural reading experience, or make your own notes on a page.

➡ **Print content from web pages.** When you find what you want online, such as an image or article, just use Microsoft Edge's Print feature to generate a hard copy.

➡ **Customize your web-browsing experience.** You can modify some Microsoft Edge features such as the default home page to make your online work easier.

Learn More about Microsoft Edge

With Windows 10, Microsoft introduces a brand new browser: Microsoft Edge.

Microsoft Edge was designed to load web pages more quickly than its predecessor, Internet Explorer. It also features a less-cluttered screen (see **Figure 12-1**); no drop-down menus and dialog boxes for making settings, just a few simple buttons and an address bar along the top of the screen. You can use tabs to open additional pages. And, with settings you manage from the More Actions button menu, you can change what appears when you first open Edge and more.

Internet Explorer will still be available behind the scenes. It will open automatically whenever you try to browse to a page that's not up-to-date enough to open in Microsoft Edge. Most likely, you won't see that happen often. That's why this chapter teaches you how to handle a variety of tasks in Microsoft Edge only.

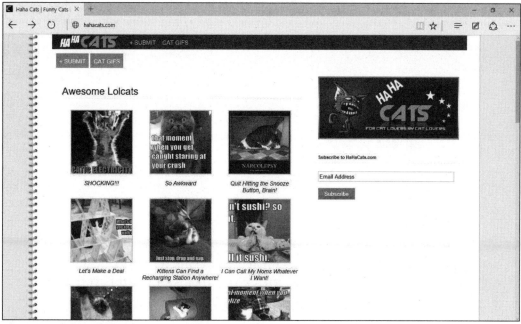

Figure 12-1

Search the Web

1. You can use words and phrases to search for information on the web using a search engine no matter which browser you use. In this example, you'll use Microsoft Edge and Google, a popular search engine. Open Microsoft Edge by clicking its Taskbar button, enter **www.google.com** in the address bar or the Search or Enter Web Address box, and press Enter.

2. Enter a search term in the search box and then press Enter.

 To start your search in a new tab, click the New Tab button or press Ctrl+T before entering your search term.

In the search results that appear (see **Figure 12-2**), you can click a link to go to that web page. If you don't see the link that you need, drag the scroll bar to view more results.

Click a link in the results list · Options button

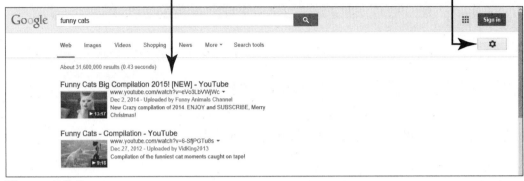

Figure 12-2

 If you don't at first see the scroll bar when you need it in Microsoft Edge, move the mouse pointer to the right edge of the screen, and the scroll bar will appear.

3. Click the Options button near the top-right corner (refer to Figure 12-2; it has a sprocket icon on it), and then click Advanced Search to change Search parameters.

4. In the resulting Advanced Search page, shown in **Figure 12-3,** modify the following parameters:

- **Find Pages With:** These options let you narrow the way words or phrases are searched; for example, you can find matches for only the exact wording you enter or enter words that you want to exclude from your results. For example, you could search *flu* and specify you don't want results that involve *swine flu*.

- **Then Narrow Your Results By:** Here you can select language and region. You can also limit results based on when information on the site was last updated, if you're looking for the most current information on the subject you're searching. You can specify a site address and where on the page to search. You can also search results to exclude explicit content by using the SafeSearch drop-down list, or adjust the file type, and *usage rights settings* (in other words, any copyrights that prohibit you from reusing content).

Advanced Search

Find pages with...		To do this in the search box
all these words:	Junny cats	Type the important words: tricolor rat terrier
this exact word or phrase:		Put exact words in quotes: "rat terrier"
any of these words:		Type OR between all the words you want: miniature OR standard
none of these words:		Put a minus sign just before words you don't want: -rodent, -"Jack Russell"
numbers ranging from:		to	Put 2 periods between the numbers and add a unit of measure: 10..35 lb, $300..$500, 2010..2011

Then narrow your results by...

language:	any language	Find pages in the language you select.
region:	any region	Find pages published in a particular region.
last update:	anytime	Find pages updated within the time you specify.
site or domain:		Search one site (like wikipedia.org) or limit your results to a domain like .edu, .org or .gov
terms appearing:	anywhere in the page	Search for terms in the whole page, page title, or web address, or links to the page you're looking for.
SafeSearch:	Show most relevant results	Tell SafeSearch whether to filter sexually explicit content.

Figure 12-3

5. When you're done with the settings, scroll down and click the Advanced Search button to run the search again with the new criteria.

You can perform a more simplified search that uses Bing Search in Microsoft Edge. Click in the Microsoft Edge address bar, type the search term, and press Enter. Bing doesn't offer as many advanced search options. However, if you pause as you type, you will see a list of Search Suggestions. You can click one to speed up your search. If you're starting on a fresh tab, you also can type your search term in the Search or Enter Web Address box and press Enter.

Knowing how search engines work can save you time. For example, if you search by entering *golden retriever*, you typically get sites that contain both words or either word. If you put a plus sign between these two keywords (*golden+retriever*), you get only sites that contain both words.

Search the Web with Cortana

1. Windows 10 includes Cortana, a built-in search assistant that can find files and apps on your computer and information on the web. Even better, if you have a microphone attached to your computer's sound input jack, you can use your voice to search with Cortana rather than typing. Click in the Cortana Search field on the taskbar, and begin typing a search term or phrase.

2. Notice that if you type a single letter or short phrase (see the left side of **Figure 12-4**), Cortana might at first show a list of matches from multiple categories, such as Apps, Settings, Documents, and Web. Continue typing a search phrase to make the search more specific (see the right side of **Figure 12-4**) and narrow it to fewer categories. For example, the right side of **Figure 12-4** shows only Web matches.

3. Click an item in the list of matches. Cortana opens the Microsoft Edge browser and displays a list of matching Bing search results.

4. Click a link in the search results to go to that web page.

Searching by voice works very naturally. With your mic connected and ready to go, click the microphone icon at the right end of the Cortana search box or say, *Hey Cortana*. (If the Set Up Your Mic dialog box appears, follow the prompts to repeat a phrase to help your mic work better.) Then ask a question like *What's the weather?* or *How many feet in a mile?* The answers to such simple questions appear in Cortana's window. If you say a search phrase, such as *blueberry muffin recipe*, Cortana launches Microsoft Edge and displays matching Bing search results.

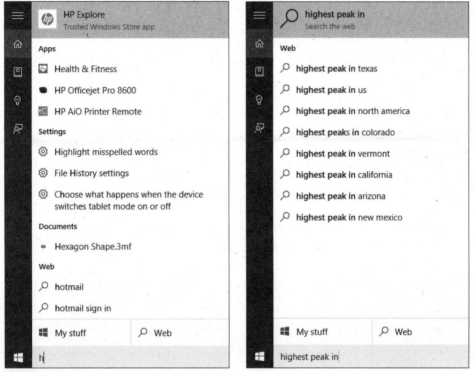

Figure 12-4

 If you come across a phrase or term on a web page that you want to learn more about, drag over it with your mouse to select it. Then right-click it and click Ask Cortana in the shortcut menu. A pane filled with helpful information about the topic appears to the right. After you finish reading, click back on the web page to close the pane. If you select more content on the page, such as a paragraph or table, you can use the Share button (a circle with three smaller circles on it) at the right end of the address bar to share the selected content to another app.

Use Reading View

1. Microsoft Edge's Reading view provides a more comfortable, clean way to view a web page. It reformats page text to a more narrow width and larger font size and removes distractions like navigation links and ads. To change to Reading view after starting Microsoft Edge and displaying a compatible page, click the Reading View button (with the book on it) toward the right end of the address bar in Microsoft Edge.

 If the Reading View button is grayed out (disabled), that means the current page has formatting or elements that prevent it from displaying properly in Reading view.

2. The page displays in the Reading view, as shown in **Figure 12-5.** You can move your mouse pointer to the right edge of the screen to display the scroll bar, and then scroll down and up as needed.

3. Click the Reading View button to return to the regular view.

Reading view

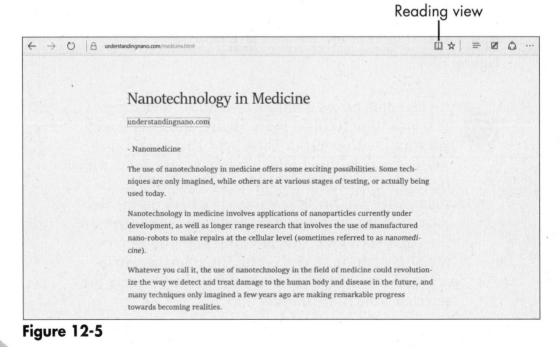

Figure 12-5

Find Content on a Web Page

1. After starting Microsoft Edge, enter a URL in the Search or Enter Web Address box or address bar, and press Enter. Click the More Actions button (it has a row of three dots on it), and choose Find on Page.

2. In the resulting Find on Page toolbar that appears below the address bar, as shown in **Figure 12-6,** enter the word that you want to search for. As you type, all instances of the word on the page are highlighted.

| Find on page | nanomedicine | ✕ | 1 of 10 | ‹ › | Options ⌄ | | ✕ |

Figure 12-6

3. Click the Next button and you move from one highlighted instance of the word to the next (see **Figure 12-7**). If you want to move to a previous instance, click the Previous button.

| Find on page | nanomedicine | | 2 of 10 | ‹ › | Options ⌄ | | ✕ |

Figure 12-7

4. When you're done searching on a page, click the Close button at the right end of the Find on Page toolbar.

 Many websites have a Search This Site feature that allows you to search not only the displayed web page but also all the web pages on a website, or to search by department or category of item in an online store. Look for a search text box and make sure that it searches the site — and not the entire Internet.

Add Your Own Notes to a Web Page

1. You can add your own highlighting and notes to a web page. For example, you might do this to capture your own experience with a recipe or instructions for a project.

After you start Microsoft Edge and display the web page that you want to make notes on, click the Make a Web Note button on the address bar.

2. In the toolbar that appears, click the lower-right corner of the pen or highlighter button, and then click the color to use (see **Figure 12-8**), or a size/shape option at the bottom.

Pick a color

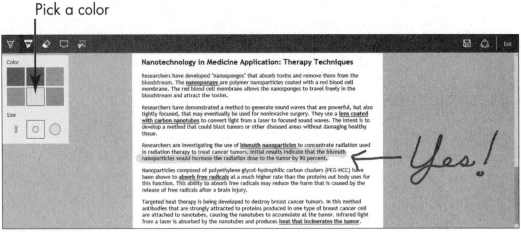

Figure 12-8

3. Drag with the mouse to write or draw on the page (refer to Figure 12-8). Release the mouse button whenever you want to stop marking, and press it again to restart your note taking.

4. Click the Save Web Note button on the toolbar. An Add To dialog box appears. Click either Favorites or Reading List at the top, and then click the Add button.

5. Click the Exit button on the Web Notes toolbar.

 Writing and drawing onscreen with a regular mouse can be awkward. You can get a drawing tablet and stylus that connects to your computer via USB. After you plug it in and set it up, if needed, you can use the stylus to write and draw just like a pencil. Using one of these tablets makes adding web notes feel the same as doodling on paper.

 When you view your page with web notes from your Favorites list at a later time, a toolbar appears below the address bar. It offers Hide Notes and Go To Original Page buttons. The later section "Use Favorites" explains how to view a page from Favorites.

Add a Web Page to the Reading List

1. You can add a web page to a reading list in Microsoft Edge so that you can come back to it later. Open Microsoft Edge, go to the news or information website, and click the link to the article that you want to read later.

2. Click the Add to Favorites or Reading List button (with a star on it) on the address bar.

3. In the pane that appears (see **Figure 12-9**), click Reading List.

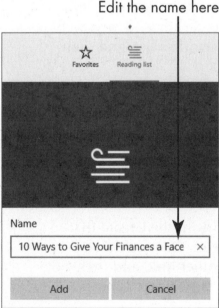

Edit the name here

Figure 12-9

4. Edit the Name for the reading list item, if you want.

5. Click the Add button.

 Microsoft Edge stores all your reading list items and favorites in the Hub. Other browsers store marked pages in a Favorites list or Bookmarks folder.

 Windows 10 computers and devices also include a Reading List app. The Microsoft Edge reading list items do not sync to this app. To share a web page from Microsoft Edge to the Reading List app, click the Share button at the right of the address bar, click Reading List, and click the Add button. Then you can read the item using the Reading List app on any Internet-connected Windows 10 device.

Add a Website to Favorites and Create a Folder

1. If there's a site you intend to revisit, you may want to save it to Microsoft Edge's Favorites list in the Hub so you can easily go there again. To use this feature, open Microsoft Edge from the desktop, enter the URL of a website that you want to add to your Favorites list, and then press Enter.

2. Click the Add to Favorites or Reading List button on the address bar. In the pane that opens, click Favorites at the top.

3. Modify the name of the Favorite listing to something easily recognizable, as shown in **Figure 12-10.**

4. If you wish, choose another folder from the Create In drop-down list to store the favorite in. Or, to create a new folder, click the Create New Folder link, and then type a name in the Folder Name text box that appears.

5. Click the Add button to add the site.

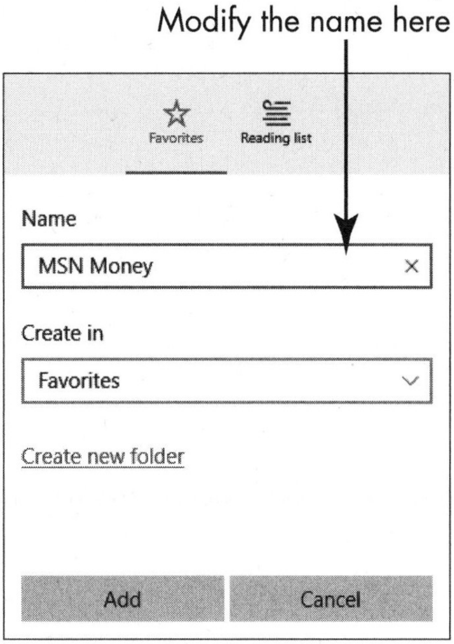

Modify the name here

Figure 12-10

Use Favorites

1. You can go back to one of your favorites at any time from the Hub. With Microsoft Edge open from the desktop, click the Hub button (a set of three jagged horizontal lines) on the address bar.

2. In the Hub pane that appears (see **Figure 12-11**), click the Favorites (star) button.

3. If you saved the favorite in a folder, click the folder in the list. (Click Favorites above the folder contents if you click the wrong folder.) When you see the favorite to open, click it. The Hub pane closes, and the favorite appears in the current tab. Additionally, the Add to Favorites or Reading List button changes to show a filled yellow star.

Favorites button   Hub button

Figure 12-11

 Regularly cleaning out your favorites or reading list is a good idea — after all, do you really need the sites that you used to plan last year's vacation? With the Hub displayed, right-click any item and then choose Remove to delete it. In some cases, the shortcut menu has a Rename command, too. Click it to rename the item.

 If you created new folders when adding other favorites, you can manually transfer other favorites into those folders. To do this, just display the Hub and click and drag a favorite listed there onto a folder. To move a favorite from within a folder back to the main favorites list, open the folder in the Hub, and then drag the favorite onto the word Favorites above the folder content.

View Your Browsing History

1. If you went to a site recently and want to return there but can't remember the name, you might check your browsing history in the Hub to find it. In Microsoft Edge, click the Hub button in the address bar and then click the History button (with the clock face on it) in the Hub pane to display the History list (see **Figure 12-12**).

2. As the History list accumulates items, it groups them by date, such as Last Hour, Today, and Last Week. You can click any of the time category labels to expand or collapse the entries in the group (see **Figure 12-13**).

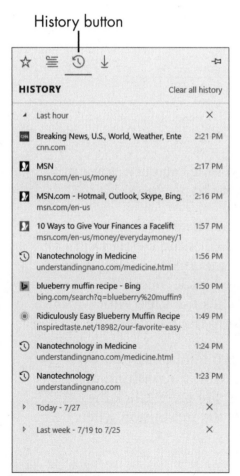

History button

Figure 12-12

Click time category to
expand or collapse it

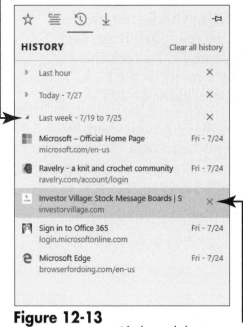

Figure 12-13

Click to delete entry

3. Once you've expanded the desired time category, you can
click an item to go to it. The History pane closes.

 To delete a single item from the History list, move
the mouse pointer over it, and click the Delete (X)
that appears at the right. (Refer to Figure 12-13.) You
can also right-click the item and click Delete. To
remove all the history items, click the Clear All
History link at the upper right in the History pane.

 You can pin the Hub pane open temporarily by clicking the Pin This Pane button (with the pushpin on
it) in the upper-right corner of the pane. Click the
Close (X) button that replaces the pin button when
you want to unpin the pane.

View Your Reading List

1. Finding your reading list items works like using favorites and your browsing history. Open Microsoft Edge, click the Hub button on the address bar, and then click the Reading List button (with a stack of papers on it) in the Hub pane.

2. In the list that appears, click the item to read (see **Figure 12-14**). The Hub pane closes, and the reading list item opens in the current tab.

Reading list

Figure 12-14

Print a Web Page

1. If a web page includes a link or button to print or display a print version of a page, click that and follow the instructions.

2. If the page doesn't include a link for printing, click the More Actions button on the Microsoft Edge address bar, and then click Print in the menu that appears.

3. In the resulting Print window (see **Figure 12-15**), choose a printer from the Printer drop-down list, if needed. Then click the plus button beside the Copies text box to print multiple copies.

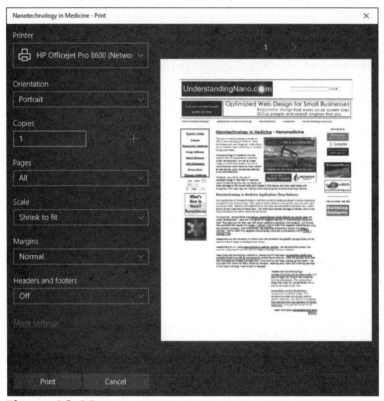

Figure 12-15

4. Change the Orientation and other settings if needed.

 Note that clicking the More Settings link usually opens another window with more settings for the printer selected in the main Print window. These settings might include different paper sizes, duplex (two-sided) printing, color mode, or resolution. After you chose any settings here, click OK to return to the main Print window.

5. After you adjust all settings you need, click Print.

Adjust Microsoft Edge Settings

1. You can work with a variety of settings that adjust how
Microsoft Edge works. Click the More Actions button at
the far-right end of the Microsoft Edge address bar, and
then click Settings in the menu that appears.

2. In the Settings pane that appears (see **Figure 12-16**),
make selections for the settings such as these:

SETTINGS	⫟
Choose a theme	
Light	⌄
Show the favorites bar	
⬤‍◯ Off	
Import favorites from another browser	
Open with	
◉ Start page	
◯ New tab page	
◯ Previous pages	
◯ A specific page or pages	
Open new tabs with	
Top sites	⌄
Clear browsing data	
Choose what to clear	
Reading	
Reading view style	

Figure 12-16

- **Choose a Theme:** Choose the Light or Dark theme from this drop-down list.

- **Show the Favorites Bar:** Use the On/Off slider to control whether an additional favorites bar appears below the address bar.

- **Open With:** As described in Chapter 11, the choices here determine what displays when you start Microsoft Edge.

- **Open New Tabs With:** This drop-down list controls the content for new browser tabs. Chapter 13 provides more details about these choices.

- **Clear Browsing History:** Click the Choose What To Clear button here to delete various types of browsing data. Chapter 13 covers this in more detail.

- **Reading View Style and Reading View Font Size:** Make choices from these drop-down lists to change the colors and text size for the Reading view.

3. Move the mouse to the right edge of the screen to display the scroll bar, and then scroll down. Clicking the View Advanced Settings button under Advanced Settings displays an additional pane of Microsoft Edge settings.

4. When you finish your changes, click the More Actions button again or click a blank area of the current web page to close the Settings pane.

Staying Safe While Online

*G*etting active online carries with it certain risks, like most things in life. But, just as you know how to drive or walk around town safely when you know the rules of the road, you can stay relatively safe online.

In this chapter, you discover some of the risks and safety nets that you can take advantage of to avoid risk, including

➡ **Understand what risks exist.** Some risks are human, in the form of online predators wanting to steal your money or abuse you emotionally; other risks come from technology, such as computer viruses. For the former, you can use the same common sense you use when interacting offline to stay safe. For the latter, there are tools and browser settings to protect you.

➡ **Be aware of what information you share.** Abuses such as ID theft occur most often when you or somebody you know shares information about you that's nobody's business. Find out how to spot who is exposing information (including you) and what information to keep private, and you'll become much safer online.

Get ready to . . .

➡️ **Avoid scams and undesirable content.** Use various privacy settings in Windows 10 to limit the undesirable information, such as blocking pop-ups. Also, find out how to spot various email scams and fraud so you don't become a victim.

➡️ **Create safe passwords.** Passwords don't have to be hard to remember, just hard to guess. I provide some guidance in this chapter about creating passwords that are hard to crack.

Understand Technology Risks on the Internet

When you buy a car, it has certain safety features built in. Sometimes after you drive it off the lot, you might find that the manufacturer slipped up and either recalls your car or requests that you go to the dealer's service department for replacement of a faulty part. In addition, you need to drive defensively to keep your car from being damaged in daily use.

Your computer is similar to your car in terms of the need for safety. It comes with an operating system (such as Microsoft Windows) built in, and that operating system has security features. Sometimes that operating system has flaws — or new threats emerge after it's released — and you need to install an update to keep it secure. And as you use your computer, you're exposing it to dangerous conditions and situations that you have to guard against.

Threats to your computer security can come from a file you copy from a disc you insert into your computer, but most of the time, the danger is from a program that you download from the Internet. These downloads can happen when you click a link, open an attachment in an email, or download a piece of software without realizing that *malware* (malicious software) is attached to it.

You need to be aware of these three main types of dangerous programs:

➡️ A *virus* is a little program that some nasty person thought up to spread around the Internet and infect computers. A virus can do a variety of things but, typically, it attacks your data by deleting files, scrambling data, or making changes to your system settings that cause your computer to grind to a halt.

➠ *Spyware* consists of programs responsible for tracking what you do with your computer. Some spyware simply helps companies you do business with track your activities so that they can figure out how to sell things to you; other spyware is used for more insidious purposes, such as stealing your passwords.

➠ *Adware* is the computer equivalent of telemarketing phone calls at dinnertime. After adware is downloaded onto your computer, you'll see annoying pop-up windows trying to sell things to you all day long. Beyond the annoyance, adware can quickly clog up your computer. The computer's performance slows down, and it's hard to get anything done at all.

To protect your information and your computer from these various types of malware, you can do several things:

➠ **You can buy and install an antivirus, antispyware, or anti-adware program.** It's critical that you install an antivirus program, such as those from McAfee, Symantec, or Trend Micro, or the freely downloadable AVG Free (see **Figure 13-1**).

➠ People come up with new viruses every day, so it's important that you use software that's up to date with the latest virus definitions and that protects your computer from the latest threats. Many antivirus programs are purchased by yearly subscription, which gives you access to updated virus definitions that the company constantly gathers throughout the year. Be sure to update the definitions of viruses on your computer regularly using this software, and then run a scan of your computer on a regular basis. For convenience, you can use settings in the software to activate automatic updates and scans. Consult your program's Help tool for instructions on how to use these features.

Figure 13-1

⇒ **Install a program that combines tools for detecting adware and spyware.** Windows 10 has a built-in program, Windows Defender, which includes an antispyware feature. (I cover Windows Defender tools in Chapter 20.) You can also purchase programs such as Spyware Doctor (from PC Tools) or download free tools such as Spybot or Spyware Terminator.

⇒ **Use Windows tools to keep Windows up to date with security features, and fixes to security problems.** You can also turn on a firewall, which is a feature that stops other people or programs from accessing your computer over an Internet connection without your permission. (I cover Windows Defender and firewalls in Chapter 20.)

⇒ **Use your browser's privacy and security features,** such as the Suggested Content and InPrivate Browsing features in Microsoft Edge.

Use Suggested Content

1. To allow Microsoft Edge to suggest sites you might like that are similar to the sites you visit most, open Edge, click the More Actions button, and then click Settings in the menu that appears.

2. Click the box below Open New Tabs With, and click Top Sites and Suggested Content, as shown in **Figure 13-2**. Click outside the Settings pane to close it.

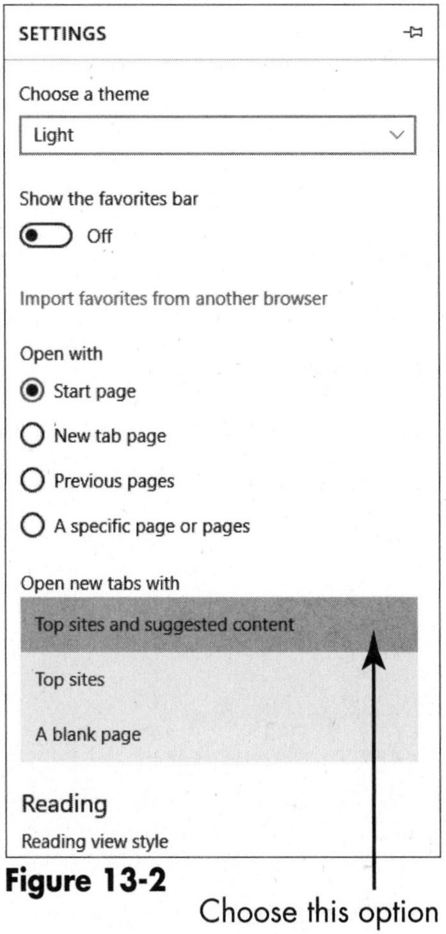

Figure 13-2

Choose this option

3. Click the New Tab button or press Ctrl+T. Tiles for Top Sites appear (see **Figure 13-3**), as well as a My News Feed section with suggested content.

Top sites tiles

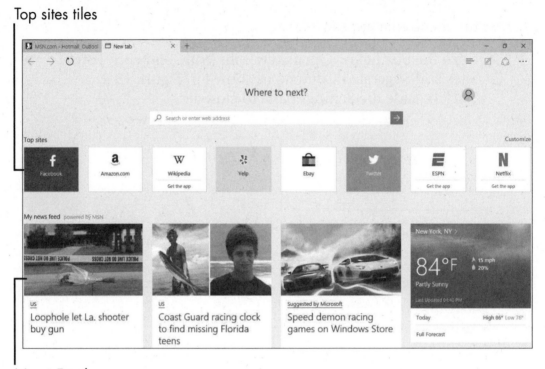

News Feed
Figure 13-3

4. Click a site tile to open its website or click an article to view it.

 The Top Sites feature uses your browsing history to come up with later suggestions, so when you first activate it, it may take a little while before the feature comes up with useful suggestions. You can customize what topics appear at the top of your news feed by clicking the Customize link above the Top Sites tiles, clicking favorite categories at the bottom, and clicking Save.

If you don't want to see the news feed, you can click Top Sites in Step 2 to see the Top Sites tiles only. To open new tabs without any content, click A Blank Page.

Download Files Safely

1. The two tricks to downloading files while staying safe from malware are to only download from sites you trust and to never download file attachments to emails that you aren't completely sure are safe. The most dangerous files to download are executable files that sport an .exe extension at the end of the filename. Clicking on these will run a program of some kind, and could therefore pose an active threat. Open a trusted website that contains downloadable files. Typically, websites offer a Download button or link that initiates a file download.

If you don't know of a file to download but want to practice these steps, try www.adobe.com. From that site, you can search for and download the free Adobe Acrobat Reader DC, a handy and popular utility program. (If the Adobe website only shows a version for Windows 8.1, it's okay to download and install that one.)

2. Click the appropriate link or button to proceed. (This button often is called Download, but on the Adobe site, it may be called Install.) Windows might display a dialog box asking your permission to proceed with the download; click Yes. The download also might open in a separate Microsoft Edge window in some cases.

3. By default, a security scan runs during the download of the document. The toolbar that appears along the bottom of the Microsoft Edge window, shown in **Figure 13-4**, displays different choices depending on the type of file downloaded:

- **For an executable file, click Run to download the file to a temporary folder.** You can run a software installation program, for example. However, beware: If you run a program you obtained from the Internet, you could be introducing dangerous viruses to your system. You might want to set up an antivirus program to scan files before downloading them.

- **For a document file, such as a PDF file, click Open to open the file in another browser tab or the app that's installed on your computer for that type of document.** For executable files, consider using an antivirus program to scan them before opening the files.

- **For any type of file, click View Downloads.** The Hub opens and shows you recent downloads, as shown in **Figure 13-5.** You can click the Clear (X) button beside a download to remove it from the list, or click Clear All to clear the list of past downloads. Or, you can click Open Folder to open your Downloads folder to work with downloaded files. Press Esc or click elsewhere on the browser window to close the Hub pane.

| readerdc_en_ma_install.exe finished downloading. | | Run | View downloads | X |

Figure 13-4

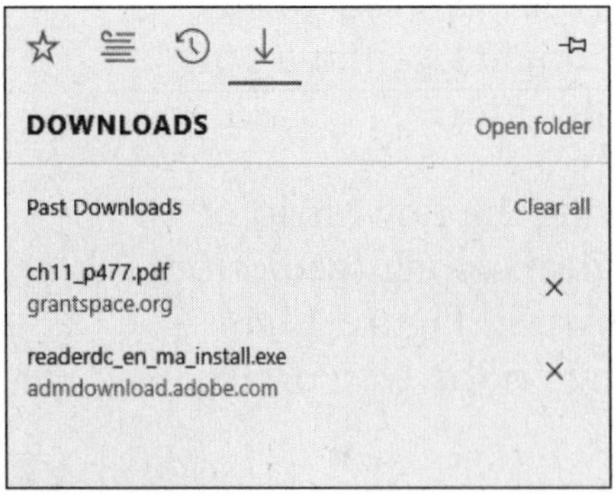

Figure 13-5

The Downloads folder is one of your default user folders. Note that you can download some website picture files by right-clicking and clicking Save Picture. Make sure you have the proper permissions to use any content you download from the Web.

 If you're worried that a particular file might be unsafe to download (for example, if it's from an unknown source, or if you discover that it's an executable file type, which could contain a virus), click Cancel in the download toolbar.

 If a particular file will take a long time to download (some can take 20 minutes or more), you may have to babysit it. If your computer goes into standby mode, it could pause the download. If your computer automatically downloads Windows updates, it may cause your computer to restart automatically as well, cancelling or halting your download. Check in periodically to keep things moving along.

Use InPrivate Browsing

1. InPrivate Browsing is a feature that stops Edge from saving information about your browsing session, such as cookies and your browsing history. InPrivate Browsing allows you to block or allow sites that automatically collect information about your browsing habits. InPrivate Browsing is not active by default when you open an Edge window. To use InPrivate Browsing, open Microsoft Edge and click the More Actions button.

2. In the menu that appears, click New InPrivate Window. As shown in **Figure 13-6,** the new Microsoft Edge browser window that appears displays InPrivate in the upper-left corner. The tab that appears is titled InPrivate and displays a description of InPrivate browsing.

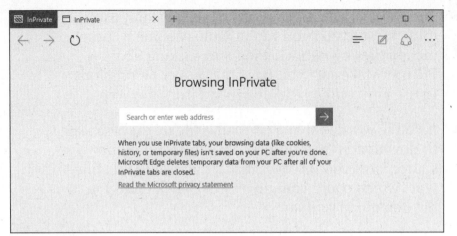

Figure 13-6

3. You can now surf the web privately by entering a search phrase or web address in the Search or Enter Web Address box and pressing Enter, or by clicking in the Address bar, typing a web address, and pressing Enter.

4. To turn off InPrivate Browsing, click the Close button in the upper-right corner of the InPrivate window.

 If you don't want to use InPrivate Browsing but would like to periodically clear your browsing history manually, with Microsoft Edge open, click the Hub button at the right side of the address bar, and then click the History button at the top of the pane. Click the triangle icon beside any date category to review your history for that date, and click the Delete (X) button if you decide to delete it. Or, you can click Clear All History to delete all history entries. Press Esc to close the Hub when you finish.

Use SmartScreen Filter

When you activate SmartScreen Filter, you allow Microsoft to check its database for information on the websites you visit. Microsoft alerts you if any of those websites are known to generate phishing scams or download malware to visitors' computers. SmartScreen Filter is on by default, but if it gets turned off, to turn it on again, open Edge and follow these steps:

1. Click the More Actions button, and then click Settings.

2. Hover your mouse over the right edge of the pane to display the scroll bar, scroll down, and then click the View Advanced Settings button under Advanced Settings.

3. Use the mouse to display the scroll bar at right again, and scroll down. Click the on/off button below Help Protect Me from Malicious Sites and Downloads with SmartScreen Filter to On. Then press Esc to close the pane.

 Once it's turned on, SmartScreen Filter automatically checks websites and will generate a warning message if you visit one that has reported problems. However, that information is updated only periodically, so if you have concerns about a particular site, avoid browsing to it.

Change Privacy Settings

1. You can modify how Microsoft Edge deals with privacy settings to keep information about your browsing habits or identity safer. In Microsoft Edge, click the More Actions button, and then click Settings.

2. Move the mouse pointer to the right edge of the Settings pane to display the scroll bar, scroll down, and click View Advanced Settings under Advanced Settings.

3. In the Advanced Settings pane, scroll down to the bottom of the pane, past the Privacy and Services heading. Click the drop-down list under Cookies, then click either Block All Cookies or Block Only Third Party Cookies (refer to **Figure 13-7**).

4. Press Esc or click outside the pane to close it.

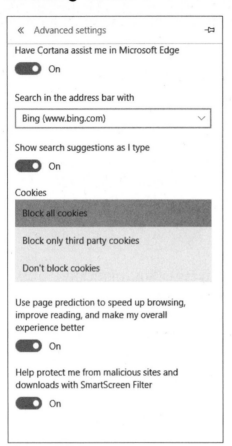

Figure 13-7

 Some sites, such as online news and magazine sites that you subscribe to, must use cookies to store your logon information. If you have cookies enabled, Remember Me or Keep Me Signed In options won't work on those pages, and you'll have to enter your logon information each time you visit the site.

 You can also use the Block Pop-Ups setting near the top of the Advanced Settings pane. When this setting is toggled on, Microsoft Edge prevents any pop-up windows from loading when you visit a site. While pop-ups generally show harmless or annoying ads, some may be associated with phishing schemes or malware, so your computer is more secure with pop-ups blocked.

Understand Information Exposure

Many people think that if they aren't active online, their information isn't exposed. However, you aren't the only one sharing your information. Consider how others might handle information about you.

➡ **Employers:** Many employers share information about employees. Consider carefully how much information you're comfortable with sharing through, for instance, an employee bio posted on your company website. How much information should be visible to other employees on your intranet? When you attend a conference, is the attendee list shown in online conference documents? And even if you're retired, there may still be information about you on your former employer's website. Review the site to determine if it reveals more than you'd like it to — and ask your employer to take down or alter the information if needed.

➡ **Government agencies:** Some agencies post personal information, such as documents concerning your home purchase and property tax (see **Figure 13-8**), on publicly available websites. Government agencies may also post birth, marriage, and death certificates, and these documents may contain your Social Security number, loan number, copies of your signature, and so on. You should check government records carefully to see if private information is posted and, if it is, demand that it be removed.

➡ **Family members and friends:** They may write about you in their blogs, post photos of you, or mention you on special-interest sites such as those focused on genealogy.

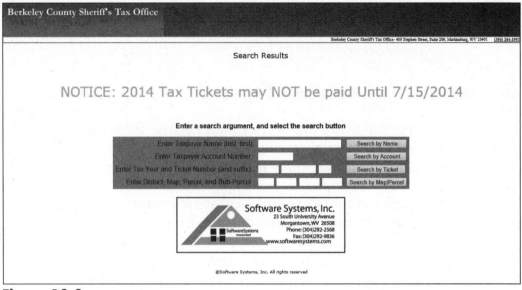

Figure 13-8

→ **Clubs and organizations:** Organizations with whom you volunteer, the church you attend, and professional associations you belong to may reveal facts such as your address, age, income bracket, and how much money you've donated.

→ **Newspapers:** If you've been featured in a newspaper article, you may be surprised to find the story, along with a picture of you or information about your work, activities, or family, by doing a simple online search. If you're interviewed, ask for the chance to review the information that the newspaper will include, and be sure that you're comfortable with exposing that information.

→ **Online directories:** Services such as www. whitepages.com, shown in **Figure 13-9,** or www. anywho.com, list your home phone number and address, unless you specifically request that these be removed. You may be charged a small fee associated with removing your information — a so-called privacy tax — but you may find the cost worthwhile.

➥ Online directories often include the names of members of your family, your email address, the value of your home, your neighbors' names and the values of their homes, an online mapping tool to provide a view of your home, driving directions to your home, and your age. The record may also include previous addresses, schools you've attended, and links for people to run background checks on you. (Background check services generally charge a fee.) A smart con person can use all that information to convince you that he's a friend of a friend or even a relative in distress who needs money.

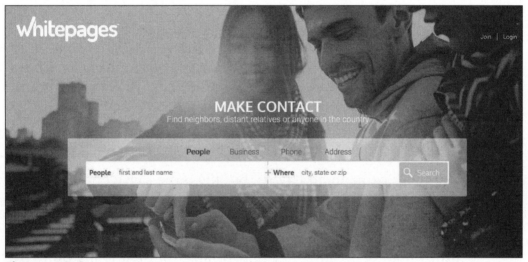

Figure 13-9

 Because services get new information from many sources, you'll need to check back periodically to see if your information has again been put online — if it has, contact the company or go through its removal process again.

 Try entering your home phone number in any browser's address line; chances are you'll get an online directory listing with your address and phone number (although this doesn't work for cellphone numbers).

Many web browsers not only track browsing data, but also save the personal data you enter into online forms so that information can be reused later to fill forms automatically. In Microsoft Edge, you can delete saved form data for safety and privacy. Click the More Actions button, and click Settings. Under Clear Browsing Data, click the Choose What to Clear Button. Click the Form Data check box to check it, and check or uncheck other options as needed. (The other items you can clear are Browsing History, Cookies and Saved Website Data, Cached Data and Files, Download History, and Passwords.) Click Clear, then press Esc to close the pane after the data clears.

Keep Your Information Private

Sharing personal information with friends and family enriches your relationships and helps you build new ones. The key is to avoid sharing information online with the wrong people and shady companies because, just as in the real world, exposing your personal information is one of your biggest risks.

Criminals come in all flavors, but the more savvy ones collect information in a very systematic way. Each piece of information is like a series of brushstrokes that, over time, form a very clear picture of your life. And after criminals collect and organize the information, they never throw it away because they may be able to use it many times over.

Fortunately, information exposure is a risk you have a great deal of control over. Before sharing information, such as your date of birth, make sure you're comfortable with how the recipient will use the information.

➡ **Address and phone number:** Abuse of this information results in you receiving increased telemarketing calls and junk mail. Although less common, this information may also increase a scammer's ability to steal your identity and make your home a more interesting target for break-ins.

➡ **Names of husband/wife, father, and mother (including mother's maiden name), siblings, children, and grandchildren:** This information is very interesting to criminals, who can use it to gain your confidence and then scam you, or use it to guess your passwords or secret-question answers, which often include family members' names. This information may also expose your family members to ID theft, fraud, and personal harm.

➡ **Information about your car:** Limit access to license plate numbers; VINs (vehicle identification numbers); registration information; make, model, and title number of your car; your insurance carrier's name and coverage limits; loan information; and driver's license number. The key criminal abuse of this information includes car theft (or theft of parts of the car) and insurance fraud. The type of car you drive may also indicate your financial status, and that adds one more piece of information to the pool of data criminals collect about you.

➡ **Information about work history:** In the hands of criminals, your work history can be very useful for "authenticating" the fraudster and convincing people and organizations to provide him or her with more about your financial records or identity.

➡ **Information about your credit status:** This information can be abused in so many ways that any time you're asked to provide this online, your answer should be "No." Don't fall for the temptation to check your credit scores free through sites that aren't guaranteed as being reputable. Another frequent abuse of credit information is found in free mortgage calculators that ask you to put in all kinds of personal information in order for them to determine what credit you may qualify for.

Many people set automatic responders in their email, letting people know when they'll be away from their offices. This is helpful for colleagues, but exercise caution and limit whom you provide the information to. Leaving a message that says, "Gone 11/2–11/12. I'm taking the family to Hawaii for ten days," may make your house a prime target for burglary. And you'll probably never make the connection between the information you exposed and the offline crime.

 You may need to show your work history, particularly on resumes you post on Internet job or business-networking sites. Be selective about where you post this information, create a separate email account to list on the resume, and tell what kinds of work you've done rather than give specifics about which companies and what dates. Interested, legitimate employers can then contact you privately, and you won't have given away your life history to the world. After you've landed the job, take down your resume. Think of it as risk management — when you need a job, the risk of information exposure is less than the need to get the job.

Spot Phishing Scams and Other Email Fraud

As in the offline world, the Internet has a criminal element. These cybercriminals use Internet tools to commit the same crimes they've always committed, from robbing you to misusing your good name and financial information. Know how to spot the types of scams that occur online and you'll go a long way toward steering clear of Internet crime.

Before you click a link that comes in a forwarded email message or forward a message to others, ask yourself:

➥ **Is the information legitimate?** Sites such as www.truthorfiction.com, www.snopes.com

(see **Figure 13-10**), or `http://urbanlegends.
about.com` can help you discover if an email is
a scam.

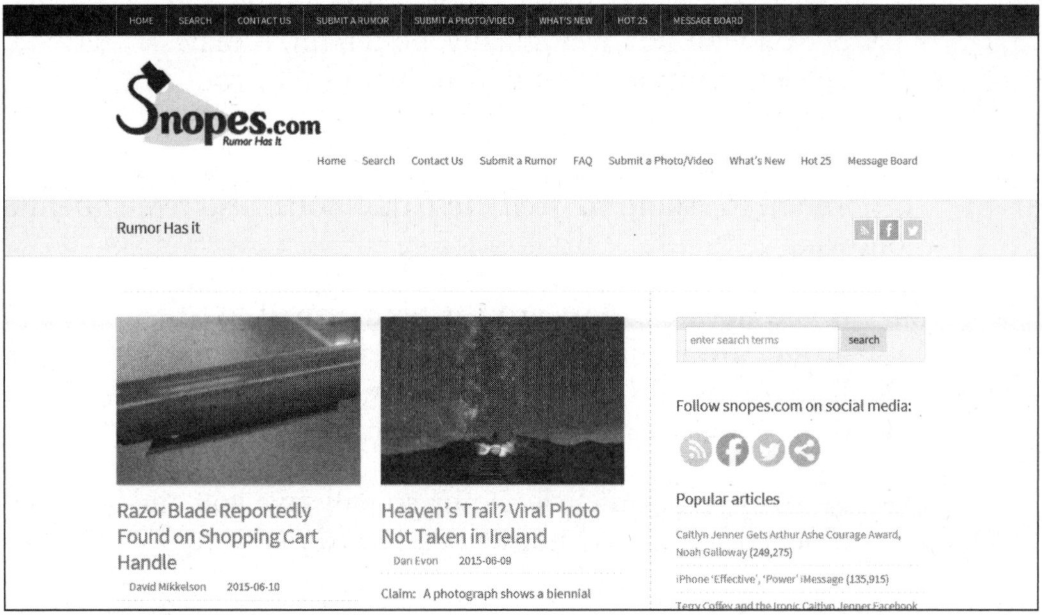

Figure 13-10

➠ **Does a message ask you to click links in email or
instant messages?** If you're unsure whether a message is genuinely from a company or bank that you
use, call it, using the number from a past statement
or the phone book.

Don't call a phone number listed in the email; it
could be a fake. To visit a company's or bank's website, type the address in yourself if you know it or
use your own bookmark rather than clicking a link.
If the website is new to you, search for the company
online and use that link to visit its site. Don't click
the link in an email, or you may land on a site that
looks right — but is in reality a good fake.

➠ **Does the email have a photo or video to download?** If so, exercise caution. If you know the person who sent the photo or video, it's probably fine to download, but if the photo or video has been forwarded several times and you don't know the person who sent it originally, be careful. It may deliver a virus or other type of malware to your computer.

In addition to asking yourself these questions, also remember the following:

➠ **If you decide to forward (or send) email to a group, always put their email addresses on the Bcc: (or Blind Carbon Copy) line.** This keeps everyone's email safe from fraud and scams.

➠ **Think** *before* **you click.** Doing so will save you and others from scams, fraud, hoaxes, and malware.

Create Strong Passwords

A strong password can be one of your best friends in protecting your information in online accounts and sites. Never give your password to others, and change passwords on particularly sensitive accounts, such as bank and investment accounts, regularly.

Table 13-1 outlines five principles for creating strong passwords.

Table 13-1	Principles for Strong Passwords
Principle	*How to Do It*
Length	Use at least ten characters.
Strength	Mix it up with upper- and lowercase letters, characters, and numbers.

Principle	How to Do It
Obscurity	Use nothing that's associated with you, your family, your company, and so on.
Protection	Don't place paper reminders near your computer.
Change	The more sensitive the information, the more frequently you should change your password.

Look at Table 13-2 for examples of password patterns that are safe but also easy to remember.

Table 13-2	Examples of Strong Passwords
Logic	**Password**
Use a familiar phrase typed with a variation of capitalization and numbers instead of words (text message shorthand).	L8r_L8rNot2day = Later, later, not today 2BorNot2B_ThatIsThe? = To be or not to be, that is the question.
Incorporate shortcut codes or acronyms.	CSThnknAU2day = Can't Stop Thinking About You today 2Hot2Hndle = Too hot to handle
Create a password from an easy-to-remember phrase that describes what you're doing, with key letters replaced by numbers or symbols.	1mlook1ngatyahoo = I'm looking at Yahoo (I replaced the Is with 1s.) MyWork@HomeNeverEnds
Spell a word backward with at least one letter representing a character or number.	$lidoffaD = Daffodils (The $ replaces the s.) y1frettuB = Butterfly (The 1 replaces the l.) QWERTY7654321 = This is the six letters from left to right in the top row of your keyboard, plus the numbers from right to left across the top going backward.
Use patterns from your keyboard. (See **Figure 13-11.**) Make your keyboard a palette and make any shape you want.	1QAZSDRFBHU8 is really just making a W on your keyboard. (Refer to Figure 13-11.)

Figure 13-11

 Microsoft Edge includes a new feature to remember passwords for you. Click the More Actions button, and then click Settings. Scroll down, and click View Advanced Settings. Under Privacy, click the button below Offer to Save Passwords to turn that setting On. (After it's active, when you enter a password, a prompt appears at the bottom of the browser window; click Yes to save the password.) You can then use the Manage My Saved Passwords link just below Offer to Save Passwords to remove saved passwords, if needed.

Keeping in Touch with Mail

An email app is a tool you can use to send messages to others. These messages are delivered to the recipient's email inbox, usually within seconds. You can attach files to email messages and even put images within the message body. You can get an email account through your Internet provider or through sites such as Yahoo! and Microsoft Outlook.com. These accounts are typically free.

When you have one or more email accounts, you can set them up in the Mail app in Windows 10, and then use that app to send and receive email for all your Outlook.com and Gmail accounts in one place. Mail uses the information you store in the People app for addressing your emails, and it can sync contacts from your individual accounts to People if you choose.

Chapter 14

Get ready to . . .

With Windows 10, setting up Yahoo!, AOL, and many other types of email accounts is available in addition to Outlook and Google. If you prefer, you can instead use your provider's email interface in your Internet browser. Some of these programs provide more tools for working with email, such as more sophisticated tools to format message text or add a signature (for example, your company name and phone number) to every message you send.

To make your emailing life easy, this chapter looks at these tasks:

➡ **Choose an email provider.** Find out how to locate email providers and what types of features they offer.

➡ **Set up your email accounts in the Mail app.** Make settings to access your Outlook.com or Gmail account from within the Mail app so you can check all your messages in one place. This is useful if you use both work and home email accounts, for example. If you do access work email from home, you can use the Microsoft Exchange type of account to do so (check with your work network administrator about how to do this).

➡ **Receive, send, and forward messages.** Deal with the ins and outs of receiving and sending email.

➡ **Make settings for each account.** Set up how often content is downloaded, and whether to sync your email, contacts, and calendar information from each account.

Sign Up for an Internet-Based Email Account

Your Internet service provider (ISP) — whether that's your cable or phone company or a local provider — probably offers you a free email account along with your service. You can also get free accounts from many online sources, such as Yahoo!, AOL, Gmail, and Outlook.com.

The Mail app in Windows 10 can work with these types of online accounts — as well as Microsoft Exchange accounts, which are typically business accounts such as the one that your company provides. By default, the email address that's part of the Microsoft account you use to sign in to Windows is already set up for you in the Mail app. You're free to get and set up more email accounts in Mail, say if you want to have one email address that's public and one that's more private.

Here are some tips for getting your own email account:

➡ **Using email accounts provided by an ISP:** Check with your ISP to see whether an email account comes with your connection service. If it does, your ISP should provide instructions on how to choose an *email alias* (that's the name on your account, such as `SusieXYZ@aol.com`) and password, and instructions on how to sign into the account.

➡ **Searching for an email provider:** If your ISP doesn't offer email, or you prefer to use another service because of the features it offers, use your browser's search engine to look for what's available. Don't use the search term *free email* because results for any search with the word *free* included are much more likely to return sites that will download bad programs like viruses and spyware onto your computer. Besides, just about all email accounts today are free! Alternatively, you can go directly to services such as Yahoo!, AOL, or Gmail (Google's email) by entering their addresses in your browser's address field (for example, `www.gmail.com`).

➡ **Finding out about features:** Email accounts come with certain features that you should be aware of. For example, each account includes a certain amount of storage for your saved messages. (Look for one that provides 10 gigabytes or more. Some providers charge extra for anything beyond a minimal amount of storage space.) The account should also include an easy-to-use address book feature to save your contacts' information. Some services provide better formatting tools for text, as well as calendar and to-do list features.

Whatever service you use, make sure it has good junk-mail filtering to protect you from unwanted emails. You should be able to modify junk-mail filter settings so that the service places messages from certain senders or with certain content in a junk-mail folder, where you can review the messages with caution or delete them.

→ **Signing up for an email account:** When you find an email account you want to use, sign up (usually there will be a Sign Up or Get an Account button or link to click) by providing your name and other contact information and selecting a username and password. The username is your email address, in the form of `UserName@service.com`, where the *service* is, for example, Yahoo!, Outlook.com, or AOL. Some usernames might be taken, so have a few options in mind.

→ **Making sure your username is a safe one:** If possible, don't use your full name, your location, age, or other identifiers. Such personal identifiers might help scam artists or predators find out more about you than you want them to know.

Set Up Accounts in the Mail App

1. You can set up the Windows 10 Mail app to manage Outlook and other accounts so you can receive all your email messages in one place. Click the Start button on the taskbar, and then click the Mail tile on the Start menu.

The first time you start the Mail app, a Welcome screen appears. Click the Get Started button to see the Accounts screen. There, you can click Add Account to add another account or click Ready To Go to skip this step.

2. Click the Settings icon (it looks like a sprocket) and then click the Accounts link shown in **Figure 14-1**.

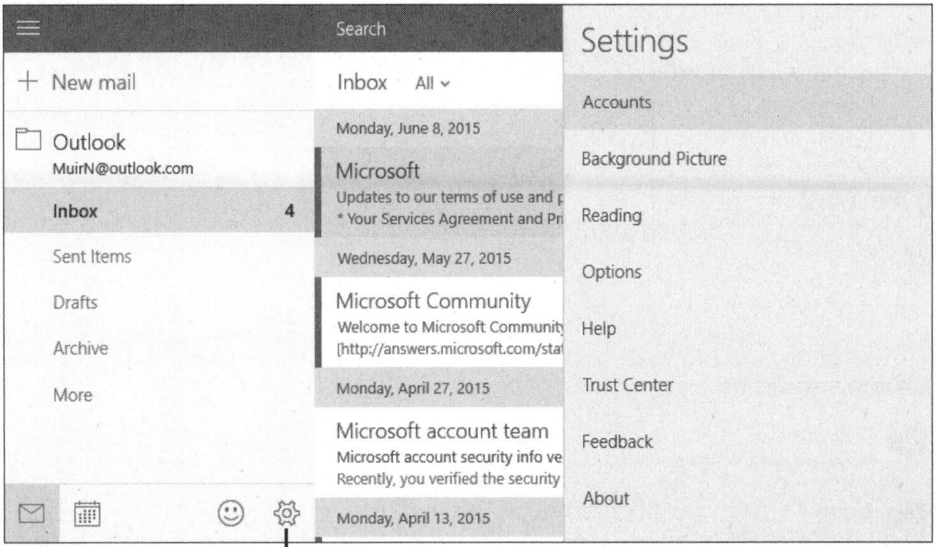

Figure 14-1

Click for Settings

3. Click the Add Account link shown in **Figure 14-2**.

4. Click a provider option as shown in **Figure 14-3**.

5. In the resulting window, enter the account email address. Click Next if needed, and then enter your password (see **Figure 14-4**). Then click Sign In. For some accounts, you may see an additional verification screen or be prompted to select account recovery information. Follow the prompts to continue.

6. At the next window, scroll down and click the Accept button.

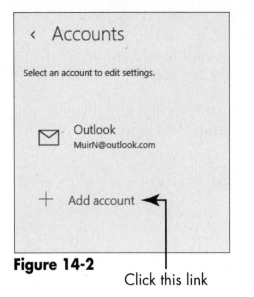

Figure 14-2

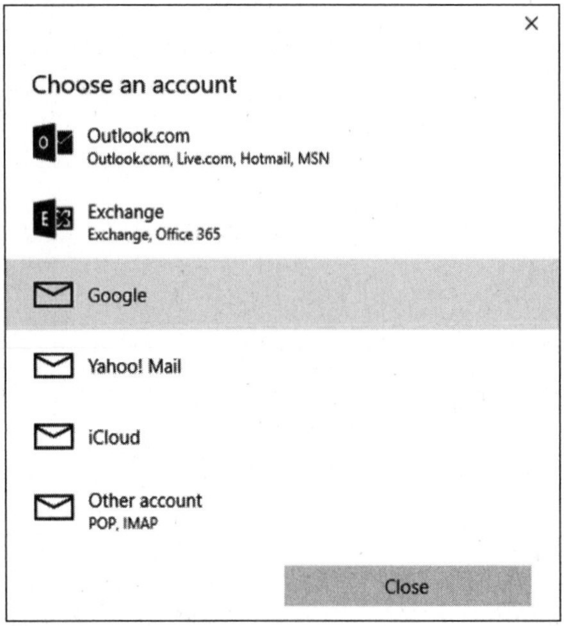

Click this link

Figure 14-3

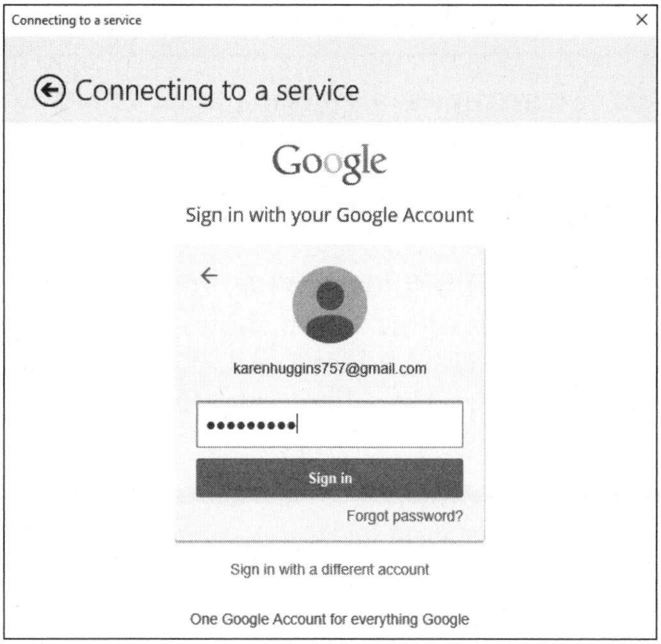

Figure 14-4

7. If you see a prompt window with a Your Name text box, type your name in it, then click the Sign-In button.

8. Mail takes a moment to set up the account, and then displays the All Done! window. Click the Done button, and press Esc twice to close the settings.

9. Click Accounts in the left side of the Mail window, and then click your new account to open its inbox and view messages.

Get to Know Mail

The Mail app (see **Figure 14-5**) may look a bit different from other email programs that use menus and tools to take actions such as deleting an email, creating a new email, and so on. Mail has a sparser, cleaner interface in line with the whole Windows 10 approach. It has a list of folders for the selected account on the left. Some typical folders are your Inbox, where most incoming mail appears; your Drafts folder, where saved drafts of emails are ready to be sent; and your Sent Items folder, where copies of sent emails are stored. You can set up any other folders by signing in at the email provider's website, such as www.outlook.com, mail.yahoo.com, or www.gmail.com, because you can't set these up in Mail.

The section on the left displays the folders. When you click Inbox or another folder, the right portion of the screen shows the list of messages in the folder. To see additional folders, click the More link to open a list of all available folders, including your Outbox, and then click the one you want.

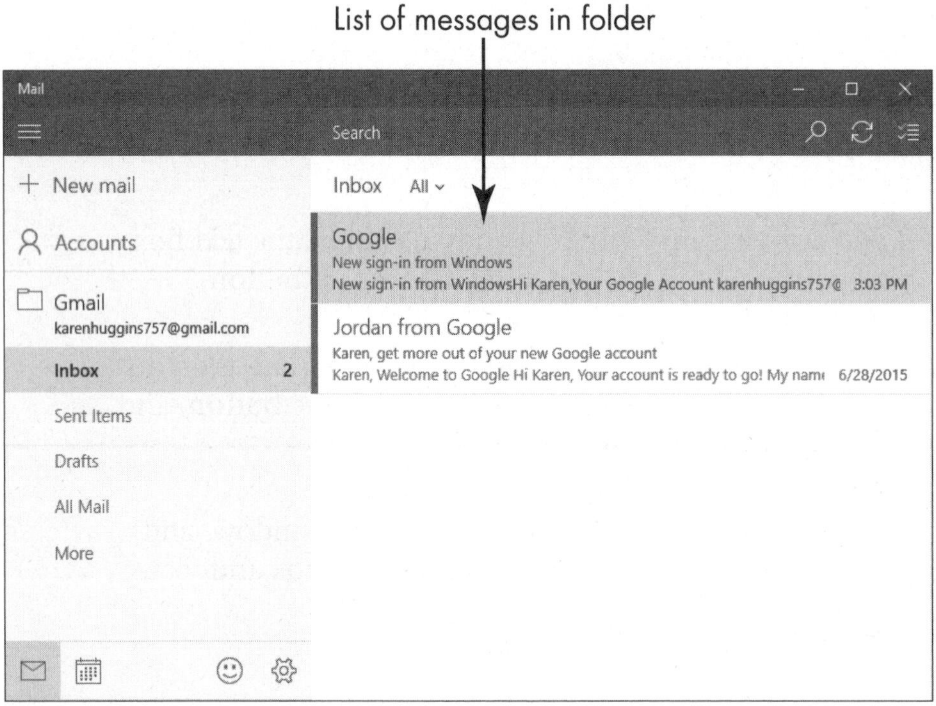

List of messages in folder

Figure 14-5

 To move a message from your Inbox, right-click it and then click the Move command in the shortcut menu that appears. Click a folder, and the message is moved there.

When you access Outlook.com and many of the other online email services using your browser, you're using a program that's hosted online, rather than software installed on your computer. That makes it easy to access your mail from any computer because your messages and folders are stored online. If you use an email client such as Outlook (part of Microsoft Office) to access your email accounts, the client software and your downloaded messages are stored on your computer.

Open Mail and Receive Messages

1. Click the Start button, and then click the Mail tile.

2. Click the Accounts choice at the left, then click the account you want to read mail from. The contents of the Inbox are displayed, as shown in **Figure 14-6**.

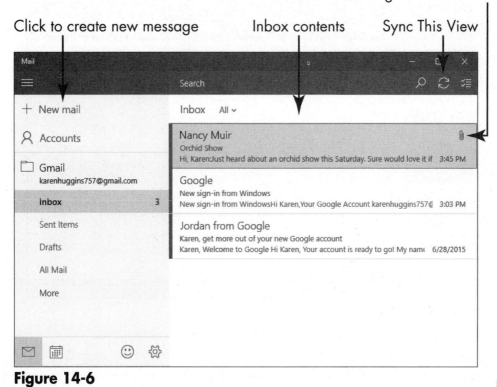

Icon indicating an attachment

Click to create new message   Inbox contents   Sync This View

Figure 14-6

3. Click a message, and its contents appear in the Mail window. Use the scroll bar to move through the message contents, if needed.

4. If the message has an attachment, you'll see a paper clip symbol (see **Figure 14-6**) next to it in the list of received files. When you open the message, an icon for the attachment appears in the message. Click the attachment once, and it displays a thumbnail for pictures or another icon for other types of attachments (see **Figure 14-7**). Right-click the thumbnail and choose one of the following options from the menu that appears:

- **Open:** The file opens in the app that Windows 10 associates it with.

- **Save:** Windows 10 opens the Documents folder, where you can enter a name and click Save to save the file in that folder.

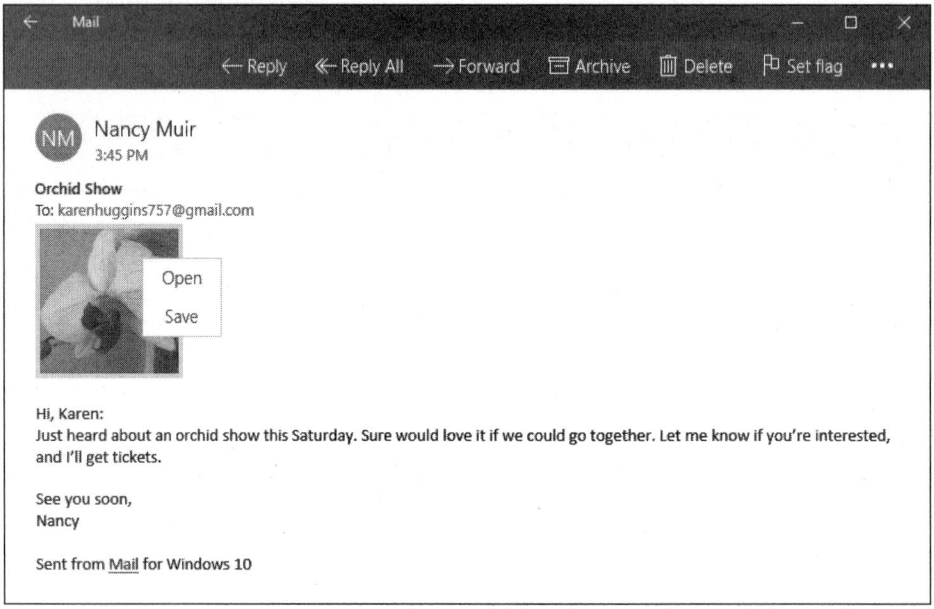

Figure 14-7

5. To return to the list of messages, click the left-arrow button beside Mail in the upper-left corner of the window.

If your mail doesn't come through, it's probably because your email provider's servers are experiencing technical problems. Just wait a little while, and try clicking the Sync This View button (refer to Figure 14-6) to check for the latest mail on the servers. If you still can't get mail, make sure your connection to the Internet is active. Mail may show in your Inbox, but if you've lost your connection, it can't receive new messages.

If you move your mouse over a message in the Inbox message list, little file box, trashcan, and flag icons appear at the right. Click the file box icon to move the message to the Archive folder for an Outlook account. (This may be a different folder for other types of accounts, such as the All Mail folder.) Click the trashcan icon to delete the message, which moves it to the Trash folder for most accounts. Click the flag icon to display a red flag on the message at all times, marking it as a priority message you may want to review again later.

Create and Send Email

1. Creating email is as simple as filling out a few fields in a form. Open Mail, click Accounts at the left, and click the account from which you want to send the email.

2. Click the New Mail link (refer to **Figure 14-6**).

3. Type the email address of the recipient(s) in the To field, using a semicolon to separate addresses. If you want to send a courtesy copy of the message to other people, click the Cc & Bcc link. Then enter addresses in the Cc field, or to send a blind copy, enter addresses in the Bcc.

4. Click in the Subject field (see **Figure 14-8**) and type a concise, descriptive subject.

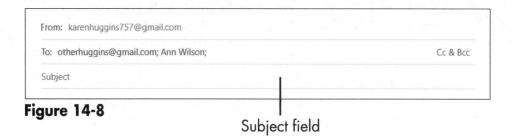

From: karenhuggins757@gmail.com

To: otherhuggins@gmail.com; Ann Wilson;   Cc & Bcc

Subject

Figure 14-8

Subject field

5. Click in the message pane beneath the subject and type your message (see **Figure 14-9**).

← Mail					— □ ×
Format	Insert	Options		🗑 Discard	▷ Send

B *I* <u>U</u> ∨   ≔ ≔ ∨   Heading 1   ∨   ↰ Undo   ↱ Redo

From: karenhuggins757@gmail.com

To: otherhuggins@gmail.com; Ann Wilson;   Cc & Bcc

Investment Club Tonight

Hi, John and Ann:
Are either of you planning to join us at Investment Club tonight? It sounds like Jim has put together a really good presentation about laddering bonds, and I'd like to hear more.

Hoping to see you this evening,
Karen

Sent from Mail for Windows 10

Figure 14-9

Don't press Enter at the end of a line when typing a message. Mail and most email programs have an automatic text-wrap feature that does this for you. Do be concise. If you have lots to say, consider sending a letter by snail mail or overnight delivery. Most people tire of reading text onscreen after a short while.

Keep email etiquette in mind as you type. For example, don't type in ALL CAPITAL LETTERS. This is called shouting, which is considered rude. Do be polite even if you're really, really angry. Your message could be forwarded to just about anybody, just about anywhere, and you don't want to get a reputation as a hothead.

6. If you want, you can use the buttons on the Format tab to change how the text looks. Drag over the text to select it. Then click one of the buttons to apply formatting. For example, you might click the Bold button or the Font Color button to make the text stand out. You can use the Bullet and Numbering buttons to create lists. You can also choose a priority for the message if you want to, by clicking the Options tab and clicking either the High Importance or Low Importance button.

7. When you finish typing your message, click the Send button. The message goes on its way!

Remember that when you're creating an email, you can address it to a stored contact in the People app. (The trick is that when you add the contact in People, you have to choose the right account type — Outlook, Gmail, and so on.) Begin to type a stored contact in an address field (To, Bcc, or Cc), and Mail provides a list of likely matches from your contacts. Just click the correct name or email address when it appears in the list to enter it.

Send an Attachment

1. It's very convenient to be able to attach a document or image file to an email that the recipient can open and view on his end. To do this, open Mail, click Accounts at the left, and click your email account. Click New Mail to create a new email message, address it, and enter a subject.

2. Click the Insert tab and click Attach (see **Figure 14-10**).

Format
Insert
Options
Discard
Send
Attach
Table
Pictures
Link

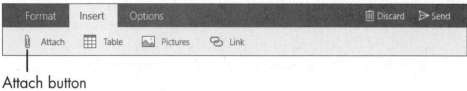

Attach button
Figure 14-10

3. The Open dialog box appears. Locate the file or files that you want and click it (or them).

4. Click the Open button. A thumbnail of the attached file appears in the message body (see **Figure 14-11**), indicating that it's uploaded. If you have other attachments from other folders on your computer, you can click the Attach button again and repeat the previous steps as many times as you like to add more attachments.

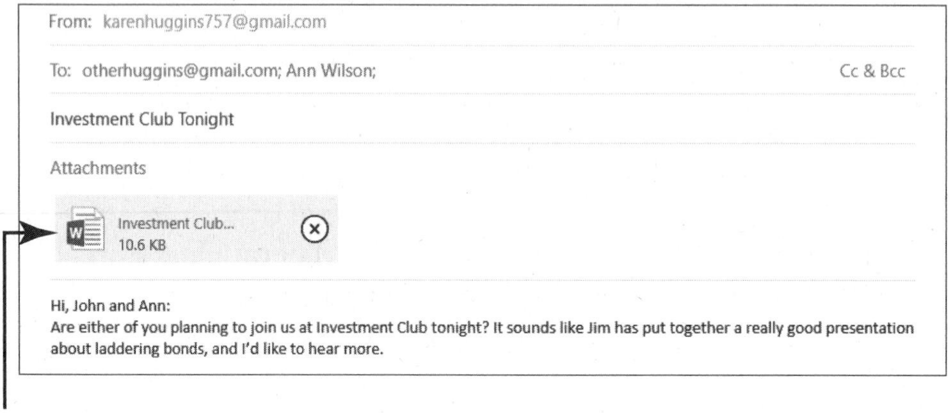
From: karenhuggins757@gmail.com
To: otherhuggins@gmail.com; Ann Wilson;
Cc & Bcc
Investment Club Tonight
Attachments
Investment Club...
10.6 KB
Hi, John and Ann:
Are either of you planning to join us at Investment Club tonight? It sounds like Jim has put together a really good presentation about laddering bonds, and I'd like to hear more.

Attached file
Figure 14-11

5. Click the Send button to send the message and attachment.

You can attach as many files as you like to a single email by repeating steps in this task. Your limitation is size. Various email providers have different limitations on the size of attachments, and some prevent you from attaching certain types of files for security reasons. If you attach several documents and your email fails to send, consider using Microsoft's OneDrive file-sharing service instead. See Chapter 15 for more about using OneDrive.

 If you change your mind about sending a message while you're creating it, just click the Discard button (it's in the top-right corner with a trashcan icon). To remove an attachment before sending a message, click the X button in the attachment thumbnail.

Read a Message

1. When you receive an email, your next step is to read it. Click an email message in your Inbox. Unread messages have a blue line to the left and messages you've read have no line.

 You can click the Sync This View (double-arrow circle) button at the upper right to check for new messages.

2. Click in the message body and use the scroll bar in the message window, if needed, to scroll down through the message and read it (see **Figure 14-12**).

3. If you want to delete the message, simply click the Delete button in the toolbar.

 If you'd like to save an attachment to a local storage drive, right-click the thumbnail of the attachment in the message, click Save, choose the location to save the file to, and then click Save.

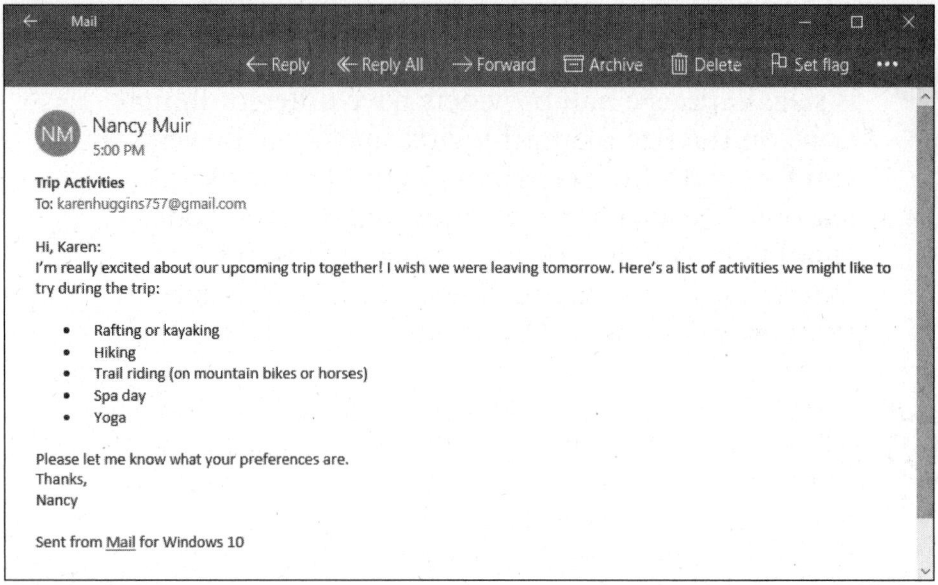

Mail — ☐ ✕

← Reply ← Reply All → Forward 🗄 Archive 🗑 Delete ⚑ Set flag •••

NM Nancy Muir
5:00 PM

Trip Activities
To: karenhuggins757@gmail.com

Hi, Karen:
I'm really excited about our upcoming trip together! I wish we were leaving tomorrow. Here's a list of activities we might like to try during the trip:

- Rafting or kayaking
- Hiking
- Trail riding (on mountain bikes or horses)
- Spa day
- Yoga

Please let me know what your preferences are.
Thanks,
Nancy

Sent from Mail for Windows 10

Figure 14-12

Reply to a Message

1. If you receive an email and want to send a message back, use the Reply feature. Open the message you want to reply to, and then click one of the following reply options, as shown in **Figure 14-13**:

- **Reply:** Send the reply to only the author.

- **Reply All:** Send a reply to the author as well as to everyone who received the original message.

Reply choices

← Reply ← Reply All → Forward 🗄 Archive 🗑 Delete ⚑ Set flag •••

Figure 14-13

2. In the resulting email window (see **Figure 14-14**), enter any additional recipient(s) in the To text boxes. To send a copy or blind copy, you can click Cc & Bcc to display the Cc and Bcc fields. Type your message in the message window.

Enter recipients here

```
←   Mail                                              —  □  ✕
 Format    Insert    Options           🗑 Discard   ➢ Send

 B   I   U   ⌄    ☰  ☰   ⌄    Heading 1    ⌄    ↶ Undo   ↷ Redo

 From:  karenhuggins757@gmail.com

 To:  Nancy Muir;

 Cc:  otherhuggins@gmail.com;

 Bcc:

 RE: Trip Activities

 Sign me up for hiking and a spa day! Thanks for making these arrangements, Nancy!
 Karen

 Sent from Mail for Windows 10


 From: Nancy Muir
 Sent: Tuesday, July 28, 2015 5:00 PM
 To: karenhuggins757@gmail.com
 Subject: Trip Activities
```

Figure 14-14

3. Click the Send button to send the reply.

 Replying to a message creates a conversation or message thread; a small triangle appears to the left of the message in the Inbox.

 If you start creating a message or reply and have it open for a few moments, Mail automatically saves it as a draft. If you click the Back button without sending the message, Mail adds a copy of the message in the Drafts folder with [Draft] added in the message listing. You can open the message later from there to finish and send it.

Forward Email

1. To share an email you receive with others, use the Forward feature. Open the email message that you want to forward in Mail.

2. Click the Forward button on the toolbar.

3. In the message that appears with FW: added to the beginning of the subject line, enter a new recipient(s) in the To and/or Cc and Bcc fields, and then enter any message that you want to include in the message window, as shown in the example in **Figure 14-15**.

4. Click Send to forward the message.

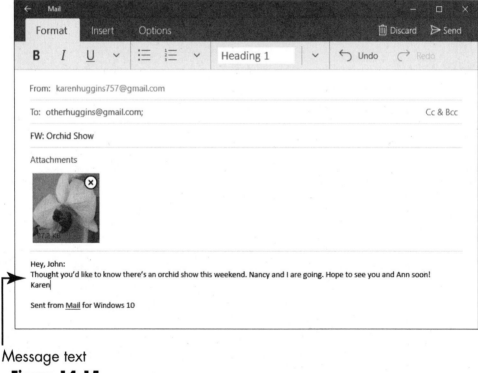

Message text

Figure 14-15

Make Account Settings in Mail

1. Each account that you set up in Mail has its own settings. Click the Mail tile on the Start menu.

2. From within Mail, click the Settings icon, and then click Accounts in the Settings panel (see **Figure 14-16**).

Click this option

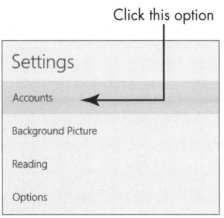

Figure 14-16

3. Click the account for which you want to change settings.

4. Edit the Account Name if you want.

5. Click Change Mailbox Sync Settings in the Account Settings window. In the window displayed in **Figure 14-17**, you can make changes including these:

- **Download New Email:** You can click this box and, from the drop-down list that appears, choose to download content when a message arrives, based on your usage, or every 15 or 30 minutes. You could choose to download messages hourly or every two hours. If you prefer, you can choose to download items only when you click the button beside the account by clicking the Manually option here.

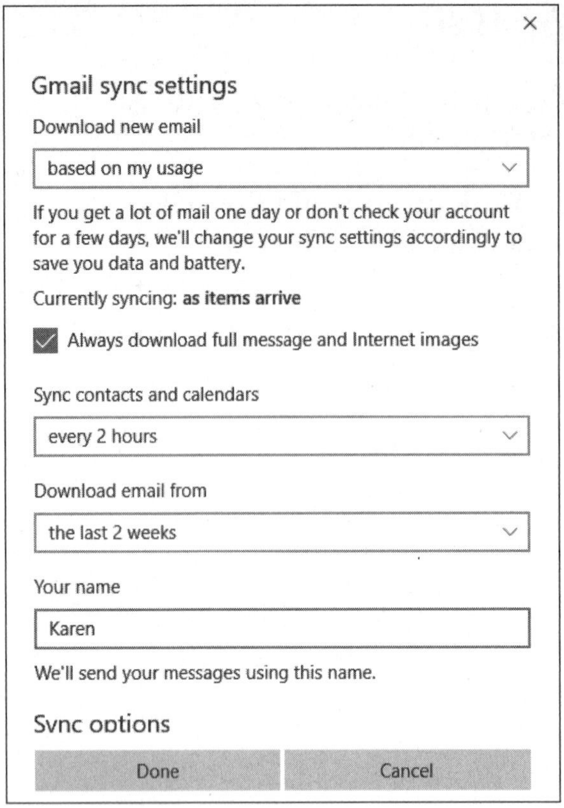

✕

Gmail sync settings

Download new email

| based on my usage ⌄ |

If you get a lot of mail one day or don't check your account for a few days, we'll change your sync settings accordingly to save you data and battery.

Currently syncing: **as items arrive**

☑ Always download full message and Internet images

Sync contacts and calendars

| every 2 hours ⌄ |

Download email from

| the last 2 weeks ⌄ |

Your name

| Karen |

We'll send your messages using this name.

Sync options

| Done | Cancel |

Figure 14-17

- **Sync Contacts and Calendars:** Syncing involves having certain actions and content delivery or deletions coordinated among different accounts and servers, such as downloading your email messages. You can choose how often to sync items using this command. The default setting is Every 2 Hours.

- **Download Email From:** This is a handy setting if you're away from Mail for a while and have been checking messages in your browser. If so, you may not want to download a month's worth of messages you've already read, so choose another setting from this drop-down list, such as The Last 7 Days.

- **Your Name:** In this text box, type the name you want displayed in messages you send.

- **Advanced Mailbox Settings:** Scroll down, click this choice, and scroll down a bit more to see specific settings that control how your email account operates, such as the Incoming Email Server. Don't change any of these settings unless your email provider tells you to; otherwise, your account may stop working in Mail.

6. Click the Done button to go back to the Account Settings window.

7. Click the Save button to finish and close the window.

 To remove an account from Mail, click Delete Account in the Account Settings window in Step 5. For the account you use to sign in to Windows 10, you'll have to perform this procedure through the Settings window (press Win+I and then click Accounts).

Controlling Notifications in Windows 10

To change notification settings for new email, press Win+I, click System, and then click Notifications & Actions at left. Scroll down to see the Mail option and make sure it is set to On (see **Figure 14-18**).

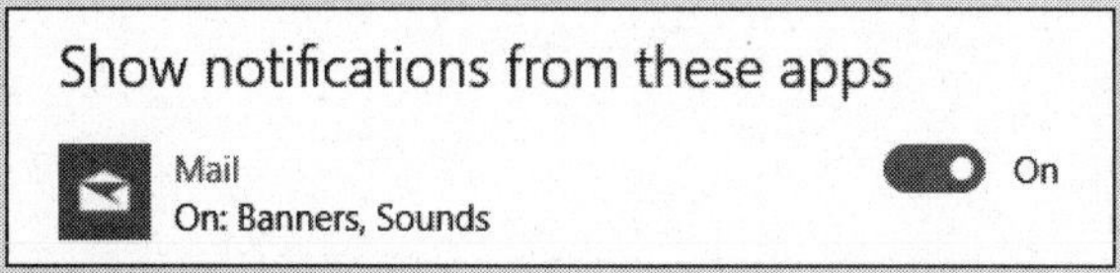

Show notifications from these apps

| Mail On: Banners, Sounds | On |

Figure 14-18

Working in the Cloud

*Y*ou may have heard the term *cloud* bandied about. The term comes from the world of computer networks, where certain functionality isn't installed on computers but resides on the network itself, in the so-called cloud.

Today, the definition of the term has broadened to include functionality that resides on the Internet. If you can get work done without using an installed piece of software — or if you store and share content online — you're working in the cloud.

In this chapter, you discover the types of applications you might use in the cloud, saving you the cost and effort of buying and installing software. In addition, I explore two Windows 10 features that help you access your own data in the cloud: OneDrive and Sync. OneDrive is a file-sharing service that has been around for a while, but with Windows 10, sharing files from your computer with others or with yourself on another computer is more tightly integrated. Sync allows you to share the settings you've made in Windows 10 on one computer with other Windows 10 computers.

Use Applications Online

Certain apps, such as Maps and People, are built into Windows 10. You may purchase or download and install other apps, such as drawing apps or television viewing apps like Netflix, or more robust applications such as Microsoft Word or Excel. Although these apps and applications may connect to the Internet to get information — such as the latest traffic info, or software help files — the software itself is installed on your computer.

Today, you have the option of using software in the cloud, meaning that you never have to install the software on your computer; instead, you simply make use of it online. Here are some examples you can explore:

➡ **Online office suites:** For example, the Google Docs suite of online software (available at `http://docs.google.com/`; see **Figure 15-1**) includes word processor, spreadsheet, and presentation software products you can use by logging into a Google account. These applications are compatible with popular office software such as Microsoft Word and PowerPoint. Your Microsoft account also enables you to work with Office Online apps, including Word Online, Excel Online, PowerPoint Online, and OneNote Online. You can access these apps after signing in to Outlook.com or OneDrive.

➡ **Email clients:** When you log into Gmail or Outlook.com, you're using software in the cloud. In addition, some email clients that can access more than one email account, such as Outlook and Gmail, connect with file-sharing sites. Rather than attaching files to email messages, you're given the option of uploading and sharing them on the file- sharing site. You can do that with Outlook.com and OneDrive, for example.

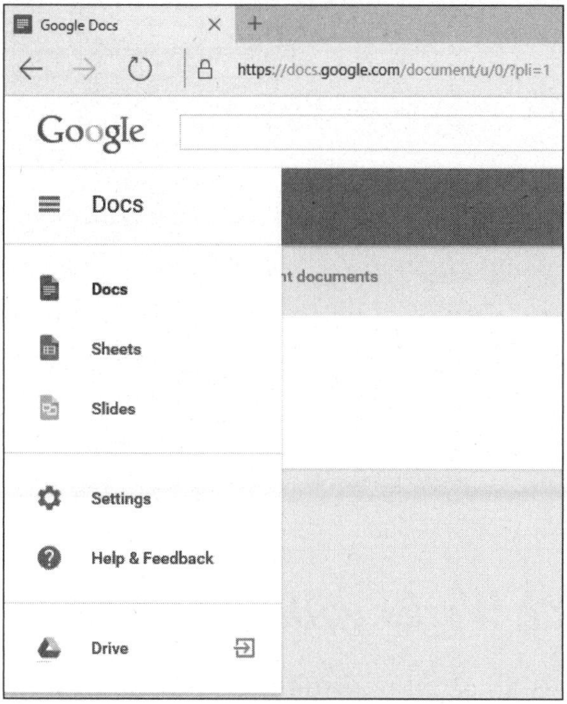

Figure 15-1

⇒ **Photo-sharing sites:** Sites such as Flickr (`www.flickr.com`), shown in **Figure 15-2,** allow you to upload and download photos to them without ever installing an app on your computer. A variation on this is a site such as Viewbook (`www.viewbook.com`), where you can create an online portfolio of art samples or business presentations to share with others.

⇒ **Financial applications:** You might use a tool such as the Morningstar® Portfolio Manager (`portfolio.morningstar.com`) to maintain an online portfolio of investments and generate charts to help you keep track of trends. You can also use online versions of popular money-management programs, such as Intuit's free online service Mint (`www.mint.com`), through which you can access your data from any computer or mobile device.

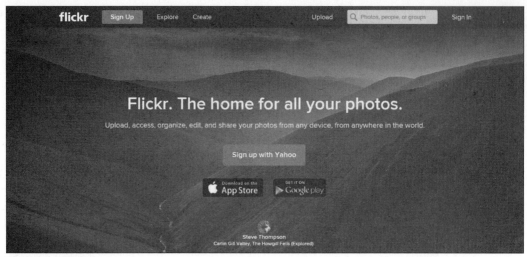

Figure 15-2

Understand How OneDrive Works with the Cloud

OneDrive from Microsoft is all about storing files and sharing them between your computer and the cloud. In Windows 10, OneDrive storage folders in File Explorer on your computer work together with the online version of OneDrive. (Sign in to `onedrive.live.com` with your Microsoft account to work with your online OneDrive.)

Any files you move or copy into a OneDrive folder in File Explorer automatically sync (or back up) to your OneDrive storage in the cloud, and vice versa. Any folder you create in OneDrive in File Explorer also appears in your cloud OneDrive.

The first time you sign in to Windows, you might have noticed a Welcome to OneDrive window. Clicking the Get Started button accepts the terms of the service agreements and privacy statements that are required to use OneDrive. The next window that appears prompts you to confirm the default OneDrive folders on your computer. Click Next, and then click Next again to accept the default setting of syncing all your OneDrive folders. Then click Done to close the window and begin using OneDrive. If you are prompted to enter an administrator password, type it and then click Yes.

After all that, File Explorer opens and shows you your OneDrive folders. These are Documents, Music, and Pictures by default (see **Figure 15-3**). Click OneDrive in the Navigation pane to see these folders any time. You also can click the OneDrive icon near the right end of the taskbar, and then click Open Your OneDrive folder in the pop-up. Use your favorite technique to move or copy files into one of the folders (for example, click and drag or select a file and copy and paste it). From there, Windows uploads your files automatically.

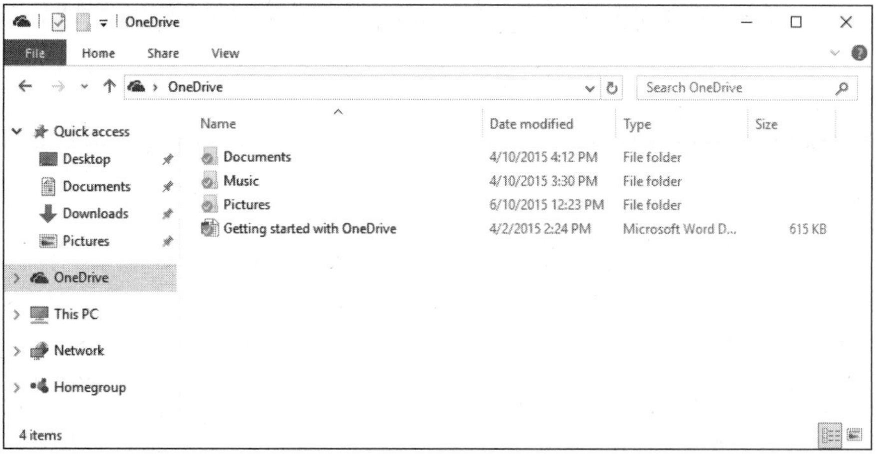

Figure 15-3

Add Files to OneDrive Online

1. You can easily add or upload files to OneDrive online at any time, from mobile devices as well as your computer. Click the Microsoft Edge button on the taskbar.

2. In the Search or Enter Web Address box or the address bar, type `https://onedrive.live.com`, and press Enter.

 If MSN.com is your browser home page, you may see a button that you can click to go to OneDrive.

3. Follow the process for signing in, if prompted, and use your Microsoft account username and password. Your default folders appear (see **Figure 15-4**). Note that the Pictures folder may already contain subfolders, indicated by the number on the folder's tile.

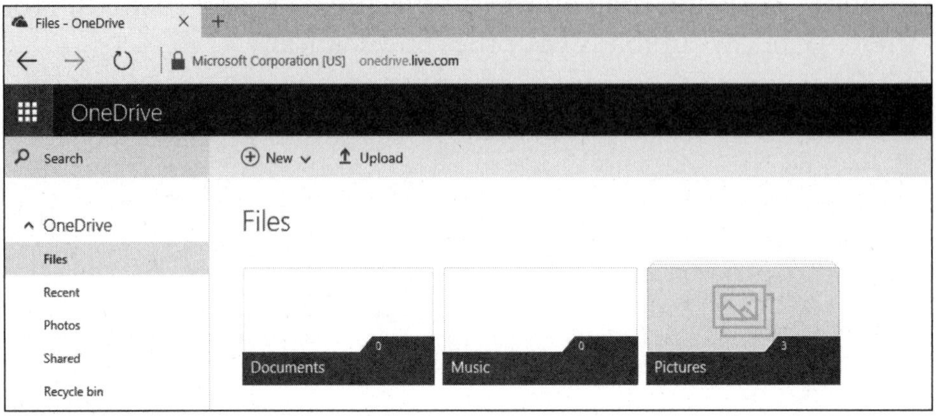

Figure 15-4

4. Click a folder, and it opens.

After you click a folder, click OneDrive in the toolbar or Files in the pane at the left to redisplay your default folders.

5. Click the Upload button in the OneDrive toolbar.

6. Use the Open dialog box that appears (see **Figure 15-5**) to locate a file or folder.

7. Click a file or folder.

8. Click Open.

You also can add a file to OneDrive by dragging it from the File Explorer window to an open OneDrive folder in your browser.

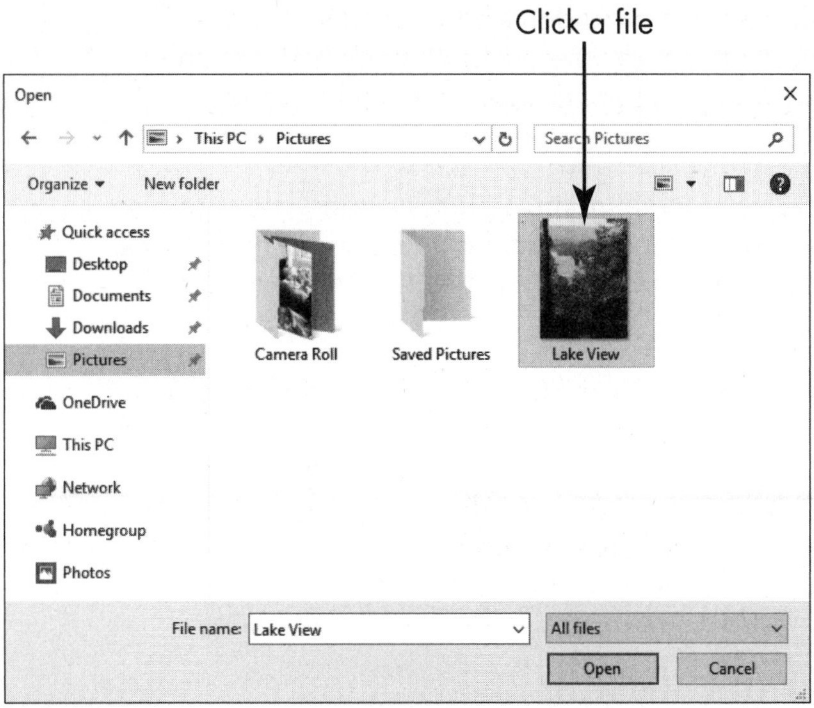

Click a file

Figure 15-5

You may want to delete a file from OneDrive, as the free storage is typically limited to 15 gigabytes (GB). First, find the file that you want to delete in OneDrive. Right-click the file, and then click Delete in the shortcut menu.

Share a Folder or File Using OneDrive

1. The OneDrive service lets you share files with others. Sharing files and folders online can be easier than sending them as attachments because email apps typically limit how much data you can send at one time. You can share a file or folder that you've already stored or created. Find the file or folder that you want to share in OneDrive (online).

2. Right-click the file or folder, and then click Share. Or, move the mouse pointer over the file, click the round check button that appears, and click Share in the toolbar.

 If you need to share multiple files, move your mouse pointer over each one first and click the round check button that appears. Then click the Share button in the toolbar.

3. Type an email address in the To field. To add another address, type a comma and space, and then type the next address. (If any email address you type in the To field matches one of your contacts, the contact name appears, and you can simply click it to select it.)

4. Click in the box below the To field, and then type a message.

5. Click Share (see **Figure 15-6**).

Type an email address

Share

Invite people to this photo

Invite people

Enter contacts to send an email with a link to this item.

Get a link

To

Ann Wilson ✕

Shared with

Only me

Here's a photo from our trip. Wish you had come with us!

Recipients can only view

Share   Close

Figure 15-6

If your account is not verified, you may be prompted to complete a security check. Click the Please Complete This Security Check link, type the characters displayed into the text box, click Continue, and then click Close. You then should be back at the Share window, where you can click the Share button.

 Click the field labelled Recipients Can Only View for more sharing options, such as allowing others to edit the shared file.

6. At the screen that confirms that the file has been shared, click the Close button. The people you shared with receive an email message with a link for viewing the shared file.

 When you share a word-processing file with another person on OneDrive and grant permission to edit it, she can edit it in Word Online (a cloud version of Microsoft Word) or open the document in Microsoft Word on her computer. This is also the case with Excel and PowerPoint files.

 You also can share a file or folder directly from the OneDrive folders on your computer (refer to Figure 15-3). Right-click the item to share, and click Share a OneDrive Link. This automatically copies the link to the Clipboard, and you can use Ctrl+V to paste it into an email message.

Create a New OneDrive Folder

1. You can keep your shared files in order by placing them in folders on OneDrive. After you've placed content in folders, you can then share those folders with others. This capability to share individual folders gives you a measure of security, as you don't have to share access to your entire OneDrive content with anybody. Open your browser, go to onedrive.live.com, and sign in with your Microsoft account if prompted.

2. If you want the new folder to be created within one of the three default folders, click a folder first.

3. On the toolbar, click New.

4. In the menu, click Folder.

5. Enter a name for the new folder (see **Figure 15-7**).

6. Click the Create button.

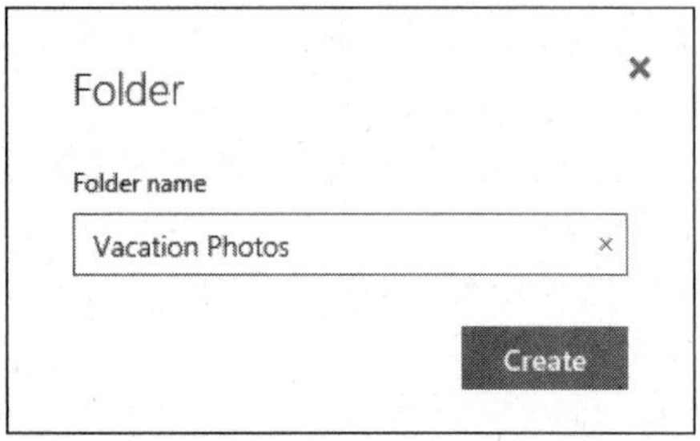

Folder ×

Folder name

Vacation Photos ×

Create

Figure 15-7

Turn On the Sync Feature

1. You can use the Sync feature to share your PC settings among Windows 10 devices so you don't have to redo the settings on each device. To sync, the Sync feature has to be turned on in Settings, which it is by default. If, for some reason, it's been turned off, you have to turn it on. To turn on the Sync feature, press Win+I.

2. Click Accounts, and then click Sync Your Settings.

3. Click the Sync Settings On/Off button (see **Figure 15-8**) if it is turned off to turn it on.

4. Click the Close (X) button to close the window and apply the settings. With the Sync feature turned on, sign in to your Microsoft account on another device, and all your settings will be synced from the cloud.

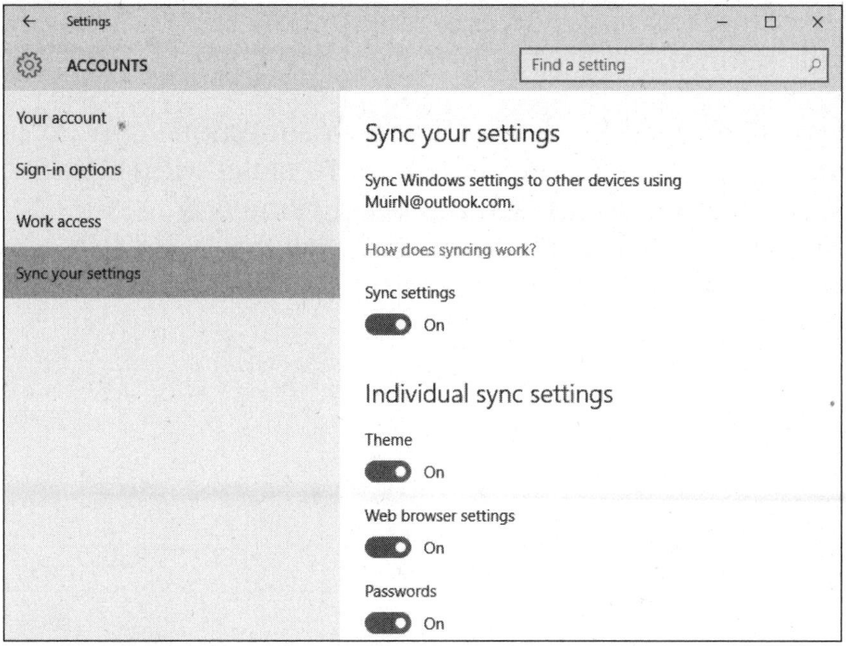

Settings

⚙ ACCOUNTS   Find a setting

Your account

Sign-in options

Work access

Sync your settings

Sync your settings

Sync Windows settings to other devices using
MuirN@outlook.com.

How does syncing work?

Sync settings

🔘 On

Individual sync settings

Theme

🔘 On

Web browser settings

🔘 On

Passwords

🔘 On

Figure 15-8

 Syncing works only with Windows 10 settings and settings for apps that you buy from the Windows Store.

Choose which Settings You Want to Sync

1. When you turn on syncing, you can choose what you want to share. For example, you can share language preferences, passwords, or Ease of Access settings — it's up to you. To set up what you want to sync, begin by pressing Win+I.

2. Click Accounts.

3. Click Sync Your Settings.

4. In the Individual Sync Settings section, click the On/Off buttons for the various settings you want to share, such as Web Browser Settings or Passwords (refer to Figure 15-8). With Sync turned on, selected settings are synced automatically among Windows 10 devices.

5. Click the Close (X) button to close the window and apply the settings.

 If you're charged for data or Internet connection time — for example, on a Windows 10 tablet with 4G — go to Devices in Settings, leave Printers & Scanners selected, scroll down, and click the On/Off button under Download over Metered Connections.

Connecting with People Online

Chapter 16

*T*he Internet offers many options for connecting with people and sharing information. You'll find discussion boards, blogs, and chat on a wide variety of sites, from news sites to recipe sites, sites focused around grief and health issues, and sites that host political- or consumer-oriented discussions.

There are some great senior chat rooms for making friends, and many sites allow you to create new chat rooms on topics at any time.

Instant messaging (IM), on the other hand, isn't a website but a service. Using software such as the Skype app in Windows 10, IM allows you to chat in real time with your contacts. You can access instant-messaging programs via your computer or your cellphone or use instant messaging features offered by some social networking services.

As with any site where users share information, such as social networks and blogs, you can stay safer if you know how to sidestep some abuses, including *data mining* (gathering your personal information for commercial or criminal intent), *social engineering* ploys that try to gain your trust and access to your money, ID theft scams, and so forth. If you're careful to protect your privacy, you can enjoy socializing without worry.

Finally, Windows 10 offers some neat sharing features that allow you to share content such as music or videos with others via services such as email or Facebook by using the Share charm.

In this chapter, I look at some ways of sharing information content and tell you how to do so safely.

Use Discussion Boards and Blogs

A *discussion board* is a place where you can post written messages, pictures, and videos on a topic. Others can reply to you, and you can reply to their postings. In a variation on discussion boards, you'll find *blogs* (web logs) everywhere you turn, and you also can post your comments about blog entries.

Discussion boards and blogs are *asynchronous*, which means that you post a message (just as you might on a bulletin board at the grocery store) and wait for a response. Somebody might read it that hour — or ten days or several weeks after you make the posting. In other words, the response isn't instantaneous, and the message isn't usually directed to a specific individual.

You can find a discussion board or blog about darn-near every topic under the sun, and these are tremendously helpful when you're looking for answers. They're also a great way to share your expertise — whether you chime in on how to remove an ink stain, provide historical trivia about button styles on military uniforms, or announce the latest breakthroughs in your given field. Postings are likely to stay up on the site for years for people to reference.

1. To try using a discussion board, enter this URL in your browser's address field: `http://answers.microsoft.com/en-us`. (Some discussion boards require that you become a member, with a username, and sign in before you can post. This site lets you sign in with the same Microsoft account that you use to sign in to Windows 10.)

2. If you scroll down to the lower-left corner of the page, the default language and region is English. You can click that link and then click another language of your choice. Then scroll up and click a topic area under Browse the Categories, such as OneDrive.

3. In the topic list that appears, click another topic, such as Working with Files and Folders on OneDrive, to see more options. Continue to click until you get to a specific discussion thread, such as the one shown in **Figure 16-1**.

Figure 16-1

4. When you click a posting that has replies, you'll see that the replies are listed down the page in easy-to-follow threads, which arrange postings and replies in an outline-like structure. You can review the various participants' comments as they add their ideas to the conversation.

5. To reply to a posting yourself, first click the posting and then click the Reply link. For this site, you then fill in a brief sign-up screen where you enter your display name, click a check box to accept the Code of Conduct, and then click Sign Up. Type your comments in the Reply box (see **Figure 16-2**), scroll down, and click Submit.

Question

Applies to OneDrive | Working with files and folders on OneDrive | Editing and viewing files and folders
 | OneDrive in Windows 10
3 views

Still have questions?

Ask the community

Uploading files to onedrive

HI higgichris asked on July 29, 2015 ⌄

what am i supposed to do about a message that tells me that I cannot upload files to onedrive because the path to a file or folder is too long?" (60)

1 person had this question

Me Too   Reply   Report abuse ⌄   Subscribe to updates

Reply
☐ Reply with quote

🔄 ↻ **B** *I* U̲ ✂ ☰ ☰ ☰ ☰ Format ▼ ☰ ☰ ☰ ∞ 🖼 ▦

I have the same question!

Figure 16-2

Participate in Chat

A *chat room* is an online space where groups of people can talk back and forth via text, audio, web camera, or a combination of media. (See **Figure 16-3,** which shows a website that links to hundreds of chat rooms.) In chat, you're having a conversation with one or more people in real time, and your entire conversation appears in the chat window. Here are some characteristics of chat that you should know about:

➡ When the chat is over, unless you save a copy, the conversation is typically gone.

➡ Interactions are in real time (synchronous), which means you can interact with others in the moment.

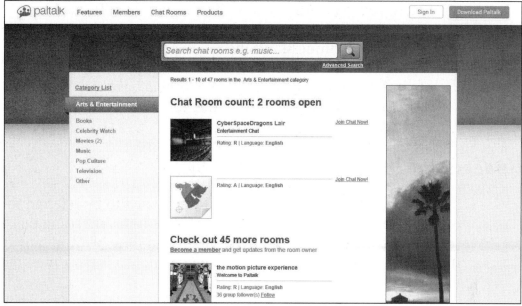

Figure 16-3

➠ Several people can interact at once, although this can take getting used to as you try to follow what others are saying and jump in with your own comments.

➠ When you find a chat you want to participate in, sign up to get a screen name, and then you simply enter the chat room, type your message, and submit it. Your message shows up in the stream of comments, and others may — or may not — reply to it.

When you're talking to someone in a chat room with multiple people, you might be able to, if you'd like, invite him to enter a private chat room, which keeps the rest of the folks who wandered into the chat room out of your conversation. Also, others can invite you into private chat rooms. Be careful whom you interact with in this way, and be sure you understand the motivations for making your conversation private. This may be entirely reasonable, or it may be that you're dealing with someone with suspect motivations.

Before you get started, check out the website's Terms of Use and privacy, monitoring, and abuse-reporting procedures to understand the safety protections that are in place. Some sites are well monitored for signs of abusive content or interactions; others have no monitoring at all. If you don't like the terms, find a different site.

Understand Instant Messages (IMs)

Instant messaging (often called just *IMing*) used to be referred to as real-time email. It used to be strictly synchronous, meaning that two (or more) parties could communicate in real time, without any delay. It still can be synchronous, but now you can also leave a message that the recipient can pick up later.

Instant messaging is a great way to stay in touch with younger generations who rarely use email. IM is ideal for quick, little messages where you just want an answer without forming a formal email, as well as for touching base and saying hi. Text messaging on cellphones is largely the same phenomena: This isn't a tool you'd typically use for a long, meaningful conversation, but it's great for quick exchanges.

Depending on the IM service you use, you can do the following:

➠ Write notes to friends, grandchildren, or whomever.

➠ Talk as if you were on the phone.

➠ Send photos, videos, and other files.

➠ Use little graphical images, called *emoticons* (such as smilies or winks), *avatars*, and *stickers* (cartoony pictures and characters), to add fun to your IM messages.

➠ See participants via web cameras.

➠ Get and send email.

➡ Search the web, find others' physical location using Global Positioning System (GPS) technology, listen to music, watch videos, play games, bid on auctions, find dates, and more.

➡ Track the history of conversations and even save transcripts of them to review later.

Instant messaging programs vary somewhat, and you have several to choose from, including the Skype app that's included in Windows 10. Other messaging apps include Yahoo! Messenger (available at `http://messenger.yahoo.com`), and AOL Instant Messenger, also known as AIM (available at `www.aim.com`). Gmail also has a built-in IM feature.

IM is one place where people use shortcut text. Some of this will be familiar to you, such as FYI (for your information) and ASAP (as soon as possible). Other short text may be less familiar. Visit `pc.net/slang` for a table of common shortcut text terms. Knowing these will make communicating with younger folks more fun.

Consider what you're saying and sharing in IM and how you'd feel if the information were made public. IM allows you to store your conversation history, which is super-useful if you need to go back and check something that was said, but it has its downside. Anything you include in an IM can be forwarded to others. If you're at work, keep in mind that many employers monitor IM (and email) conversations.

If you run across illegal content — such as child pornography — downloading or continuing to view this for any reason is illegal. Report the incident to law enforcement immediately.

You can send IMs from a computer to a mobile phone (and vice versa) and from one mobile phone to another. If you include your mobile phone number as part of your IM profile, anyone who can see your profile can view it. This is useful information for both friends and criminals, so it's important to consider whether you want your number exposed — especially if you have many people on your Contacts list whom you don't personally know.

Explore Skype and Add Contacts

1. The Skype app enables you to send IMs to friends, as well as to make voice and video calls. Skype is available as a free download. To get started using Skype, click in the Cortana search box, type **Get Skype**, and then click Get Skype at the top of the search results. In the window that appears, click Download Skype.

2. After the download and installation finishes, the Skype window remains open. You can sign in with your Microsoft account or Skype Name. If you see a Windows Security Alert dialog box, review the selected options, and then click Allow Access. (You may be prompted to enter an administrator password.) Then, follow the prompts to set up your sound, video, and profile picture.

 By default, the install process adds a desktop shortcut that you can use to open Skype at a later time. You can also use the Cortana search box on the taskbar to search for and open Skype.

3. After finishing connecting to the service, Skype then prompts you to search for contacts (see **Figure 16-4**). (You need to add your friends and family as contacts in order to message and call them. They have to be set up as Skype users, too.) You can click the Search Address Book button to add contacts. Existing contacts appear in the

Contacts list at the lower left. A green dot beside a contact's name means that person is currently available for conversations and calls.

Skype lists your contacts here

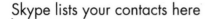

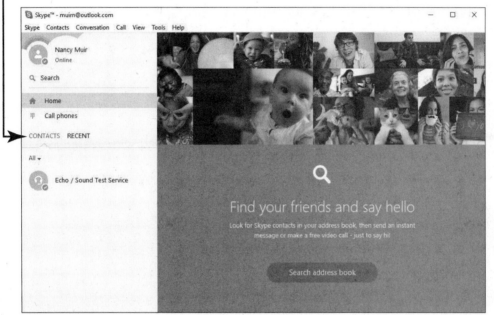

Figure 16-4

4. To add a contact later, click on Search below your user name, type a contact's Skype Name or email address, and then click the Search Skype button. In the list that appears, click the Add a Contact button (see **Figure 16-5**).

5. In the next window, click the Add to Contacts button.

Figure 16-5

6. Edit the brief message in the message field that opens
(see **Figure 16-6**) and click Send. Once your contact
receives your message and accepts the invitation, the
question mark on the contact's photo or icon in your
Contacts list changes to a green check mark. The green
check mark also indicates when a contact is online, so
the two of you can message and call on Skype.

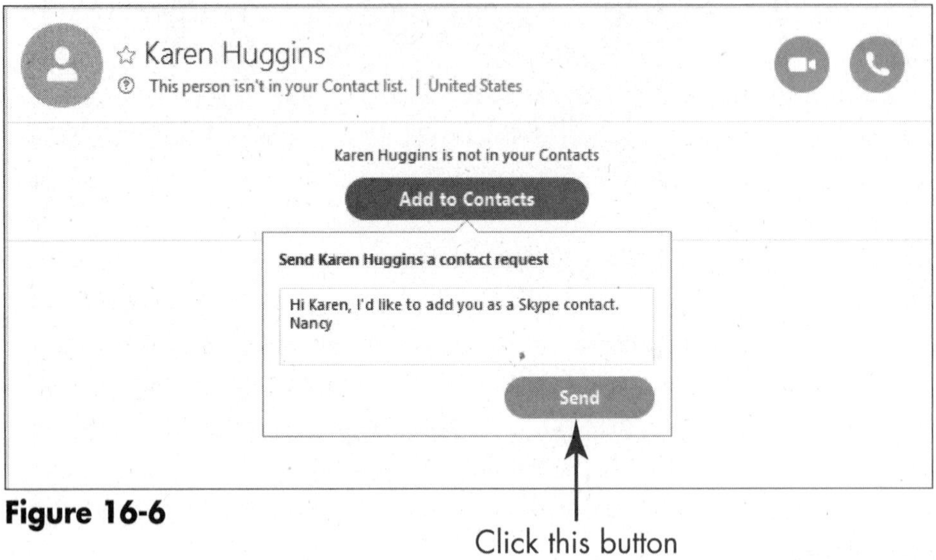

Figure 16-6

Click this button

 Click Recent on the left side of Skype to display your
contact request. When the contact accepts, you'll also
see a message that the contact has shared his or her
contact details with you.

Send and Receive Instant Messages (IMs) in Skype

1. To chat with a single user, just click Contacts in the left
pane of the Skype window, and click the available
(online) contact in the list (see **Figure 16-7**).

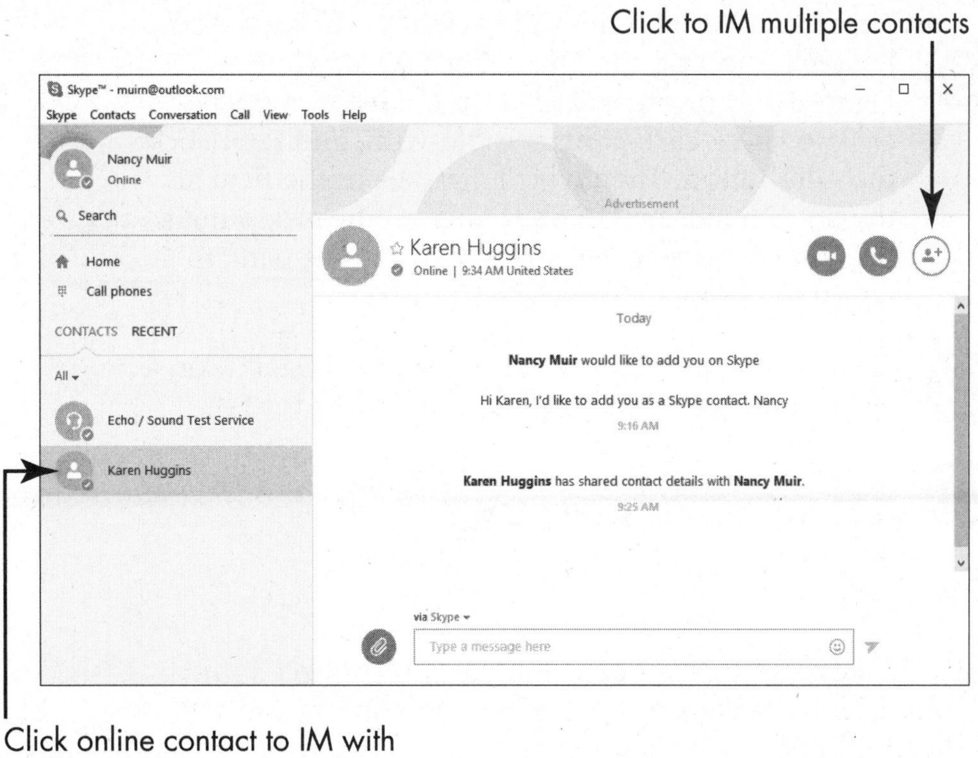

Click to IM multiple contacts

Click online contact to IM with
Figure 16-7

2. On the messaging screen, type a message in the field at the bottom of the screen (see **Figure 16-8**) and press Enter. The message appears as the first message in the conversation. Read your friend's response when it appears, and type additional comments to carry on your conversation.

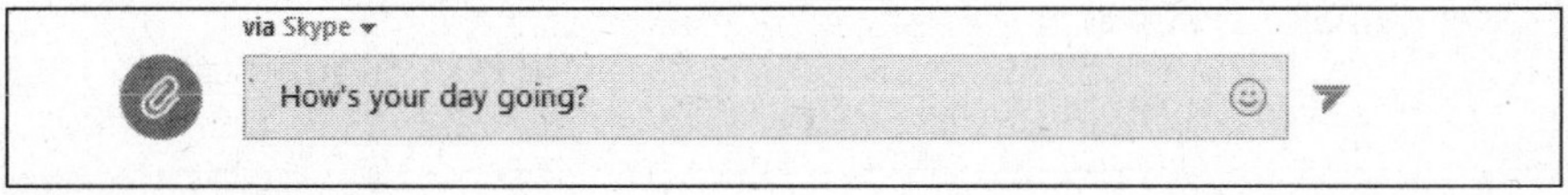

Figure 16-8

3. To return to the main Skype screen, click the Back (left arrow) button on the contact's photo.

To start an IM with multiple contacts, click the Add People button on the main Skype screen (refer to Figure 16-7) or press Ctrl+N. In the list that opens, click to check each contact to IM with, and then click the Add button. Then type a message in the field at the bottom and press Enter. After all the group members finish chatting, click Home in the left pane to return to the main Skype screen.

Skype is also available as a mobile app. Install it on a smartphone or tablet to use those devices for IM.

Some online services call messaging *direct messaging* (DM) or *private messaging* (PM).

Make a Call

1. To make a call to a contact, you have to connect a microphone and speakers to the system. Or, you can use a headset/microphone combination that's designed for making online calls. Follow the instructions that came with your computer and the devices for connecting and setting them up in Windows.

2. In the main Skype screen, click Contacts in the left pane, then the contact to call in the Contacts list.

3. Click the Call button (see **Figure 16-9**) to the right of the contact's name.

Click to place call

Figure 16-9

4. If a box with choices pops up, click Call Skype. (Charges apply if you click Call Mobile.) Your contact will see a pop-up box in Skype where he or she can click to accept or hang up the call.

5. Talk as you normally would using the microphone. Move your mouse over the contact to display buttons for working with the call. You can click the microphone button (see **Figure 16-10**) to mute and unmute your microphone. The button with the plus on it lets you add more contacts to the call, among other things.

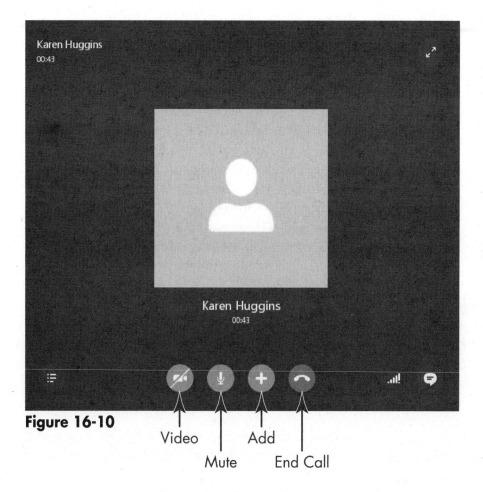

Figure 16-10

Video

Mute

Add

End Call

6. Click the End Call button at the right below the contact photo to finish the Skype call.

7. Click Home in the left pane to go back to the main Skype screen. If you're finished using Skype, click the Close button.

 To dial a phone number with Skype, click the Call Phones button (with the phone icon) on the main Skype screen. Use the onscreen keypad to enter the number, including the area code, and click the round Call button at the bottom. Note that calling fees apply. In the United States, you can pay per minute as you go, or buy a low-cost monthly subscription.

 If you simply close the Skype window, you are still signed in to Skype and will appear as Online (available for calls and messages) to your Skype contacts. If you receive any incoming IMs or calls, Skype will reopen to alert you. If you do not want to be available, you have two choices that you can make before closing the Skype window. You can either click the Skype menu and click Sign Out (in which case, you will have to sign back in when you restart Skype), or you can click the Skype menu, point to Online Status, and click a different status in the submenu.

Use Webcams

Webcams are relatively inexpensive, and laptops now come with webcams embedded in their lids. (See **Figure 16-11.**) You can use a webcam with apps like Skype to make calls over the Internet, or other apps to have face-to-face, live meetings.

A webcam can be a great way to communicate with friends and family, but it can quickly become risky when you use it for conversations with strangers.

Figure 16-11

➡ Giving your image away, especially one that may show your emotional reactions to a stranger's statements in real time, simply reveals too much information that can put you at risk.

➡ If you use a webcam to meet with someone whom you don't know online, that person may expose you to behavior you'd rather not see.

➡ Note that webcams can also be hijacked and turned on remotely. This allows predators to view and listen to individuals without their knowledge. When you aren't using your webcam, consider turning it off or disconnecting it if it isn't a built-in model.

 Teens in particular struggle to use good judgment when using webcams. If you have grandchildren or other children in your care, realize that normal inhibitions seem to fall away when they aren't physically present with the person they're speaking to — and many expose themselves, figuratively and literally. In addition to having a conversation about appropriate webcam use with children and teens, it may be wise to limit access to webcams.

Get an Overview of Collaborative and Social Networking Sites

Although you may think kids are the only active group using social networking, that isn't the case. In fact, people 35–54 years old make up a large segment of social networkers.

There are several types of sites where people collaborate or communicate socially. The following definitions may be useful:

→ **Wiki:** A website that allows anyone visiting to contribute (add, edit, or remove) content. Wikipedia, for example, is a virtual encyclopedia built by users providing information in their areas of expertise. Because of the ease of collaboration, wikis are often used when developing group projects or sharing information collaboratively.

→ **Blog:** An online journal (*blog* is short for *web log*) that may be entirely private, open to select friends or family, or available to the general public. You can usually adjust your blog settings to restrict visitors from commenting on your blog entries, if you'd like.

→ **Social networking site:** This type of website (see Figure 16-12) allows people to build and maintain a web page and create networks of people that they're somehow connected to — their friends, work associates, and/or other members with similar interests. Most social networking sites also host blogs and have social networking functions that allow people to view information about others and contact each other.

➠ **Social journaling site:** Sites such as Twitter allow people to post short notes online, notes that are typically about what they're doing at the moment. Many companies and celebrities are now *tweeting,* as posting comments on Twitter is referred to. You can follow individuals on Twitter so you're always informed if somebody you're a fan of makes a post.

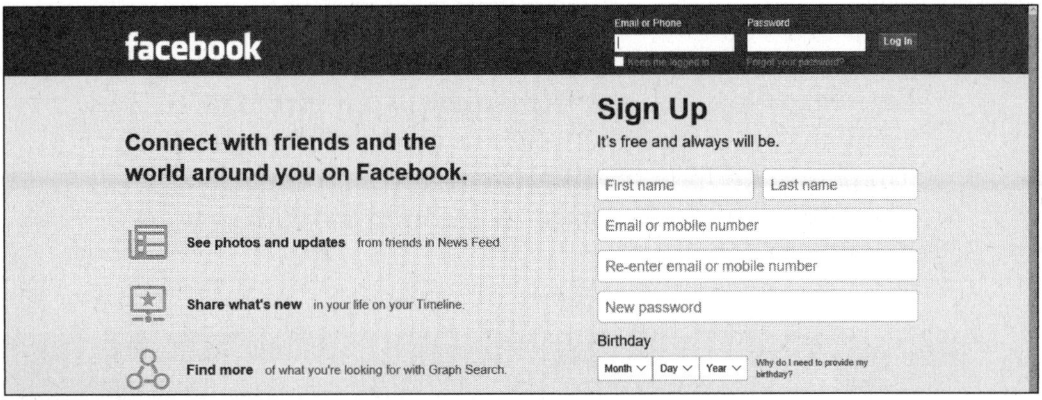

Figure 16-12

Sign Up for a Social Networking Service

Many social networking sites, such as Facebook or Pinterest, are general in nature and attract a wide variety of users. Facebook, which was begun by some students at Harvard, has become today's most popular general site, and many seniors use its features to blog, exchange virtual gifts, and post photos. Other social networking sites revolve around particular interests or age groups.

When signing up for a service, understand what is *required* information and what is optional. You should clearly understand why a web service needs any of your personally identifiable information and how it may use that information — before providing it. Consider carefully the questions that sites ask users to complete in creating a profile.

Accepting a social networking service's default settings may expose more information than you intend.

Walk through the signup process for Facebook to see the kinds of
information it asks for. Follow these instructions to do so:

1. Type this URL into your browser's address line: www.
facebook.com.

2. In the signup form that appears (see **Figure 16-13**), enter
your name, email address, a password, your gender, and
birthdate. Note that the site requires your birthdate to
verify that you are old enough to use the service, but you
can choose to hide this information from others later if
you don't want it displayed. (I recommend hiding your
birthdate.)

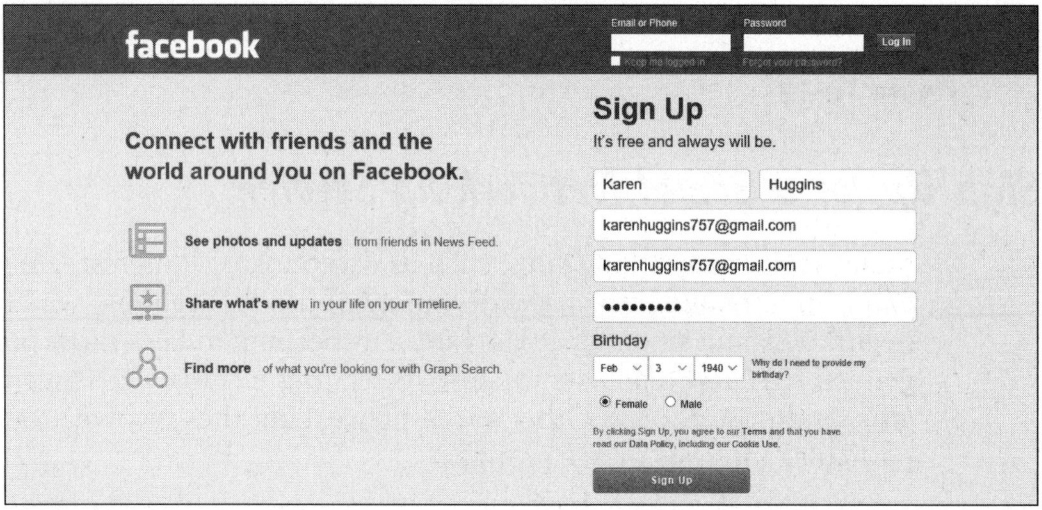

Figure 16-13

3. Click the Sign Up button. On the screen that appears (see
Figure 16-14), click the Find Friends button if you want
to find people from your contacts who are using the various services listed, or click Skip This Step and click Skip

again in the dialog box that appears to move on without adding friends if you don't want to invite everybody on your Contacts list to be your friend.

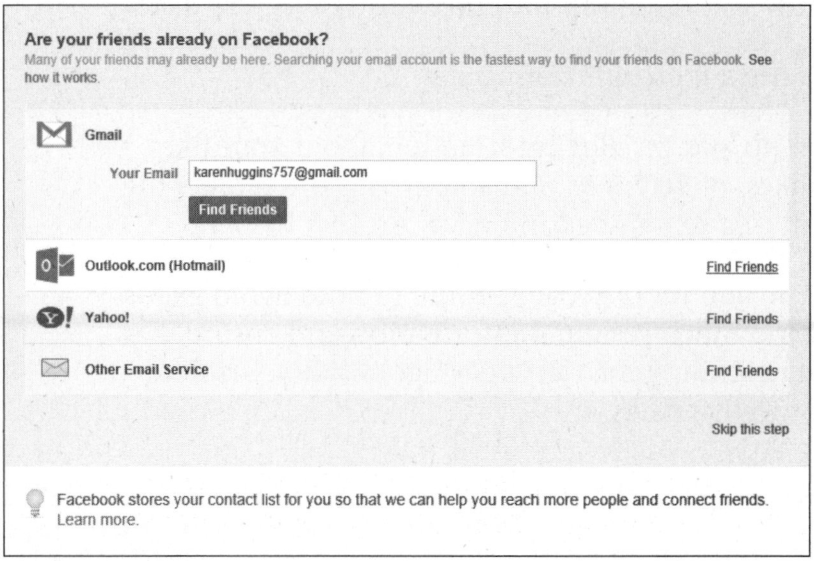

Are your friends already on Facebook?
Many of your friends may already be here. Searching your email account is the fastest way to find your friends on Facebook. **See how it works.**

Gmail

Your Email　karenhuggins757@gmail.com

Find Friends

Outlook.com (Hotmail)　　　　　　　　　　　　　　　　Find Friends

Yahoo!　　　　　　　　　　　　　　　　　　　　　　Find Friends

Other Email Service　　　　　　　　　　　　　　　　Find Friends

Skip this step

Facebook stores your contact list for you so that we can help you reach more people and connect friends. Learn more.

Figure 16-14

4. You now have a Facebook account, and can continue to fill out profile information for Facebook on the following screens, clicking Save and Continue between screens.

Remember that social networking sites sometimes ask for information during signup that they use to provide you with a customized experience that suits your needs. But sometimes the information isn't needed for the service they're providing you at all — they simply want it for marketing purposes, to show to other members, or to sell.

It's often very difficult to remove information from sites if you later regret the amount of information you've shared. It's best to be conservative in the information you share during the signup process; you can always add more later.

Understand How Online Dating Works

Many seniors are making connections with others via online dating services, and if you've been wondering if this route could be for you, here's how you can jump into the world of online dating:

➠ Choose a reputable dating site.

➠ Sign up and provide information about your likes, dislikes, preferences, and so on. This often takes the form of a self-guided interview process.

➠ Create and modify your profile to both avoid exposing too much personal information and ensure that you're sending the right message about yourself to prospective dates.

➠ Use search features on the site to find people who interest you or other people who match your profile (see **Figure 16-15**). Send them messages or invitations to view your profile.

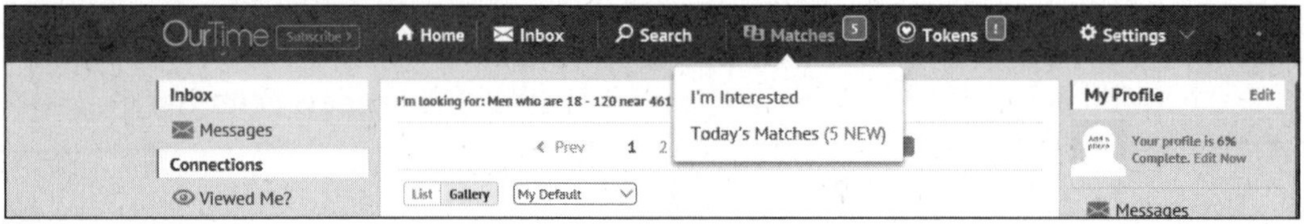

Figure 16-15

➠ You'll get messages from other members of the site, to which you can respond (or not). Use the site's chat and email features to interact with potential dates. You may also be able to read comments about the person from others who've dated him or her, if the site has that feature.

➡ When you're comfortable with the person and feel there might be a spark, decide if you want to meet the person offline.

Formal dating sites aren't the only places where people meet online, but they typically have the best safeguards in place. If you want to interact with people you meet on other sites, you should provide your own safeguards. Create a separate email account (so you can remain anonymous and abandon the email address if needed). Many dating sites screen participants and provide strong reporting measures that are missing on other types of sites, so be particularly careful. Take your time getting to know someone first before connecting.

Select a Dating Service

Select your online dating service carefully.

➡ Look for an established, popular site with plenty of members and a philosophy that matches your own.

➡ Review the site's policy regarding your privacy and its procedures for screening members. Make sure you're comfortable with them.

➡ Use a service that provides an email system (sometimes called *private messaging*) that you use for contacting other members only. By using the site's email rather than your own email address, you can maintain your privacy.

➡ Some sites, such as www.eharmony.com/senior-dating, offer stronger levels of authenticating members, such as screening to make you more confident that you know whom you're interacting with.

➡ Visit a site such as www.consumer-rankings. com/dating for comparisons of sites. Whether you choose a senior-specific dating site such as DatingForSeniors.com or a general-population site such as PerfectMatch.com, reading reviews about them ahead of time will help you make the best choice.

 If you try a site and experience an unpleasant incident involving another member, report it and make sure the service follows through to enforce its policies. If it doesn't, find another service.

Part IV

Having Fun

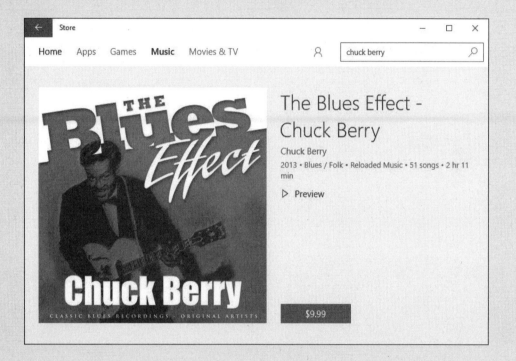

Visit www.dummies.com/extras/computersforseniors for information about creating a music playlist.

Getting Visual: Using the Video, Photos, and Camera Apps

T he world has discovered that it's fun and easy to share photos online, and that's probably why everybody is in on the digital image craze. Most people today have access to a digital camera (even if only on their cellphones) and have started manipulating and swapping photos like crazy, both online and off.

But today your phone, tablet, and computer not only let you upload and view pictures: You can use a built-in camera and the Windows 10 Camera app to take your own pictures or record videos and play them back. You can also buy videos (movies and TV shows, for example) and play them on your computer or other device, such as a tablet.

In this chapter, you discover how to buy and play video, including movies and TV shows. I also give you some guidelines for uploading photos from your digital camera, and explain how to view and share your photos.

Overview of Media Apps

Your computer is a doorway into a media-rich world full of music, digital photos, and video. It provides you with all kinds of possibilities for working with media. Windows 10 has a useful media player built right into it: the Movies & TV app. The Photos app provides another option for viewing photos. In addition, the Camera app helps you to create and view photos and video.

Here's what you can do with each of these programs:

➡ **Movies & TV app:** Just what its name suggests. As you see in **Figure 17-1,** you can use this program to watch movies, TV programs, or videos that you or others have recorded.

Movies

Search

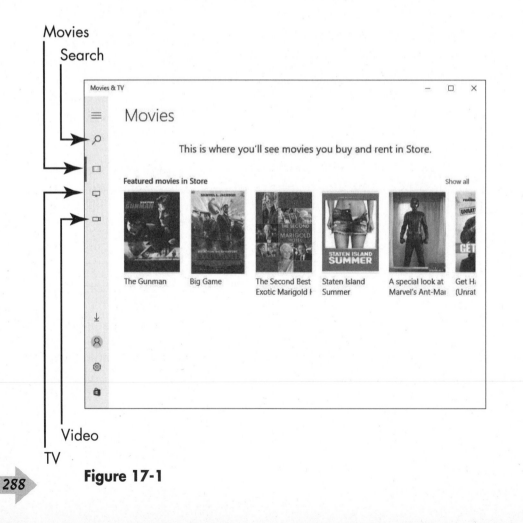

Video

TV

Figure 17-1

➡ **Photos app:** Enables you to view digital photos; it opens automatically when you double-click a photo (as shown in **Figure 17-2**) in File Explorer and when you click the Photos tile on the Start menu. You can also share photos from within the Photos app via social media sites.

Figure 17-2

➡ **Camera app:** Allows anybody who has a computer with a built-in or external camera or webcam to take photos and record videos.

Find Movies and TV Shows in the Store

1. The Windows Store offers a wonderful world of content that you can buy and play on your computer. To shop for movies and TV shows, click the Start button and then click the Store tile. Click the Music & TV link at the top of the window to get started.

2. Scroll down to view titles in categories such as New Movies, Top-Selling Movies, Featured Movies, New TV Shows, and Top Selling TV shows. Click a featured title to view details or watch a trailer.

If you're looking for a particular title or movies with a particular actor, use the search field at the upper-right corner of the window.

3. Click Buy (see **Figure 17-3**). If you click Rent at this point, you're taken through a similar sequence of steps. If requested, enter your Microsoft account password.

Figure 17-3

If you don't already have payment information associated with your Microsoft account, you'll be asked to enter payment information.

4. In the Buy Movie window, click the Buy button (see **Figure 17-4**). The movie is added to Your Video Library in the Movie & TV app.

5. Click the Close button.

Buy movie

Kingsman: The Secret Service

You'll be charged immediately. No refunds. Subject to the Microsoft Services Agreement.

DISCOVER   Nancy C Muir   **3401   4/2016
           Change

                                        $14.99 plus tax

                    Buy   Cancel

Figure 17-4

Play Movies & TV Shows

1. After you have bought a movie or TV show, from the Start menu, click the Movies & TV tile.

2. Click the Movies button or the TV button in the Navigation pane to the left.

3. In the window listing titles, click the title you want to play (as shown in **Figure 17-5**).

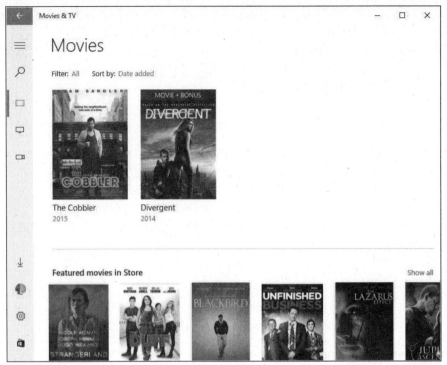

Figure 17-5

4. In the resulting window, click the Play button (if you've already played part of this video, the Play button will read Resume) to begin the playback (see **Figure 17-6**). If you've selected a TV series for which you own several episodes, select an episode before pressing the Play button.

 Movies and TV titles provide a download option. To save space on your hard drive or solid state drive, only download a title if you'll be without a WiFi connection for a time.

5. Use tools at the bottom of the screen (see **Figure 17-7**) to do the following (if they disappear during playback, just move your mouse, or tap the screen, to display them again):

- **Adjust the volume** of any soundtrack by clicking the Volume button to open the volume slider and dragging the slider left (to make it softer) or right (to make it louder). Click the megaphone-shaped

volume icon next to the slider to mute the sound
(and click it again to turn the sound back on).

- **Pause the playback** by clicking the Pause button
  in the center of the toolbar.

Figure 17-6

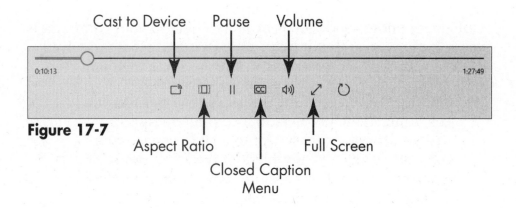

Figure 17-7

- **Enable captions** by clicking the Show Closed Caption Menu button and then clicking the language you prefer.

- **Change the proportions of the movie. Display the movie with a shadowbox effect by clicking the Aspect Ratio button.**

- **View the movie on full screen** by clicking the Full Screen button. When the movie is displayed in full screen, the Full Screen button becomes an Exit Full Screen button. Click this button to view the movie in a smaller window.

- **View the movie on a Bluetooth-enabled TV** by clicking the Cast to Device button.

6. Click the Close button to close the Movies & TV app.

You can also use the Movies & TV app to play video content. Just click the Movies & TV tile on the Start menu, locate the video in the My Videos section, and click to play it. The playback controls are almost identical to those discussed for playing movies.

Upload Photos and Videos from Your Digital Camera

Uploading photos and videos from a camera to your computer is a very simple process, but it helps to understand what's involved. (Check your manual for details.) Here are some highlights:

 Making the connection: Uploading photos and videos from a digital camera to a computer requires that you connect the camera to a USB port on your computer using a USB cable that typically comes with the camera. Power on the camera or change its setting to a playback mode as instructed by your user's manual. Some cameras are WiFi-enabled, which eliminates the need for a USB cable when you are in range of a WiFi network.

➡ **Installing software:** Digital cameras also typically come with software that makes uploading photos to your computer easy. Install the software and then follow the easy-to-use instructions to upload photos and videos. If you're missing such software, you can simply connect your camera to your computer and use File Explorer to locate the camera device on your computer and copy and paste photo or video files into a folder on your hard drive. (Chapter 3 tells you how to use File Explorer.)

➡ **Printing photos straight from the camera:** Digital cameras save photos onto a memory card, and many printers include a slot where you can insert the memory card from the camera and print directly from it without having to upload pictures first. Some cameras also connect directly to printers. However, if you want to keep a copy of the photo and clear up space in your camera's memory, you should upload the photos to your computer or an external storage medium such as a DVD or USB stick, even if you can print without uploading.

Take Photos with the Camera App

1. If your computer or computing device has a camera (in the case of a computer, what you have may be a webcam), you can use the Camera app features to take both still photos and videos. Click the Start button, click All Apps, and then scroll down and click Camera.

2. Click the More button and then click Settings. The Settings dialog box opens; click the Aspect Ratio drop-down box and choose a setting. Click outside the Settings dialog box to close it.

3. If the Camera button is larger than the Video button (see
Figure 17-8), you're in photo mode. If the Video button
is larger than the Camera button, click the Camera button to go to Photo mode. Aim your computer or computing device toward the subject of your picture and click
the Camera button. The photo is captured.

Photo App   More

Figure 17-8

Camera

Video

4. Click the Photo App button to view the photo.

 When you take a photo, you can click the Photo App
button and use the photo editing or sharing tools.
See the Edit Photos and Share a Photo sections for
more details.

Record Videos with the Camera App

1. If your computer has a camera, you can use the Camera app to take both still photos and videos. Click the Start button, click All Apps, and then scroll down and click Camera.

2. Click the More button and then click Settings. The Settings dialog box opens (see **Figure 17-9**). Scroll down to the Video Recording and Flicker Reduction drop-down boxes and adjust the resolution, frame rate, and flicker reduction frequency settings if necessary. (Most people leave these at their default settings.) Click outside the Settings dialog box to close it.

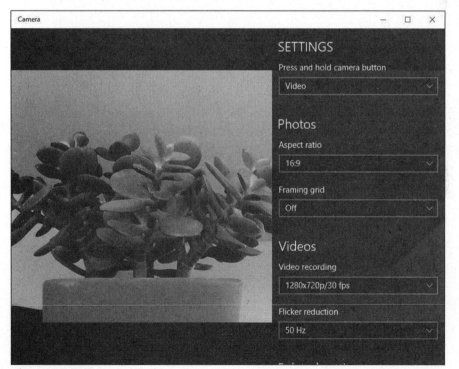

Figure 17-9

3. Click the Video button (see **Figure 17-10**) until you're in Video mode.

Figure 17-10

4. Click the Video button to begin the video recording.

5. Click the Video button in Windows again to stop recording.

 To view your video, go to the Camera Roll folder in your Pictures folder and then double-click the video file. If a list of apps that can be used to open the file appears, choose Movies & TV. The video opens in the Movies & TV app.

View Photos in the Photos App

1. To peruse your photos and open them in the Photos app, click the Photos tile on the Start menu. The Photos app opens with a thumbnail for each photo in your collection, as shown in **Figure 17-11.** Browse the thumbnails and click any thumbnail to open a photo.

Collection

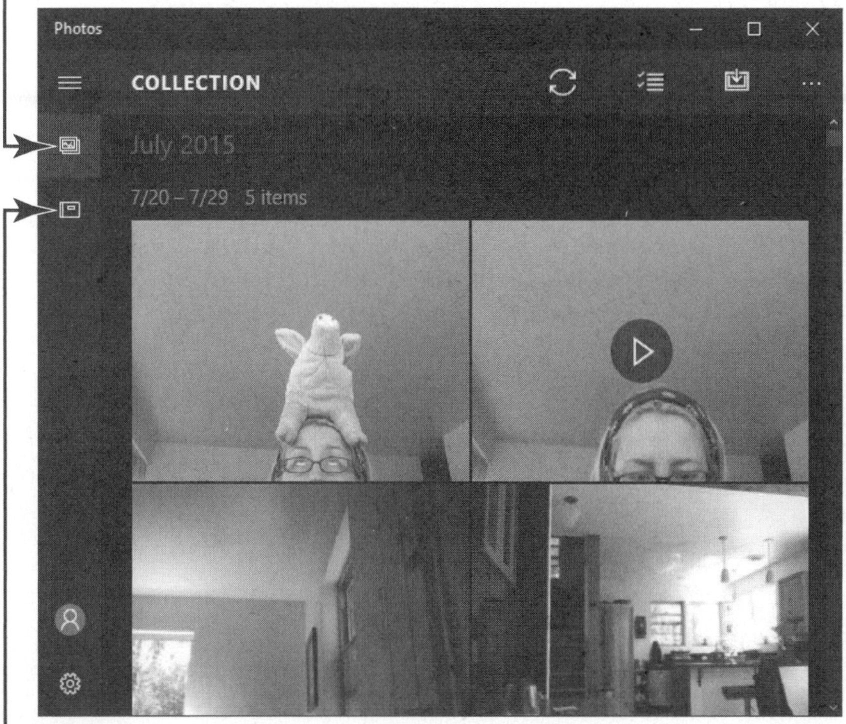

Albums
Figure 17-11

2. In the Photos app, click the Albums button. The resulting screen shows your photos organized in albums by date. Click an album to display files within it. Click a photo

and move the mouse on the picture; arrows appear on the sides (click these arrows to see the next or previous photos in the album). A -/+ symbol appears at the bottom-right corner (see **Figure 17-12**). Click these to zoom in and out.

Figure 17-12

 To change the title or content of an album, in the Photos app, click an album. Click the Edit button (the pencil-shaped icon at the top of the screen). You enter the Edit mode, which allows you to change the album title or cover image and add or remove photos from the album.

 To delete a photo, click the photo and then click the Delete button (trashcan-shaped button at the upper right). This deletes the selected image.

Edit Photos

In the Photos app, click a photo and then click the Edit button (the pencil-shaped icon at the top of the screen). Editing toolbars appear on the sides of the screen. You can use the tools shown in **Figure 17-13** to do any of the following:

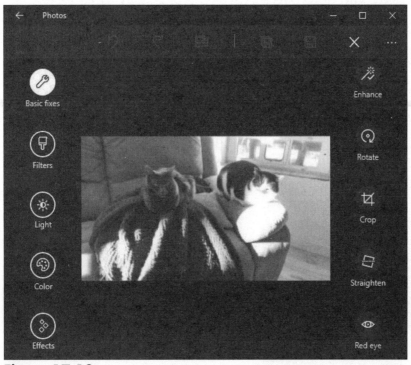

Figure 17-13

➠ The **Basic Fixes** button allows you to choose between Enhance, Rotate, Crop, Straighten, Red Eye, and Retouch.

➠ The **Filters** button allows you to choose between thumbnails of the image with different filters applied.

➩ The **Light** button lets you choose to adjust Brightness, Contrast, Highlights, or Shadows.

➩ Clicking the **Color** button lets you choose Temperature, Tint, Saturation, or Color boost.

➩ The **Effects** button lets you choose between the Vignette and Selective focus.

Share a Photo

1. Click the Photos app tile on the Start menu. Locate a photo you want to share and then click the Share button.

2. The Share screen opens, showing the apps that you can use to share the file (see **Figure 17-14**). Click any app you want to use, such as Facebook.

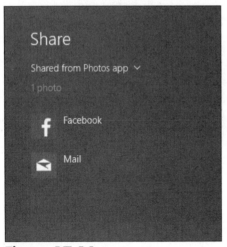

Figure 17-14

 To share a photo, you need to download the appropriate social media app, such as Facebook. From the Store, open the social media app and sign in and you can then use that social media app to share photos.

3. In the form that appears (see **Figure 17-15**), enter your message.

Write Post   Post

Shared from Photos app - 1 photo

Understanding
Nano.com

On your own timeline ▼

Figure 17-15

4. Click the Post button. The photo and message are posted on your Facebook page or other selected destination.

 If you want to set an image for your lock screen, click the More button at the upper-right corner of the screen. A menu appears that allows you to set the image to be used on the lock screen, or to copy or print the image.

Run a Slide Show in the Photos App

1. You can use the Photos app to play a slide show, which continues to run until you stop it. Click the Photos tile on the Start menu and then click a photo album to open it.

2. Click the Slide Show button shown in **Figure 17-16**.

3. Click anywhere on the screen to stop the slide show.

Click here

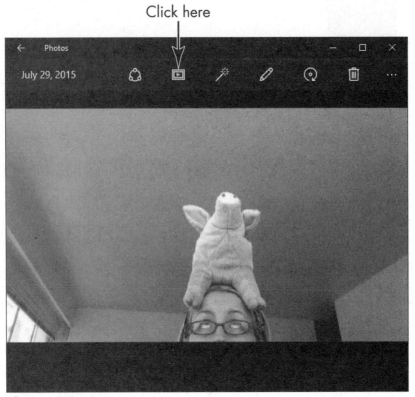

Figure 17-16

Playing Music in Windows 10

Music is the universal language, and your computer opens up many opportunities for appreciating it. Your computer makes it possible for you to listen to your favorite music, download music from the Internet, play audio CDs and DVDs, and organize your music by creating playlists. You can also access your music library on your other Windows 10 devices, such as your phone or tablet.

You can set up your speakers and adjust volume, and then use the Groove Music app to buy music, play music, and manage your music library.

Set Up Speakers

1. Attach headphones or speakers to your computer by plugging them into the appropriate connection (often labeled with a little earphone or speaker symbol) on your tower, laptop, or all-in-one monitor.

2. Right-click the Volume button (which looks like a little speaker) in the notifications area of the taskbar and in the menu that opens, click Playback Devices.

3. In the resulting Sound dialog box (see **Figure 18-1**), click the Speakers/Headphones item and then click the Properties button. *Note:* Depending on your speaker and headphone models, these settings might vary.

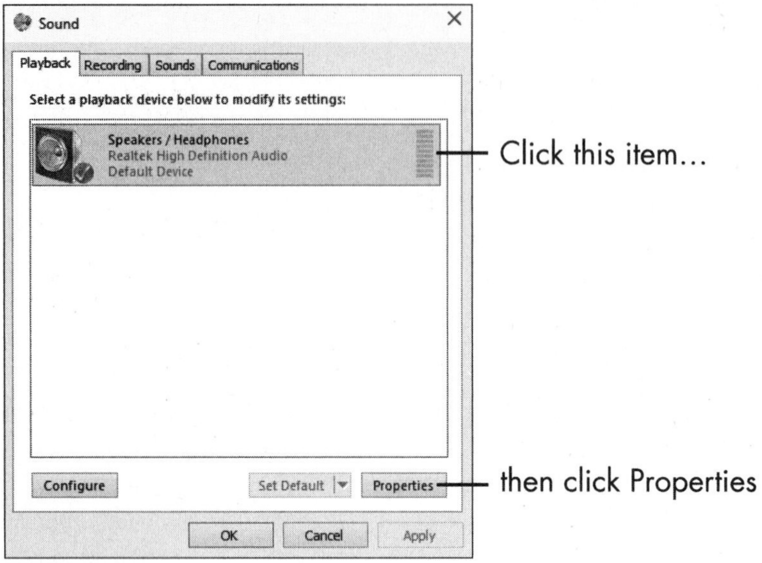

Click this item...

then click Properties

Figure 18-1

4. In the resulting Speakers/Headphones Properties dialog box, click the Levels tab, shown in **Figure 18-2**, and then use the Speakers/Headphones slider to adjust the speaker volume. *Note:* If you see a small red x on the Speaker button, click it to activate the speakers.

5. Click the Balance button. In the resulting Balance dialog box, use the L(eft) and R(ight) sliders to adjust the balance of sounds between the two speakers.

6. Click OK three times to close all the open dialog boxes and save the new settings.

 If you use your computer to make or receive phone calls, check out the Communications tab of the Sound dialog box. Here you can make a setting to have Windows automatically adjust sounds to minimize background noise.

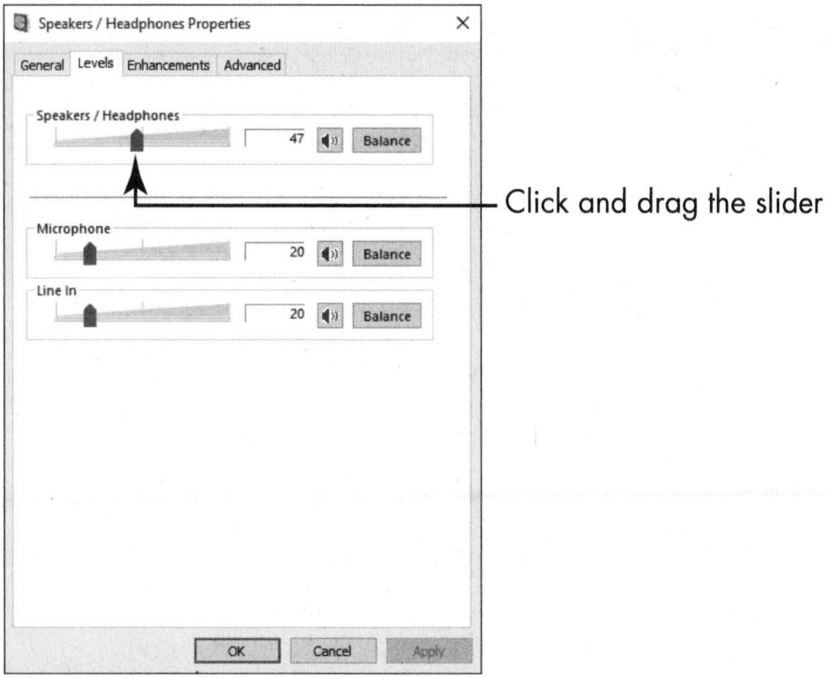

Click and drag the slider

Figure 18-2

Adjust System Volume

1. You can set the master system volume for your computer to be louder or softer. Right-click the Volume button in the notifications area of the taskbar, and in the menu that opens, click Open Volume Mixer.

2. In the resulting Volume Mixer dialog box (shown in **Figure 18-3**), make any of the following settings:

- Move the Device slider up and down to adjust the system's speaker volume.

- For sounds played by Windows (called *system sounds*), adjust the volume by moving the Applications slider.

- To mute either the main or application volume, click the speaker icon beneath either slider so that a red circle with a slash through it appears.

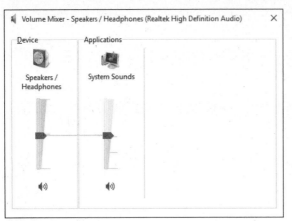

Figure 18-3

3. Click the Close button.

 Here's a handy shortcut for quickly adjusting the volume of your default sound device. Click the Volume button (the little speaker) in the notification area on the right side of the taskbar. To adjust the volume, use the slider on the Volume pop-up that appears or click the Speaker button beneath the slider to turn off sounds temporarily.

 Today, many keyboards include volume controls and a mute button to control sounds from your computer. Some even include buttons to play, pause, and stop audio playback. Having these buttons and other controls at your fingertips can be worth a little extra in the price of your keyboard.

Use Windows Media Player to Rip Music

1. If you place a CD/DVD in your disc drive, Windows Media Player can *rip* the music from the disc to your computer's Music folder. Ripping copies all the tracks on the CD/DVD on your computer. That music is then available to play with Windows Media Player or the Groove Music app. Open Windows Media Player from the All

Apps list in the Start menu. To control how ripping works, click the Organize button and choose Options.

2. Click the Rip Music tab.

3. In the Options dialog box (see **Figure** 18-4), you can make the following settings:

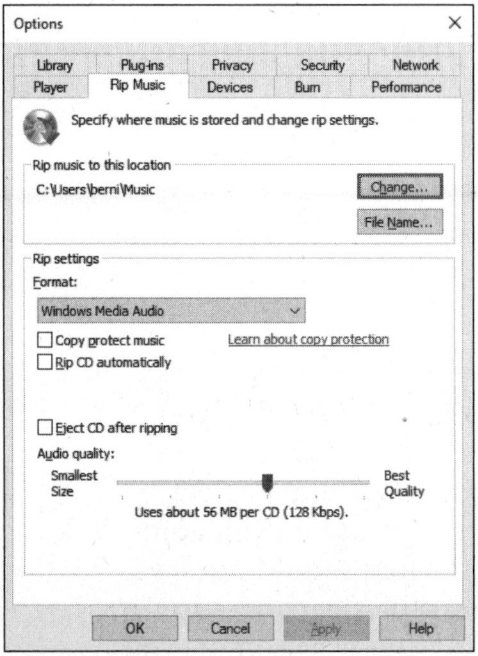

Figure 18-4

- Click the **Change** button to change the location where ripped music is stored; the default location is your Music folder.

- Click the **File Name** button to choose the information included with filenames for music that is ripped to your computer (see **Figure 18-5**).

- Choose the audio format to use by clicking the **Format** drop-down list.

Figure 18-5

- Many audio files are copyright protected. If you have permission to copy and distribute the music, you may not want to choose the **Copy Protect Music** check box; however, if you're downloading music you paid for and therefore should not give away copies of, you should ethically choose to copy-protect music so that Windows prompts you or others using your computer to download media rights or purchase another copy of the music when you copy it to another location.

- If you want music ripped automatically from CD/DVDs that you insert in your drive, select the **Rip CD Automatically** check box.

- If you want the CD/DVD to eject automatically after ripping is complete, select the **Eject CD after Ripping** check box.

4. When you finish making settings, click the OK button to save them and close the Options dialog box.

Use the Audio Quality slider to adjust the quality of the ripped music. The smallest size file will save space on your computer by compressing the data, but this causes a loss of audio quality. The Best Quality will provide optimum sound, but these files can be rather large. The choice is yours based on your tastes and your computer's capacity.

Find Music in the Store

1. The Store's search feature provides a great way to search for new music. With the Store open, click the Music tab and then type an artist name or song title in the Search box.

2. Press Enter. Results appear, as shown in **Figure 18-6**.

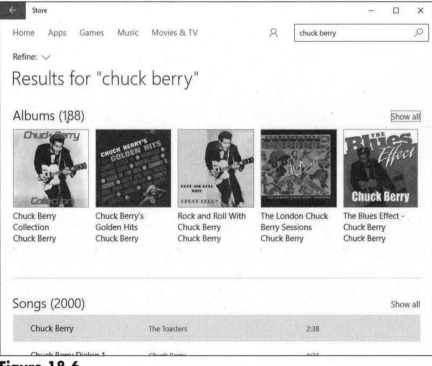

Figure 18-6

3. Hover anywhere in the row of Albums and arrows appear on one or both ends of the row. Click an arrow to scroll to the left or right to view additional albums. Click and drag the scrollbar on the right to scroll down and view more songs, and when available, apps, movies, or TV shows (in some cases even games) related to the artist or title.

4. Click an item to view more details about tracks and artist, to play a preview using the Groove Music app player, or to buy it (see **Figure 18-7**).

Figure 18-7

Buy Music

1. Purchasing music involves making your selection, entering payment information if you don't already have payment information associated with your Microsoft account, and then completing your purchase. With a

music selection displayed (see the previous task), click the Price button (the button showing the cost of the item) for an album or individual song. If requested, enter your Microsoft account password.

2. In the screen that appears, click the Add a Credit Card link and then fill in a payment method for your account and click Next.

3. In the following screen (see **Figure 18-8**), click the Buy button. The album downloads to your computer and is available to play in the Groove Music app.

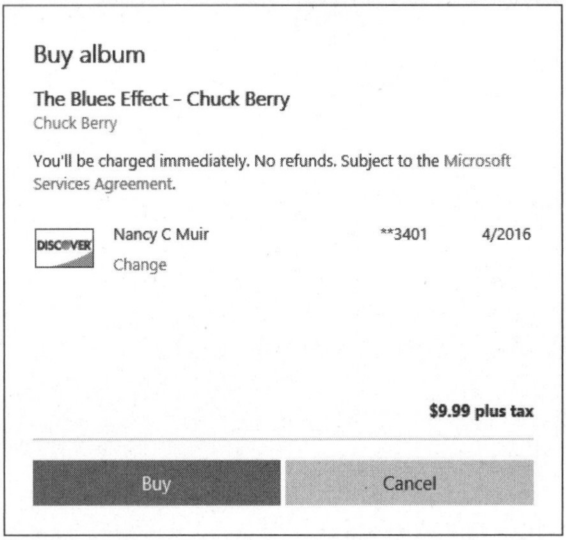

Buy album

The Blues Effect – Chuck Berry
Chuck Berry

You'll be charged immediately. No refunds. Subject to the Microsoft Services Agreement.

| DISC**VER** | Nancy C Muir Change | **3401 | 4/2016 |

$9.99 plus tax

| Buy | Cancel |

Figure 18-8

 You can purchase a Groove Music Pass that allows you, for a monthly fee, to stream or download as many titles as you like in the Music Store.

Search for Music with Cortana

1. Enter a term in the Cortana Search field or click the Microphone button and speak a search term to have Cortana search for an artist, album, or song. Results for the song "Georgia on My Mind" appear in **Figure 18-9**.

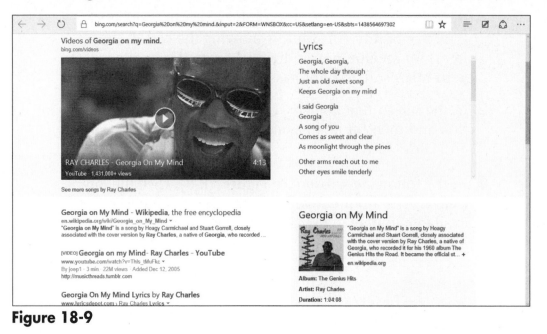

Figure 18-9

2. In the search results, you might find:

   • Videos of performances

   • Other online stores where you can purchase the music

   • Information about the song or artist

3. Click any of the items to view the results.

Create a Playlist

1. A *playlist* is a saved set of music tracks you can create yourself — like building a personal music album. From the Start menu, click the Groove Music tile: the Groove Music app shown in **Figure 18-10** appears.

2. Click the New Playlist button. In the field that appears (see **Figure 18-11**), type the name of the playlist and click Save.

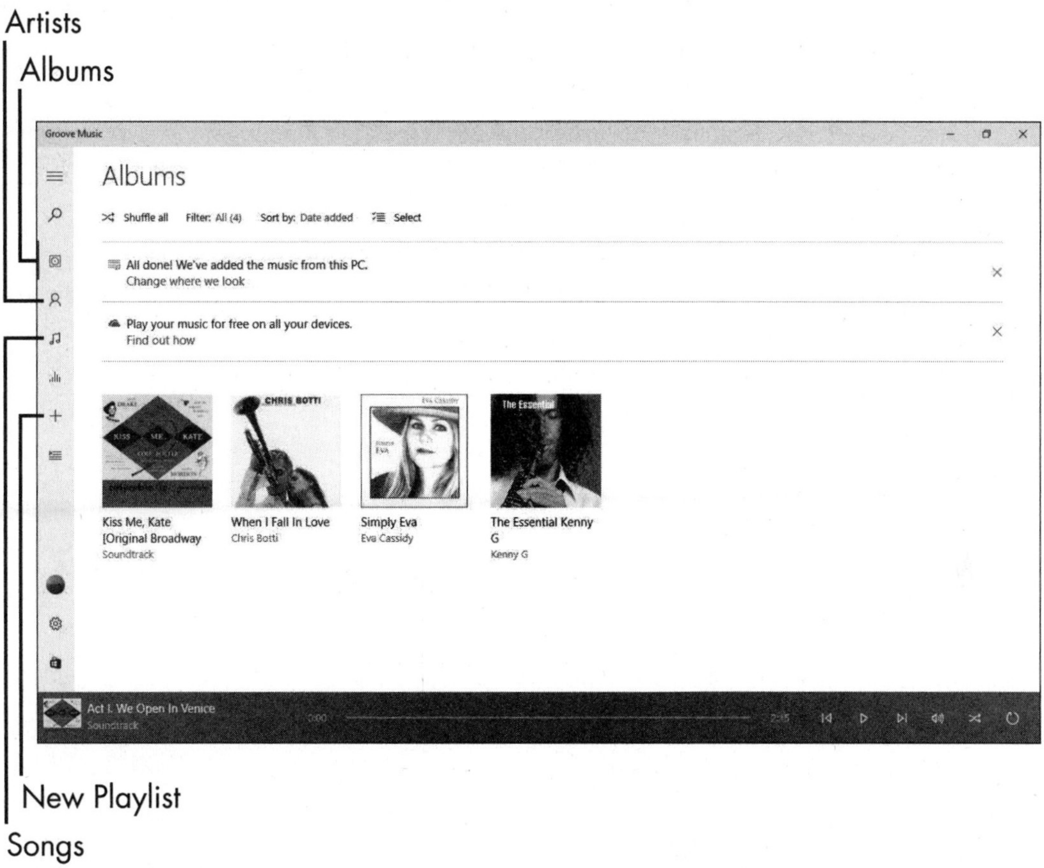

Artists

Albums

Figure 18-10

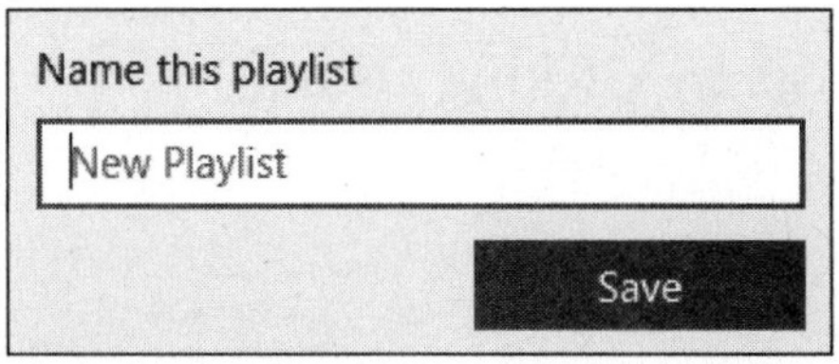

New Playlist

Songs

Figure 18-11

3. Click a tab such as Albums or Songs; the library contents appear. If you choose Albums or Artists, click an item to show the list of related songs.

4. Click a song or album and then click the Add To button (shaped like a plus sign); click the name of the playlist you want to add the song or album to from the list that

appears (see **Figure 18-12**). Repeat this step to locate
additional titles to add to the playlist.

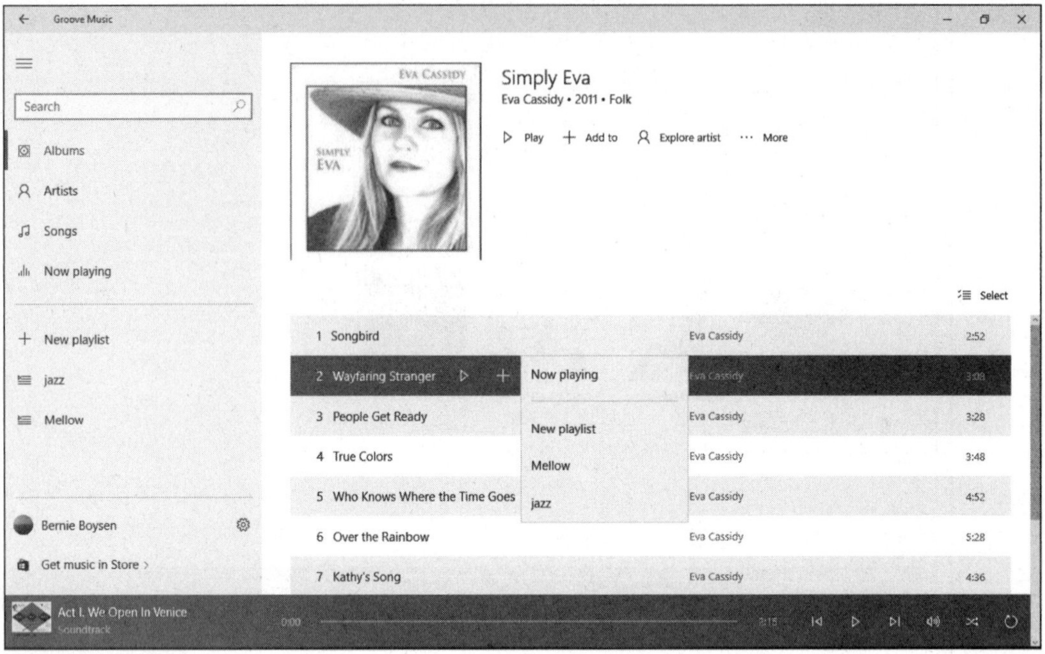

Figure 18-12

5. To play a playlist, click its name in the left pane and then
click the Play button at the top of the screen.

6. You can reorganize music in playlists by clicking a song
and dragging it to another location in the list.

Play Music

1. Open the Groove Music app by clicking the Groove
Music tile in the Start menu.

2. The Groove Music app opens with a view of the albums
in your collection. Click a library tab, such as Artists or
Songs; the library contents appear. If you choose Albums
or Artists, click an item to show the list of songs.

3. Click a song and then click the Play button that appears (see **Figure 18-13**).

←	Groove Music		− ▢ ✕

Kiss Me, Kate [Original Broadway Cast]
Soundtrack • 1949 • Soundtrack

▷ Play   + Add to   ♁ Explore artist   ⋯ More

≡ Select

1 Act I. Overture	Soundtrack	2:42
2 Act I. Another Op'nin, Another Show	Soundtrack	1:44
3 Act I. Why Can't You Behave? ▷ +	Soundtrack	
4 Act I. Wunderbar	Soundtrack	3:37
5 Act I. So In Love	Soundtrack	3:35
6 Act I. We Open In Venice	Soundtrack	2:15
7 Act I. Tom, Dick Or Harry	Soundtrack	2:06

Figure 18-13

4. Use the buttons on the bottom of the Groove Music app (as shown in **Figure 18-14**) to do the following:

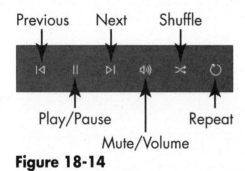

Figure 18-14

- Click the **Play** button to play a song. When a song is playing, this button changes to the **Pause** button.

- Click the **Next** or **Previous** button to move to the next or previous track in an album or playlist.

- Use the **Mute/Volume** control to pump the sound up or down without having to modify the Windows volume settings.

- Use the **Repeat** button to repeat an album or playlist.

 Tired of the order in which your songs play? You can click the Shuffle button (it sports wavy arrows) to have the Groove Music app move among the songs on your album randomly. Click this button again to turn off the Shuffle feature.

 To jump to another track, rather than using the Next and Previous buttons, you can double-click a track in a list in the Groove Music app. This can be much quicker if you want to jump several tracks ahead or behind the currently playing track.

Part V
Windows Toolkit

Visit www.dummies.com/extras/computersforseniors for information about creating strong passwords.

Working with Networks

A computer network allows you to share information and devices among computers.

You can connect your computer to other computers by setting up a wired or wireless network, for example. Devices connected to a group of computers on a network called a Homegroup can share hardware such as a printer, an Internet connection, and more.

In addition to a computer network, you can use Bluetooth technology to connect to devices without wires at a short range. For example, you might use your computer's built-in Bluetooth capability to connect to a Bluetooth mouse that sits near your computer on your work surface.

You can also use your mobile phone's 3G or 4G cellular network to go online through a process called *tethering*.

In this chapter, you explore several options for getting connected to other devices and sharing information.

Get ready to . . .

Join a Homegroup

1. When you set up a network, you have to arrange to include each computer on the network in a Homegroup so that all of them can connect to each other, a single Internet connection, and shared hardware such as printers. If somebody has set up a Homegroup on another computer, you can join that network with a few steps. Start by pressing Win+I.

2. Click Network & Internet.

3. With the WiFi category selected on the left, scroll down the right panel and click Homegroup, click the Join Now button, and then click Next.

4. Click the various drop-down lists to choose what to share with the Homegroup on the network (see **Figure 19-1**).

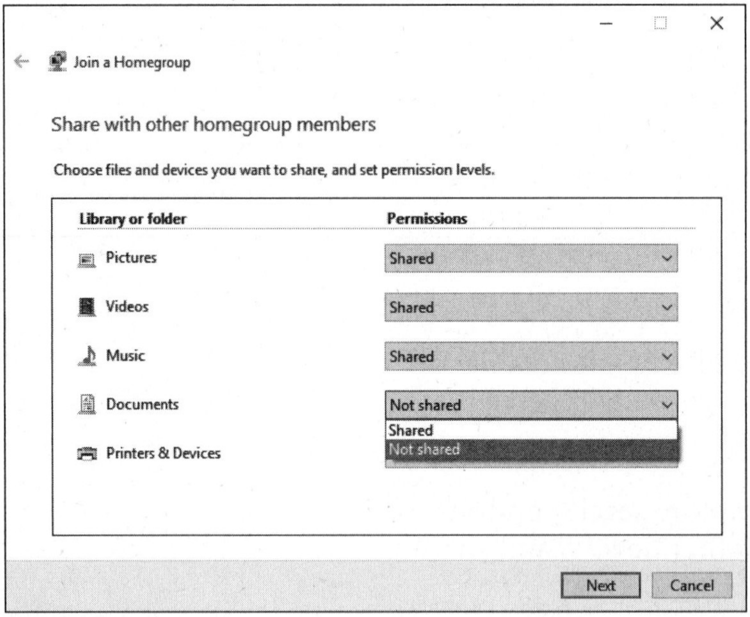

Figure 19-1

5. Click Next and enter a Homegroup password. Click Next again to make your computer part of that Homegroup.

To locate the password for the Homegroup, you need to sign in as a user with administrator status. Then, open the Start menu and choose Settings ⇨ Network and Internet ⇨ Homegroup. Click View or Print the Homegroup Password.

Make a Connection to a Network

If you take a computing device with you around town or on the road, you'll find that you often need to connect to networks in locations such as airports, coffee shops, or hotels. These public network connections are called *hotspots*.

1. When you're in range of a hotspot, click the Network Settings button on the taskbar, which looks like graph bars ascending.

2. Click an available network in the list, as shown in **Figure 19-2.**

Figure 19-2

3. Click the Connect button, as shown in **Figure 19-3.**

TP-LINK_2.4GHz_90F707
Connected

TP-LINK_2.4GHz_90F707_EXT

☐ Connect automatically

Connect

CHEZSTEIN2.4GHz

Far Reaches Farm

Far Reaches Guest

Network settings

TP-
LINK_2.4GHz_9   Airplane mode

Figure 19-3

4. If you want your computer to disconnect from a network, you can click the Disconnect button for that network. Note that you'll be disconnected from it just by moving out of range of the network.

 In many cases, you're asked to enter a password for a network after you click Connect in Step 3. You have to ask somebody for this password; it may be publicly posted — for example, in a coffee shop — or you may have to ask for the password, for example, when you check into a hotel.

Specify What You Want to Share over a Network

1. Many people use networks to share content such as word-processing documents or pictures, or even a printer connection. When you're using a network, you might not want to share your valuable data with others, so you may want to modify your sharing settings. Be sure you are part of the Homegroup (see the previous "Join a Homegroup" task) and then press Win+I.

2. Click Network & Internet.

3. Click Homegroup and then Change What You're Sharing with the Homegroup.

4. Click the drop-down list for any item that is currently Shared and click Not Shared to change the setting (see **Figure 19-4**).

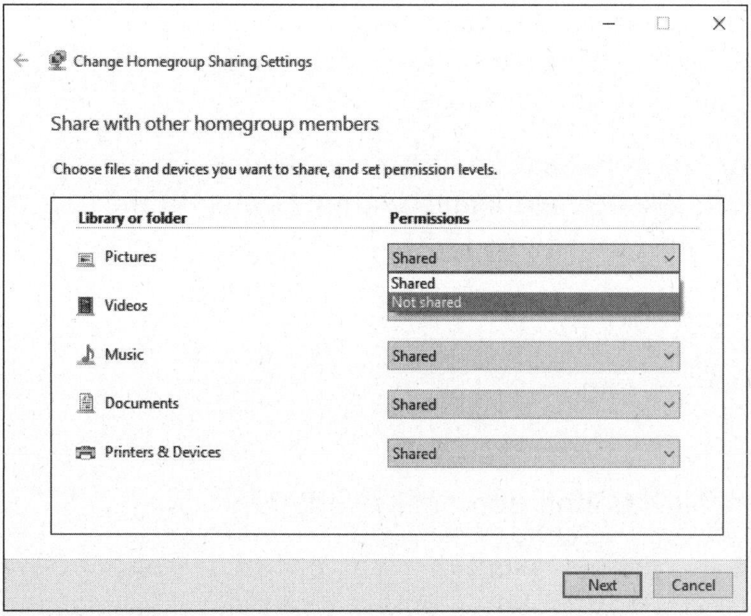

Figure 19-4

If you decide you don't want to participate in the network anymore, you can leave it by scrolling down in the Homegroup window that appears in Step 3 and clicking the Leave the Homegroup link.

 You can also share documents using a service such as Microsoft's OneDrive. You can upload and share files using this service, and a small amount of online storage is free. You can then access this content from any computer, connected to your network or not. See Chapter 15 for more about OneDrive.

Set Up a Wireless Network

1. If you have several computers in your home, you'll find you can save yourself steps by connecting them to each other through a wireless network. No more will you have to walk upstairs to print from a single computer; all your computers on every floor and in every room can share that printer, as well as an Internet connection and documents. Start by connecting a router or other access point hardware to one of your computers.

2. Right-click the Network Settings button on the taskbar and then select Open Network and Sharing Center on the menu that appears (see **Figure 19-5**).

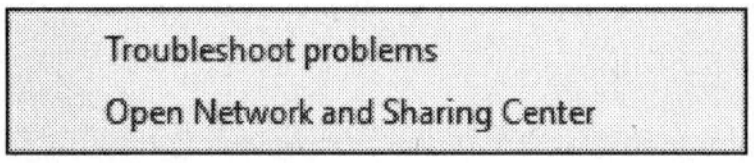

Troubleshoot problems
Open Network and Sharing Center

Figure 19-5

3. Click Set Up a New Connection or Network (see **Figure 19-6**).

4. Click Set Up a New Network (see **Figure 19-7**) and then click Next.

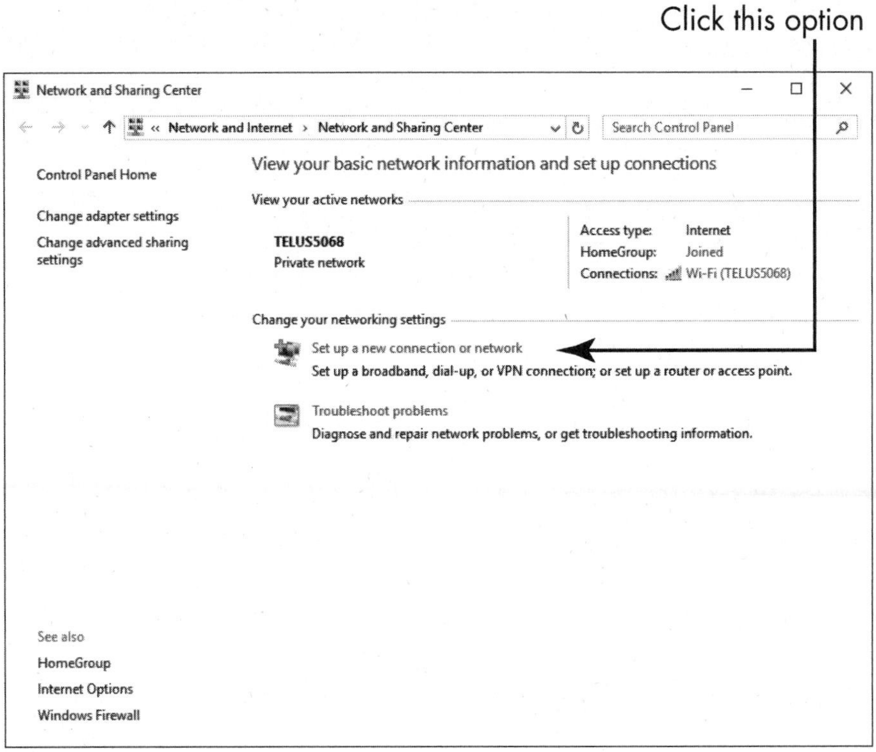

Click this option

Figure 19-6

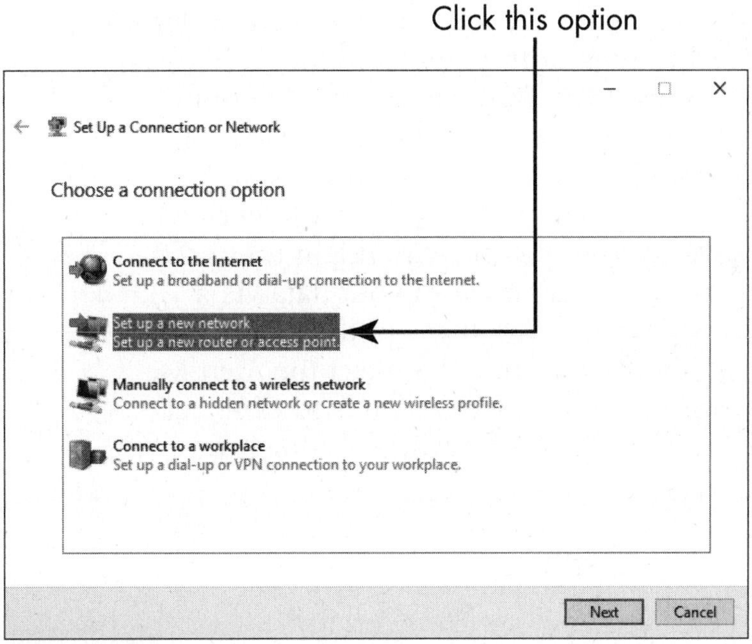

Click this option

Figure 19-7

5. Click the router or access point to set up and then click Next.

6. In the window that appears, enter the PIN number located on the router label and then click Next.

7. Enter a network name and click Next. Windows completes your network setup. Click the Close button to close the window.

Make Your Computer Discoverable to Bluetooth

1. Making a Bluetooth connection involves ensuring that both devices are Bluetooth compatible (check your device specs for this) and making both devices discoverable. Press Win+I.

2. Click Devices.

3. Click Bluetooth in the left panel and then click the On/Off switch labelled Bluetooth (see **Figure 19-8**).

 If you're travelling out of your home with your laptop, click More Bluetooth Options in the dialog box shown in **Figure 19-8**. In the resulting Bluetooth Settings dialog box, make sure the check box for Allow Bluetooth Devices to Find this PC is not selected. That step will protect your computer's contents or settings from people who might try to connect to your computer and steal your data via a Bluetooth connection. Another option is to leave your computer discoverable but select the Alert Me When a New Bluetooth Device Wants to Connect check box in the Bluetooth Settings dialog box.

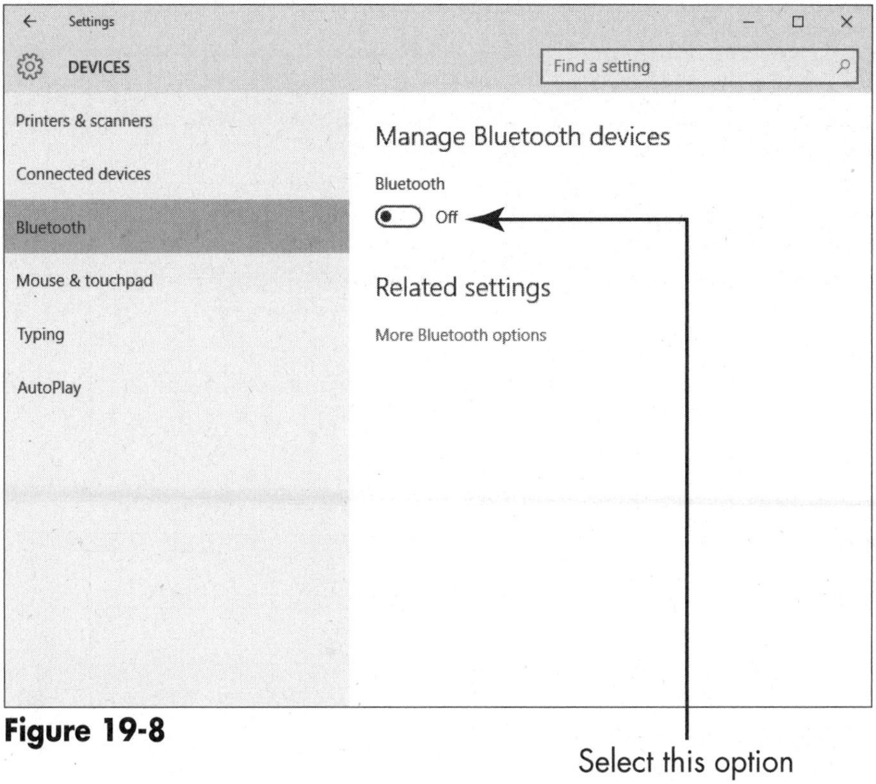

Figure 19-8

Select this option

Connect to Bluetooth Devices

1. After you make your computer discoverable, you can connect to another Bluetooth device that is turned on. Begin by pressing Win+I.

2. Click Devices.

3. In the dialog box that appears, click Bluetooth and then check that Bluetooth is set to On.

4. Your computer searches for nearby Bluetooth devices. When the one you want to pair your computer with appears (see **Figure 19-9**), click it and then click Pair.

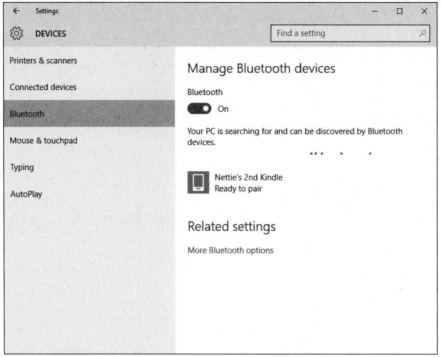

Figure 19-9

With some devices, a code will appear on your computer and device screen asking you to verify the pairing. With other devices, such as a Bluetooth mouse, the device is simply paired.

5. Click Close.

 Bluetooth devices are improving, but you may find that connections are spotty. If a Bluetooth device such as a headset isn't dependable, consider having a USB or wireless version of the device available as a backup.

Go Online Using Your Cellular Network

1. It's possible to use a smartphone's 3G or 4G connection to connect to the Internet. Usually you have to pay your phone service provider a monthly fee for this service, called *tethering* or *personal hotspot*. In addition, your computer has to be WiFi capable (today they all are). Start by turning on the hotspot feature on your phone (typically this is found in Network settings).

2. On your computer, press Win+I, and then click the Network & Internet.

3. Click your phone's WiFi connection, like the one shown in **Figure 19-10**.

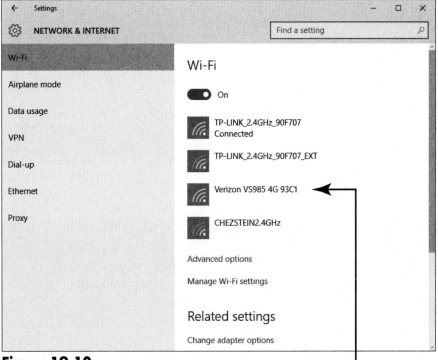

Figure 19-10

Click your phone's connection

4. Click Connect and enter the security key.

5. Click Next.

 Be aware of the drain on your phone's battery when tethering. Connect your phone to a power source when tethering, if possible, and turn off the hotspot when you're not using it.

Protecting Windows

*Y*our computer contains software and files that can be damaged in several different ways. One major source of damage is from malicious attacks that are delivered via the Internet.

Microsoft provides security features within Windows 10 that help to keep your computer and information safe, whether you're at home or travelling with a laptop computer.

In this chapter, I introduce you to the major concepts of computer security and cover Windows 10 security features that allow you to do the following:

➡ Run periodic updates to Windows, which install security solutions and patches (essentially, *patches* fix problems) to the software.

➡ Enable a *firewall*, which is a security feature that keeps your computer safe from outsiders and helps you avoid several kinds of attacks on your data.

➡ Change the password used to protect your computer from others.

➡ Protect yourself against spyware.

Understand Computer Security

Every day you carry around a wallet full of cash and credit cards, and you take certain measures to protect its contents. Your computer also contains valuable items in the form of data, and it's just as important that you protect it from thieves and damage.

Some people create damaging programs called *viruses* specifically designed to get into your computer's hard drive and destroy or scramble data. Companies might download *adware* on your computer, which causes pop-up ads to appear, slowing down your computer's performance. Spyware is another form of malicious software that you might download by clicking a link or opening a file attachment; *spyware* sits on your computer and tracks your activities, whether for use by a legitimate company in selling products to you or by a criminal element to steal your identity.

Your computer comes with an operating system (such as Microsoft Windows) preinstalled, and that operating system has security features to protect your valuable data. Sometimes the operating system has flaws or new threats emerge, and you need to get an update to keep your computer secure. You can use Windows security tools such as Windows Defender, or third-party antivirus or antispyware programs (see **Figure 20-1**) to protect your computer from dangerous computer programs collectively known as *malware*. See Chapter 13 for more detail about threats and protections from malware.

Figure 20-1

Understand Windows Update Options

When a new operating system such as Windows 10 is released, it has been thoroughly tested; however, when the product is in general use, the manufacturer begins to get feedback about a few problems or security gaps that it couldn't anticipate. For that reason, companies such as Microsoft release updates to their software, both to fix those problems and deal with new threats to computers that appear after the software release.

Windows Update is a tool you can use to make sure your computer has the most up-to-date security measures in place. You can set Windows Update to work by following these steps:

1. In the Start menu, click Settings ➪ Update & Security ➪ Windows Update.

2. Click the Advanced Options link. In the resulting Advanced Options dialog box (see **Figure 20-2**), click the

Choose How Updates Are Installed drop-down list and you find these settings:

➡ **Automatic:** With this setting, Windows Update will restart your computer automatically to install updates when it's not in use. If you've turned off your computer, the automatic update will start when you next turn on your computer.

➡ **Notify to Schedule Restart:** You can set up Windows Update to download updates and have Windows will notify you through messages in the Action Center when they're available, but you get to decide when the updates are installed and when your computer restarts to complete the installation. This is my preferred setting because I have control and won't be caught unaware by a computer reboot.

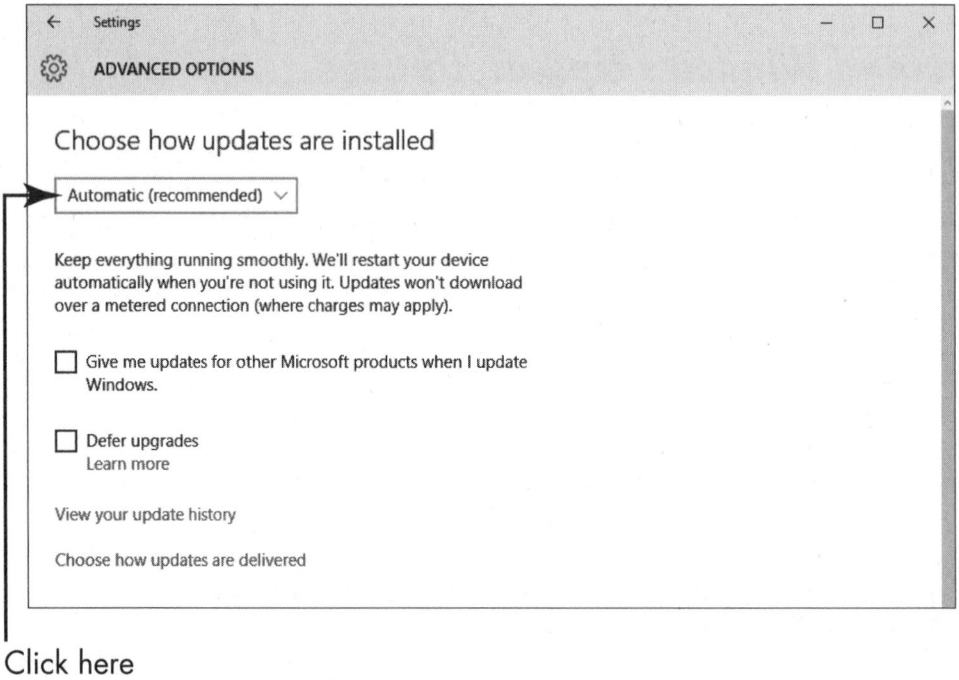

Click here
Figure 20-2

Checking for Windows Updates

1. In the Start menu, click Settings ➪ Update & Security ➪ Windows Update.

2. In the resulting window, as shown in **Figure 20-3**, click the Check for Updates link to see all updates.

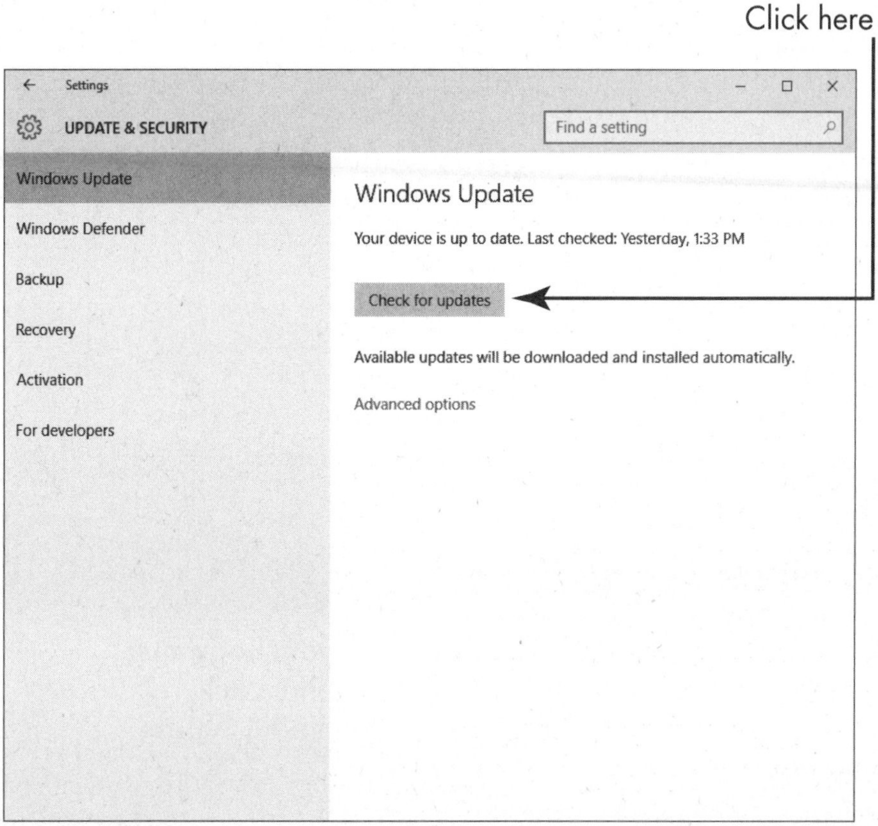

Click here

Figure 20-3

3. The following window shows the available updates (see **Figure 20-4**) and begins downloading and installing them in most cases. If instead you're presented with an Install Now button, click it.

4. If a restart is required, a screen opens that allows you to either choose a restart time or click a Restart Now button.

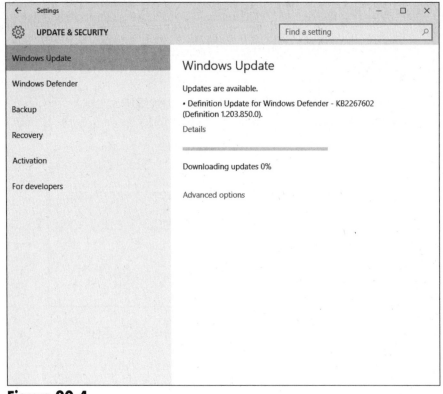

Figure 20-4

Enable Windows Firewall

1. A firewall keeps outsiders from accessing your computer via an Internet connection. In the Start menu, click Settings, and then enter "Firewall" in the Find a Setting search box.

2. Click Windows Firewall in the search results.

3. In the Windows Firewall window that appears (see **Figure 20-5**), make sure that Windows Firewall is on. If it isn't, click the Turn Windows Firewall On or Off link in the left pane of the window.

Make sure this is set to On

Windows Firewall

← → ↑ « System and Security › Windows Firewall   Search Control Panel

Control Panel Home

Allow an app or feature
through Windows Firewall

Change notification settings

Turn Windows Firewall on or
off

Restore defaults

Advanced settings

Troubleshoot my network

Help protect your PC with Windows Firewall

Windows Firewall can help prevent hackers or malicious software from gaining access to your PC
through the Internet or a network.

Private networks   Connected ⌃

Networks at home or work where you know and trust the people and devices on the network

Windows Firewall state: On

Incoming connections: Block all connections to apps that are not on the
                                     list of allowed apps

Active private networks: TELUS5068

Notification state: Notify me when Windows Firewall blocks a new
                                     app

Guest or public networks   Not connected ⌄

See also

Security and Maintenance

Network and Sharing Center

Figure 20-5

4. In the resulting Customize Settings window (see **Figure 20-6**), select the Turn on Windows Firewall radio button for Private Networks (such as your home network) and/or Public Networks (such as a coffee shop) and then click OK.

5. Click the Close button to close the Windows Firewall window.

A *firewall* is a program that protects your computer from the outside world. This is generally a good thing, unless you use a Virtual Private Network (VPN), often used in a corporate setting.

Using a firewall with a VPN can restrict you from sharing files and using some other VPN features.

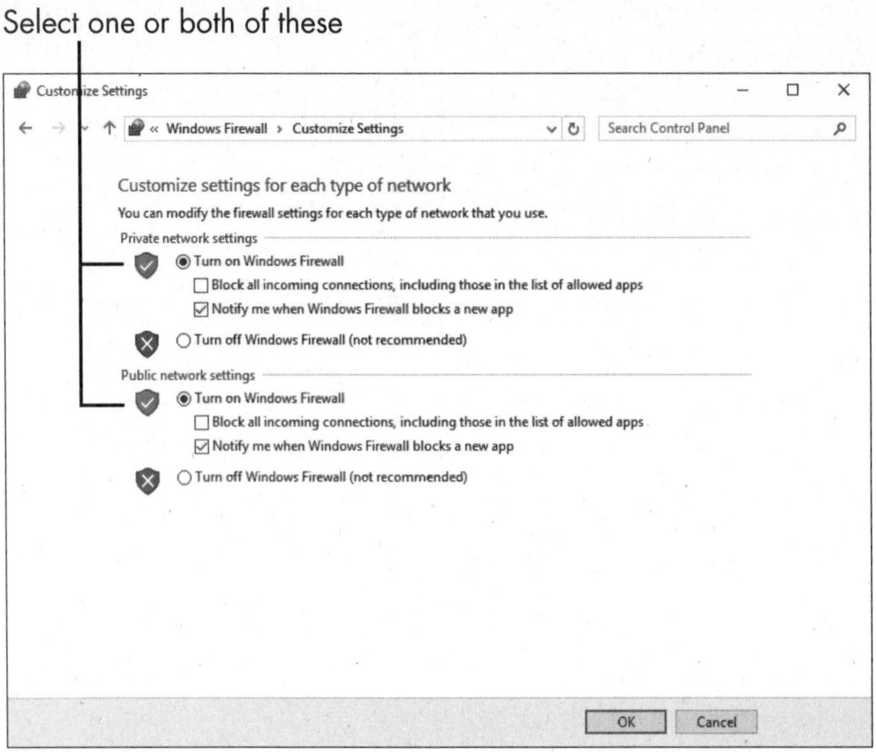

Select one or both of these

Figure 20-6

Antivirus and security software programs may offer their own firewall protection and may display a message asking if you want to switch. Check their features against Windows and then decide, but usually most firewall features are comparable. The important thing is to have one activated.

Run a Scan with Windows Defender

1. In the Notification section of the taskbar, click the Show Hidden Icons button, click the Windows Defender button (shaped like a small castle), and then click Open.

2. In the Windows Defender dialog box that appears (see **Figure 20-7**), click a Scan Option in the right pane: Quick, Full, or Custom.

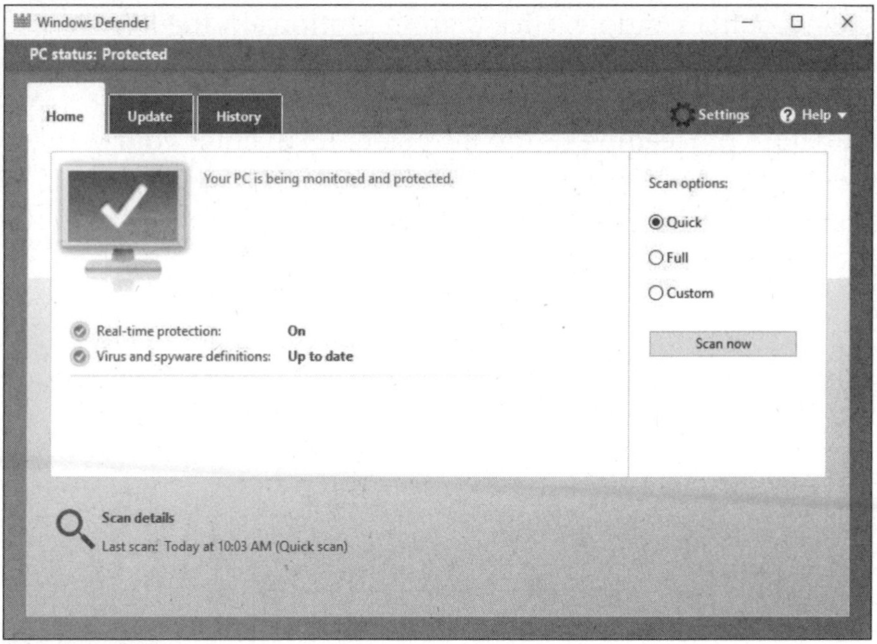

Figure 20-7

3. Click the Scan Now button to start a Quick or Full scan, depending on which option is selected. Windows Defender scans your computer and reports any findings.

4. Click check boxes to choose which drives and folders to scan for a Custom scan and then click OK. Windows Defender scans your computer and reports any findings.

Change Your Password

1. If you log into Windows using an online account, your password is the password associated with your Windows Live account. If you set up a local account not associated with an online account, you create a password when you set up the account. To change a password, in the Start menu click Settings, and then click Accounts.

2. In the Accounts window, click Sign-in Options in the left pane. In the resulting window, shown in **Figure 20-8,** click the Change button. You may be asked for your password before proceeding to the next step. If so, enter your password and click Next.

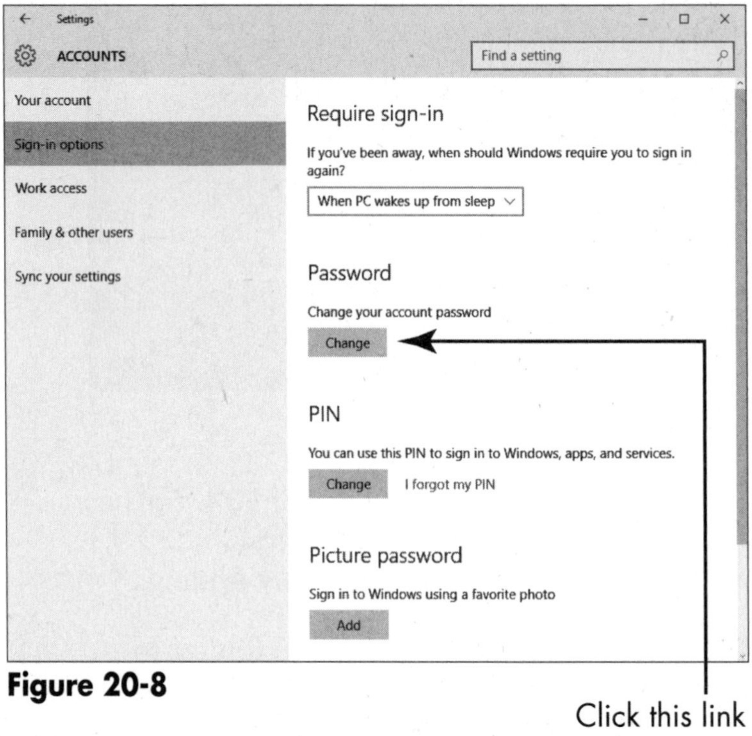

Figure 20-8

Click this link

3. In the Change Your Password screen, shown in **Figure 20-9,** enter your current password, and then enter the new password and confirm it.

4. Click Next.

5. Click Finish.

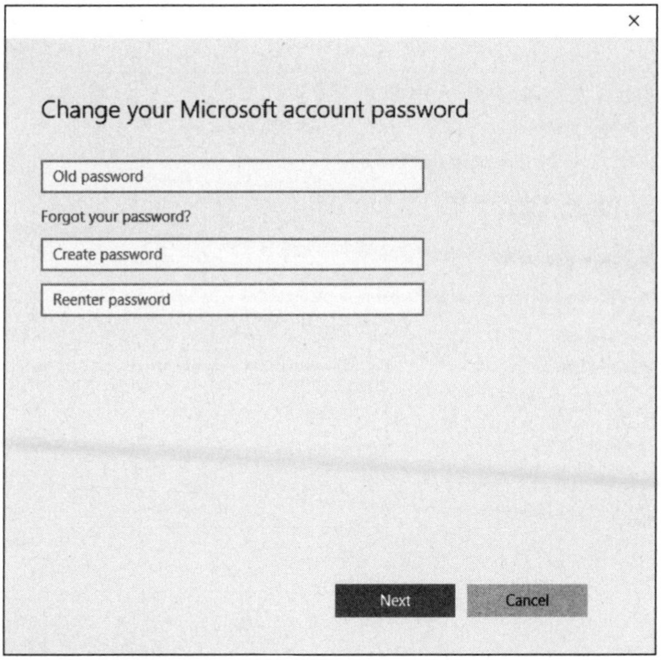

×

Change your Microsoft account password

Old password

Forgot your password?

Create password

Reenter password

Next   Cancel

Figure 20-9

 After you create a password, you can change it at any time by going to the Sign-in Options in the Account settings and clicking the Change button under the Password setting.

Allow Firewall Exceptions

1. When you have a firewall active, you can allow certain programs to communicate through that firewall. For example, you might want to allow live apps such as Weather or Video to send information or content to your computer. In the Start menu click Settings, and then type **Firewall** in the Find a Setting search box.

2. Click Windows Firewall in the search results. In the resulting Windows Firewall window (see **Figure 20-10**), click Allow an App or Feature through Windows Firewall.

Click this option

Figure 20-10

3. In the Allowed Apps window that appears (see
   Figure 20-11), click the Change Settings button, and then
   select the check box for apps on your computer that you
   want to allow to communicate over the Internet without
   being stopped by Firewall.

4. Click the Private and Public check boxes to narrow down
   whether you want just networks that are secure to allow
   this communication, or also public and non-secure networks to do so.

5. Click OK and then click the Close button to close the
   System and Security window.

Figure showing the "Allowed apps" window:

Allowed apps — □ ×

← → ∨ ↑ « Windows Firewall › Allowed apps ∨ ↻ Search Control Panel 🔎

Allow apps to communicate through Windows Firewall
To add, change, or remove allowed apps and ports, click Change settings.
What are the risks of allowing an app to communicate? 🛡Change settings

Allowed apps and features:

Name	Private	Public
☑ @{C:\Windows\WinStore\resources.pri?ms-resource://WinStore/resources/D...	☑	☐
☑ @{C:\Windows\WinStore\resources.pri?ms-resource://WinStore/resources/D...	☑	☐
☑ @{Microsoft.AAD.BrokerPlugin_1000.10158.0.0_neutral_neutral_cw5n1h2txye...	☑	☐
☑ @{Microsoft.AAD.BrokerPlugin_1000.10159.0.0_neutral_neutral_cw5n1h2txye...	☑	☐
☑ @{Microsoft.AAD.BrokerPlugin_1000.10162.0.0_neutral_neutral_cw5n1h2txye...	☑	☐
☑ @{Microsoft.AAD.BrokerPlugin_1000.10166.0.0_neutral_neutral_cw5n1h2txye...	☑	☐
☑ @{Microsoft.MicrosoftEdge_20.10158.0.0_neutral__8wekyb3d8bbwe?ms-reso...	☑	☐
☑ @{Microsoft.MicrosoftEdge_20.10159.0.0_neutral__8wekyb3d8bbwe?ms-reso...	☑	☐
☑ @{Microsoft.MicrosoftEdge_20.10162.0.0_neutral__8wekyb3d8bbwe?ms-reso...	☑	☐
☑ @{Microsoft.MicrosoftEdge_20.10166.0.0_neutral__8wekyb3d8bbwe?ms-reso...	☑	☐
☑ @{Microsoft.MicrosoftOfficeHub_17.6018.23501.0_x64__8wekyb3d8bbwe?ms-...	☑	☑
☑ @{Microsoft.Windows.CloudExperienceHost_10.0.10166.0_neutral_neutral_cw...	☑	☐

Details... Remove

Allow another app...

OK Cancel

Figure 20-11

If you allow apps to communicate across your fire-wall, it's very important that you do have antivirus and antispyware software installed on your computer, and that you run updates to them on a regular basis. These types of programs help you avoid down-loading malware to your computer that could cause advertising pop-ups, slow your computer's perfor-mance, damage computer files, or even track your keystrokes as you type to steal your identity and more. If you don't want to pay for such a program, consider a free solution such as Spyware Terminator (www.spywareterminator.com).

Maintaining Windows

Chapter

21

A ll the wonderful hardware that you've spent your hard-earned money on doesn't mean a thing if the software driving it goes flooey. If any program causes your system to *crash* (meaning it freezes up and you have to take drastic measures to revive it), you can try a variety of steps to fix it. You can also keep your system in good shape to help avoid those crashes. In this chapter, you find out how to take good care of your programs and operating system in these ways:

➡ When a program crashes, you can simply shut that program down by using Windows Task Manager. This utility keeps track of all the programs and processes that are running on your computer.

➡ If you have problems and Windows isn't responding, sometimes it helps to restart in Safe Mode, which requires only basic files and drivers. Restarting in Safe Mode often allows you to troubleshoot what's going on, and you can restart Windows in its regular mode after the problem is solved.

➡ Use the System Restore feature to first create a *system restore point* (a point in time when your settings and programs all seem to be humming along just fine), and then restore Windows to that point when trouble hits.

➠ You can clean up your system to delete unused files, free up disk space, and schedule maintenance tasks.

Shut Down a Nonresponsive Application

1. If your computer freezes and won't let you proceed with what you were doing, press Ctrl+Alt+Delete.

2. In the Windows screen that appears, click Task Manager.

3. In the resulting Task Manager dialog box, click More Details, click the Processes tab (see **Figure 21-1**), and select the application that you were in when your system stopped responding.

Click this tab

Task Manager						— ☐ ✕
File Options View						
Processes Performance App history Startup Users Details Services						
			5%	80%	0%	0%
Name		Status	CPU	Memory	Disk	Network
Apps (5)						
🎵 Groove Music			0%	0.1 MB	0 MB/s	0 Mbps
e Microsoft Edge			0%	5.0 MB	0 MB/s	0 Mbps
> 📋 Task Manager			0.4%	11.9 MB	0 MB/s	0 Mbps
☀ Weather (32 bit)			0%	0.1 MB	0 MB/s	0 Mbps
> 📁 Windows Explorer (2)			0.3%	22.0 MB	0 MB/s	0 Mbps
Background processes (69)						
⬆ AcroTray (32 bit)			0%	0.1 MB	0 MB/s	0 Mbps
> ☐ Adobe Acrobat Update Service			0%	0.1 MB	0 MB/s	0 Mbps
🖼 Adobe CEF Helper (32 bit)			0%	0.5 MB	0 MB/s	0 Mbps
🖼 Adobe CEF Helper (32 bit)			0%	0.4 MB	0 MB/s	0 Mbps
☁ Adobe Creative Cloud (32 bit)			0%	3.3 MB	0.1 MB/s	0 Mbps
📄 Adobe IPC Broker (32 bit)			0%	0.8 MB	0 MB/s	0 Mbps
🖥 Application Frame Host			0%	5.8 MB	0 MB/s	0 Mbps
⌃ Fewer details						End task

Figure 21-1

4. Click the End Task button.

5. The app shuts down. Click the Close button to close Task Manager.

If pressing Ctrl+Alt+Delete doesn't bring up the Task Manager, you're in bigger trouble than you thought. You might need to press and hold your computer's power button to shut down. Note that some applications use an AutoSave feature that keeps an interim version of the document that you were working in. You might be able to save some of your work by opening that last-saved version. Other programs don't have such a safety net, and you simply lose whatever changes you made to your document since the last time you saved it. The moral? Save, and save often.

You may see a dialog box appear when an application shuts down that asks if you want to report the problem to Microsoft. If you say yes, information is sent to Microsoft to help it provide advice or fix the problem down the road.

Create a System Restore Point

1. You can back up your system files, which creates a restore point you can later use to return your computer to earlier settings if you experience problems. Enter **Create a restore point** in Cortana's search field and then press the Enter key on your keyboard.

2. In the System Properties dialog box that appears (see **Figure 21-2**) on the System Protection tab, click the Create button.

3. In the System Protection dialog box that appears, enter a name to identify the restore point, such as the name of a program you are about to install, and click Create.

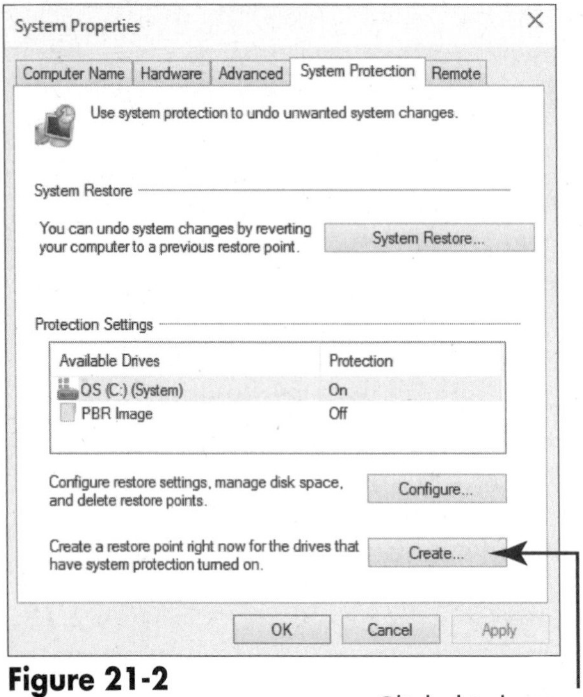

System Properties   ✕

| Computer Name | Hardware | Advanced | System Protection | Remote |

Use system protection to undo unwanted system changes.

System Restore

You can undo system changes by reverting your computer to a previous restore point.

     System Restore...

Protection Settings

Available Drives	Protection
OS (C:) (System)	On
PBR Image	Off

Configure restore settings, manage disk space, and delete restore points.

     Configure...

Create a restore point right now for the drives that have system protection turned on.

     Create... ◄

     OK   Cancel   Apply

Figure 21-2

Click this button

4. Windows displays a progress window. When the restore point is created, the message shown in **Figure** 21-3 appears. Click Close to close the message box and click the Close button to close the System Properties dialog box.

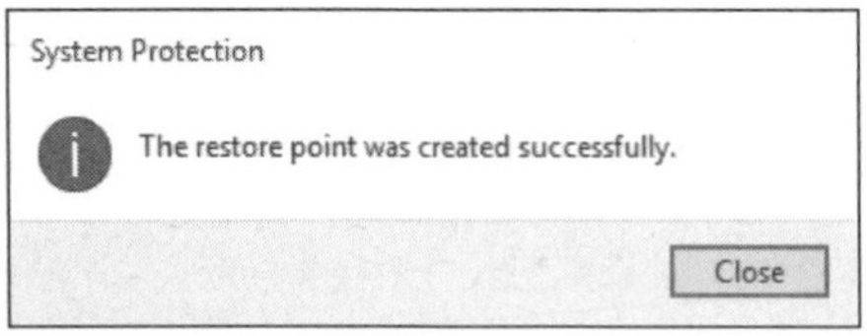

System Protection

ⓘ The restore point was created successfully.

     Close

Figure 21-3

Every once in a while, when you install a piece of software and make some new settings in Windows, and when things seem to be running just fine, create a system restore point. It's good computer practice, just like backing up your files, only you're backing up your settings. Once a month or once every couple of months works for most people, but if you frequently make changes, create a system restore point more often.

Restore Your PC

1. Enter **System restore** in Cortana's search field and then press Enter.

2. In the System Properties dialog box that appears, click the System Protection tab and then click the System Restore button, as shown in **Figure 21-4.**

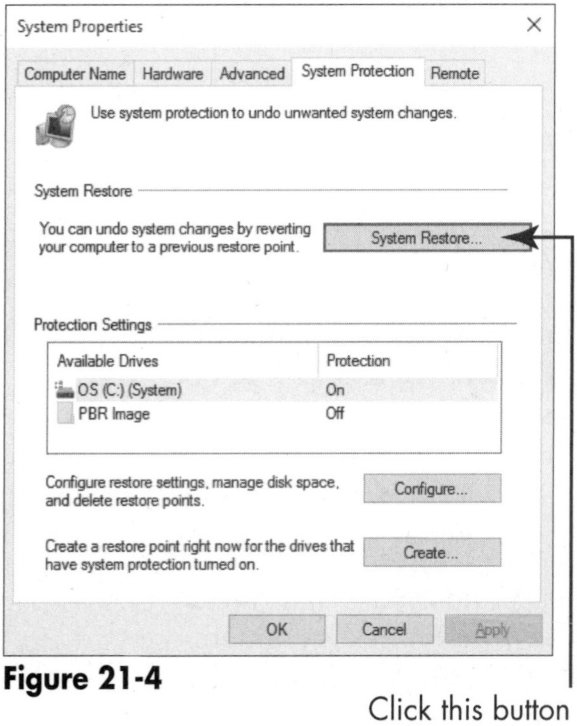

Figure 21-4

Click this button

3. In the System Restore window, click Next. In the window that appears, choose the date and time of the restore point (see **Figure 21-5**), and then click Next.

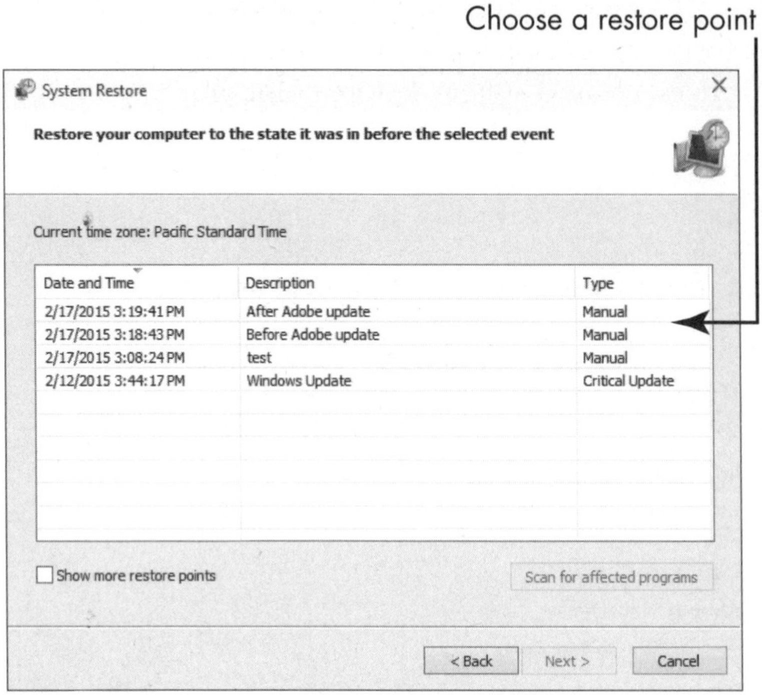

Choose a restore point

Figure 21-5

4. Click the Finish button to start the restore.

5. A dialog box confirms that you want to run System Restore and informs you that System Restore can't be interrupted — and in most cases can't be undone. Close any open files or programs, and then click Yes to proceed. The system goes through a shutdown and restart sequence.

System Restore doesn't get rid of files that you've saved, so you don't lose your Ph.D. dissertation. System Restore simply reverts to Windows settings as of the restore point. This can help if you or some piece of installed software made a setting that's causing some conflict in your system, making your computer sluggish or prone to crashes. If you're concerned about what changes will happen, click the Scan for Affected Programs button shown in the window displayed in **Figure 21-6.**

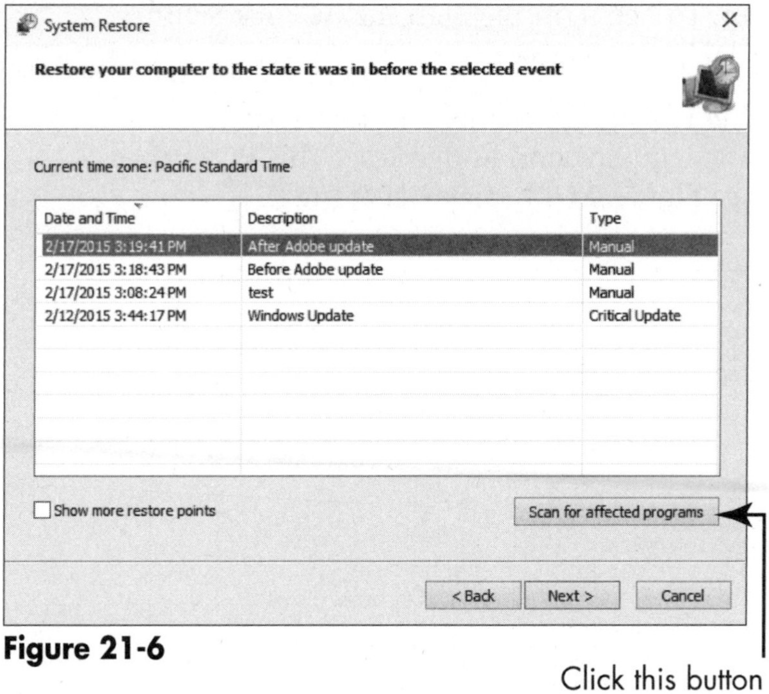

Figure 21-6

Click this button

System Restore doesn't always solve the problem. Your very best bet is to be sure you create a set of backup discs for your computer when you buy it. If you didn't do that, and you can't get things running right again, contact your computer manufacturer. The company may be able to send you a set of recovery discs, though it may charge a small fee. These discs restore your computer to its state when it left the factory, and in this case, you lose applications you installed and documents you created, but you can get your computer running again.

Reset Your PC

1. Whereas refreshing a PC resets system files to factory defaults and retains all your files and some apps, resetting your PC not only resets system files, it gets rid of all your personal files and apps you installed. Resetting is for those times when nothing else has gotten your computer working again. To begin, in the Start menu, click Settings, and then click Update & Security.

2. In the resulting Update & Security window, click Recovery in the left pane and under Reset This PC in the right pane (see **Figure 21-7**), click Get Started.

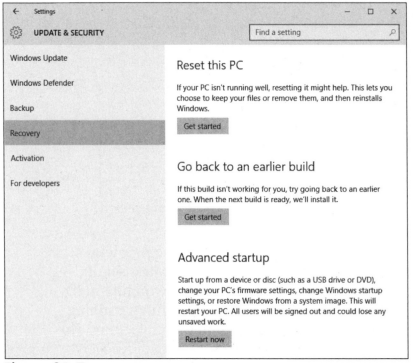

Figure 21-7

3. In the following screen, shown in **Figure 21-8**, choose Keep My Files, Remove Everything, or Restore Factory Settings.

4. In the following screen, if you're positive you want to proceed, click the Next button.

 The Reset procedure is a somewhat drastic step that will remove any apps you installed and files you saved. Remember, you can back out of the Reset procedure at any time up until you hit the Reset button. Just click Cancel.

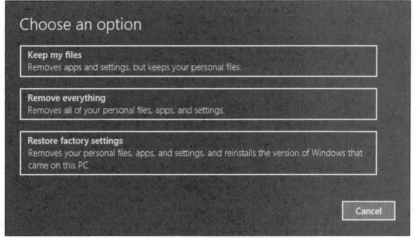

Choose an option

Keep my files
Removes apps and settings, but keeps your personal files.

Remove everything
Removes all of your personal files, apps, and settings.

Restore factory settings
Removes your personal files, apps, and settings, and reinstalls the version of Windows that came on this PC.

Cancel

Figure 21-8

Optimize a Hard Drive

1. To clean up unused or obsolete files on your hard drive, enter **Optimize a Drive** in Cortana's search field and then press Enter.

2. In the resulting Optimize Drives window (see **Figure** 21-9), to the left of the Optimize button is the Analyze button. Use this to check whether your disk requires defragmenting. When the analysis is complete, click the Optimize button. A notation appears (see **Figure 21-10**) showing the progress of optimizing your drive.

3. When the optimizing process is complete, the Optimize Drives window shows that your drive no longer requires optimizing. Click Close to close the window.

 Disk optimizing can take a while. If you have energy-saving features active (such as a screen saver), they can cause the optimize feature to stop and start all over again. Try running your optimization overnight while you're happily dreaming of much more interesting things. You can also set up the procedure to run automatically at a preset period of time — such

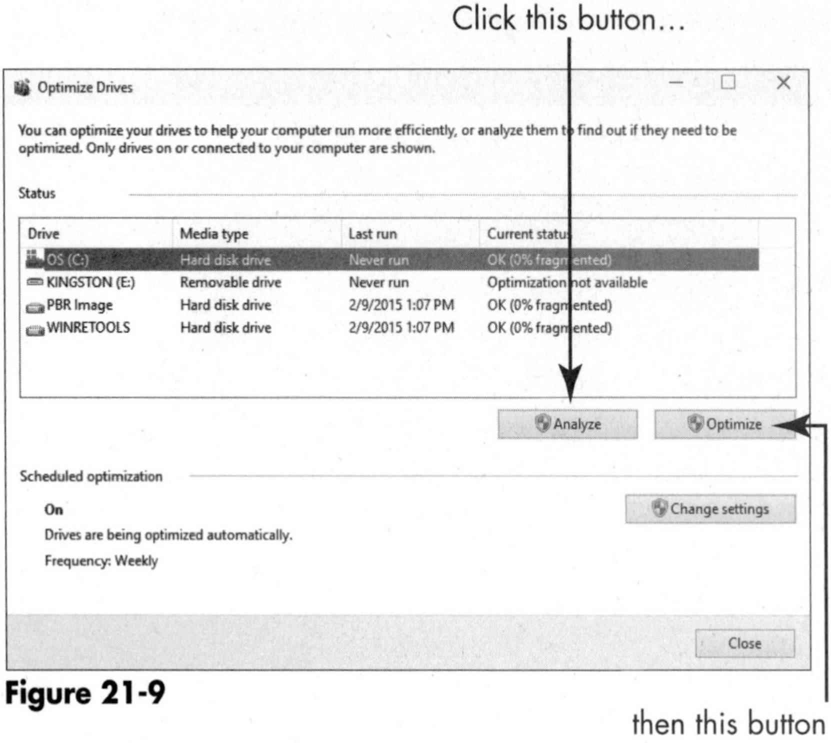
Click this button…
Optimize Drives
You can optimize your drives to help your computer run more efficiently, or analyze them to find out if they need to be optimized. Only drives on or connected to your computer are shown.
Status
Drive
Media type
Last run
Current status
OS (C:)
Hard disk drive
Never run
OK (0% fragmented)
KINGSTON (E:)
Removable drive
Never run
Optimization not available
PBR Image
Hard disk drive
2/9/2015 1:07 PM
OK (0% fragmented)
WINRETOOLS
Hard disk drive
2/9/2015 1:07 PM
OK (0% fragmented)
Analyze
Optimize
Scheduled optimization
On
Drives are being optimized automatically.
Frequency: Weekly
Change settings
Close
then this button

Figure 21-9

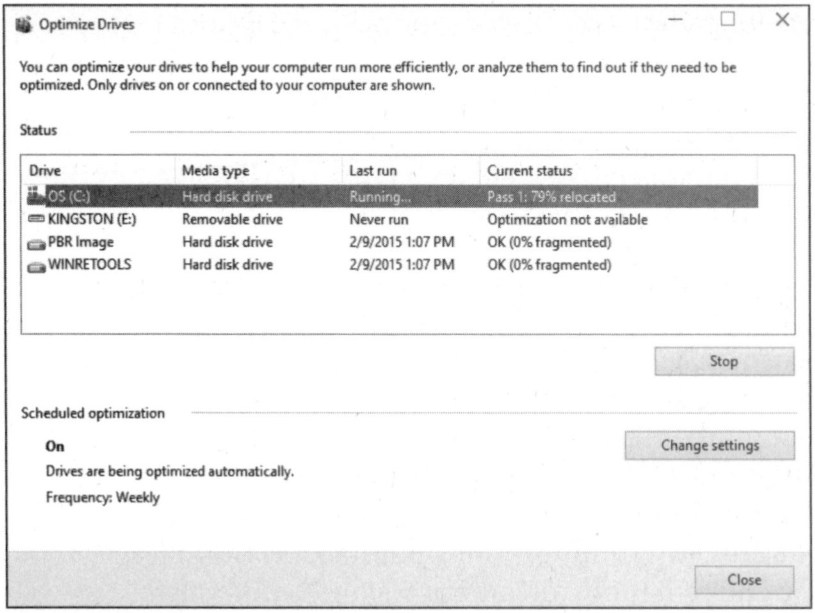
Optimize Drives
You can optimize your drives to help your computer run more efficiently, or analyze them to find out if they need to be optimized. Only drives on or connected to your computer are shown.
Status
Drive
Media type
Last run
Current status
OS (C:)
Hard disk drive
Running...
Pass 1: 79% relocated
KINGSTON (E:)
Removable drive
Never run
Optimization not available
PBR Image
Hard disk drive
2/9/2015 1:07 PM
OK (0% fragmented)
WINRETOOLS
Hard disk drive
2/9/2015 1:07 PM
OK (0% fragmented)
Stop
Scheduled optimization
On
Drives are being optimized automatically.
Frequency: Weekly
Change settings
Close

Figure 21-10

as once every two weeks — by using the Change Settings button in the Optimize Drives window and choosing a frequency in the dialog box that appears.

Free Disk Space

1. To run a process that cleans unused files and fragments of data from your hard drive to free up space, type **Disk Cleanup** in Cortana's search field and then press the Enter key on your keyboard.

2. In the Disk Cleanup: Drive Selection dialog box that appears, choose the drive you want to clean up from the drop-down list and click OK. Disk Cleanup calculates how much space you will be able to free up.

 If your computer only has one drive, the Disk Cleanup: Drive Selection dialog box will not appear. Your computer will go straight to calculating how much space you will be able to free up.

3. The resulting dialog box, shown in **Figure 21-11**, tells you that Disk Cleanup calculated how much space can be cleared on your hard drive and displays the suggested files to delete in a list (those to be deleted have a check mark). If you want to select additional files in the list to delete, click to place a check mark next to them.

4. After you select all the file types to delete, click OK. A message appears asking if you are sure that you want to permanently delete the files. Click Delete Files to proceed. The selected files are deleted.

 Click the View Files button in the Disk Cleanup dialog box to see more details about the files that Windows proposes to delete, including the size of the files and when they were created or last accessed.

Figure 21-11

Index

About the Author

Nancy C. Muir is the owner of a writing and consulting company that specializes in business and technology topics. She has authored more than 100 books, including *Laptops For Seniors For Dummies* and *iPhone For Seniors For Dummies*. Nancy holds a certificate in Distance Learning Design and has taught Internet safety at the college level.

Dedication

To my husband Earl for going above and beyond in supporting me while writing these books. Honey, you're the best.

Author's Acknowledgments

Thanks to Katie Mohr, who has been a loyal and supportive acquisitions editor through the years. Also my gratitude to Brian Walls, book juggler supreme, for very ably handling all the many details of several of my books this year. Thanks to Sharon Mealka for tech editing the book to keep me on track.

Publisher's Acknowledgments

Acquisitions Editor: Katie Mohr

Project Editor: Brian H. Walls

Technical Editor: Sharon Mealka

Sr. Editorial Assistant: Cherie Case

Cover Image: ©Getty.com/Comstock

Production Editor: Siddique Shaik